gourmetpilgrim Spain

Recipes, culture and *historias* from the kitchen tables of Spain.

Gourmet Pilgrim would like to thank the many Spanish cooks who so willingly contributed their recipes for the pages of this book, and were so proud to share their rich and unique culinary heritage with the world.

Acknowledgement

Contents

The evolution of Spanish food — 4

Ensaladas (Salads) — 12

Sopas (Soups) — 42

Tapas (Tapas) — 76

Salsas (Sauces) — 144

Frutas y verduras (Fruit & vegetables) — 162

Pescado y marisco (Fish & seafood) — 202

Carne (Meat) — 266

El Pan (Bread) — 330

El Queso (Cheese) — 358

Postres (Desserts) — 370

Dulces y galletas (Sweets & biscuits) — 416

Vino y bebidas (Wine & beverages) — 444

Referencias (Reference) — 480

  Glosario (Glossary) — 482

  Pesos y medidas (Weights & measures) — 490

  Índice (Index) — 491

La evolución de la cocina Española
(The evolution of Spanish food)

For a basic lesson in the evolution of Spanish cuisine, look no further than the country's most famous dish – *paella*.

This Valencian invention tells a story of conquests, commerce and a fertile culinary exchange spanning centuries – and it began when the early Phoenician and Greek settlers arrived around 800BC bringing olives and the know-how to make olive oil. When the Romans turned up a few hundred years later they ramped up olive oil production to export all over their empire, a legacy that remains today with Spain being the world's largest producer of olive oil. The Romans also, crucially, introduced rice and salt cultivation.

The Moors arrived from Africa in the 8th century and during their 700-year reign stocked the Spanish pantry with all manner of exotic spices and flavours. They brought new crops such as aubergines as well as citrus fruits, pomegranates, almonds and a fragrant legacy of cumin, cinnamon, nutmeg and that vital *paella* ingredient, saffron. The Arabs also introduced sophisticated agricultural techniques that established orchards and rice plantations all along the Mediterranean seaboard.

Moorish tastes – a defining legacy

The Moors left an indelible imprint on Iberian cuisine that even today sharply distinguishes Spanish cooking from the rest of Europe. Isolated by the Pyrenees and ruled for seven centuries by Muslims, Spain's European neighbours generally viewed her as being part of 'the other' – of Africa – rather than belonging to the Christian continent. Thanks to the Arabs, Spain has known the pleasures of melons and figs, exotic nuts and the perfumed spices of the Orient for many centuries. It's also highly likely the Spanish inherited their sweet tooth from their Moorish rulers, given their weakness for anything involving honey, almonds and sugar – another inspired Moorish import.

The Moorish influence is still obvious in any Spanish word beginning with the prefix 'al', like *almendras* (almonds), and in the names of vegetables like aubergine (*berenjena*) and carrot (*zanahoria*), which are Arabic. *Aceite*, the Spanish word for oil, is derived from the Arabic words for 'from the olive'.

A unique history that's as complex as it is epic. A fertile land that's as diverse as it is abundant. A restaurant scene that strives for culinary excellence and a culture that promotes a passion for life. The sum of these parts combine to make the Spain of today a food lover's paradise.

Opposite: *el toro* – the bull – is a Spanish icon. This giant silhouette stands in a field of wild flowers in Andalucia.

Many cultures have left their indelible mark on both the Spanish cuisine and the architectural landscape.

Top: The Roman Aqueduct, Segovia, Castilla y Leon – built in 1AD, is one of the world's most perfectly preserved Roman aqueducts.

Right: King Ferdinand and Queen Isabella farewell Columbus at Palos, Andalucia, on his 1st voyage of discovery to the New World, 3rd August 1492.

Culinary treasures from the New World

During the Age of Discovery, explorer Christopher Columbus and his fellow conquistadors returned home to Spain with a wealth of unfamiliar foods. From 1520, new produce began arriving on Spanish shores and ingredients such as tomatoes, potatoes, sweet peppers and chillis, corns, zucchini (courgette), beans and chocolate very soon became indispensable in the local *cocina*. It is difficult to imagine how any contemporary Spanish cookery would be possible without these now-staple tastes. And *paella*, certainly, would not exist without rice, oil, salt, paprika, saffron, tomatoes, peppers and beans.

Many of the foods we think of today as typically Spanish are a melting pot of foreign influences and tastes. Even before the Phoenicians, the ancient Iberians were responsible for bringing wheat west of the Pyrenees. The fondness for meat and fish pies in the northwest around Galicia is a hangover from the Celts while the Jews, who thrived on the Iberian Peninsula under the benevolent Moorish, left behind *adafinas* – a precursor of the *cocido*, which is arguably the commonest dish in Spain.

Cocido – convenience born of necessity

Cocidos are one-pot stews that barely need a recipe. The cook just throws in whatever is to hand, an age-old practice that has spawned such regional delicacies as Extremadura's *cocido extremeño* of bacon, hen, ham, various other meats and vegetables. Castilla-La Mancha's *tojunto*, meaning *todo junto* – everything thrown in together – is a hotchpotch of rabbit, green peppers, garlic and onion simmered in olive oil.

Once prepared, *cocidos* are the ultimate convenience food, which is why the Jews invented *adafinas* in the first place. Forbidden from cooking on the Sabbath by their religion, these stews were made on Fridays for feasting on Saturdays. It's like the Jewish version of a Sunday roast, prepared in advance.

Spaniards are so passionate about cooking and food that an entire lexicon has emerged to describe the sophistication of their cuisine and eating habits. The day's meals are carefully compartmentalised into *desayuno* (breakfast), then lunch – *almuerzo* – around 2, a late-afternoon snack – *la merienda* – or *tapas* after work and *cena*, dinner, sometime after 9pm. When your national cuisine is this deliciously diverse, you want to make the most of it.

The bounty of land and sea

Spain is blessed with the perfect topography to assimilate all the foreign foods that have reached its shores. Today, its abundant river valleys support massive orchards and *huertas*, or market gardens, that supply fresh food to all of Europe. Rice, wheat, livestock, game and spices also thrive here but perhaps the most common food group in the Spanish diet is fish and seafood.

Surrounded by sea on three sides with major fishing industries in the Cantabrian and Mediterranean seas and the Atlantic Ocean, it is hardly surprising that Spain is the biggest fish market in Europe. Various studies have put annual seafood consumption at almost 40 kilograms per person, a year-long banquet that would ordinarily comprise cod (a peculiarly Iberian addiction), anchovies and sardines, hake and bream, octopus, squid, clams, mussels of every persuasion, goose barnacles and an entire kingdom of crabs.

A visionary heritage

The Iberian Peninsula has usually been receptive to ideas and influences from the outside world, readily assimilating them into its own culture. This willingness to engage with the rest of the world helps explain the current ascendancy of avant-garde Spanish cuisine. Spanish chefs have turned everything on its head and imagined a completely new way to prepare food by marrying their own incomparable dedication to produce with a French precision of detail and mastery of technique while throwing in other ideas from wherever they might come.

The groundbreaking molecular gastronomy of Ferran Adrià – the 'father of foam' – and Juan Mari Arzak's tireless efforts at his self-named restaurant in San Sebastián have turned the global spotlight firmly on the Iberian kitchen. So much so that Spanish food has become the new global guard in the kitchen. Ferran Adrià's unmistakable *elBulli* was ranked the best restaurant in the world five times in the past decade and Adrià himself was recently crowned Chef of the Decade. Another three Spanish restaurants – including Arzak – round out the current top 10. No other country comes close to that level of excellence.

While *la nueva cocina* has thrust Spain to the forefront of global gastronomy, this is not how Spanish people eat every day. For the best expression of Iberian eating habits look no further than that other phenomenon now sweeping the globe – *tapas*.

Nothing expresses the generosity and hospitality of the Spanish like the evening ritual known as *tapeo*, hopping from bar to bar, snacking on exquisite morsels. Everyday delights like bite-sized *bocadillo* rolls stuffed with flash-fried calamari, sizzling garlic shrimp or the sweetest anchovy on top of tomato-smeared toast showcase a original and tantalising cuisine. But *tapas* is much more than just fabulous tidbits of food – it is about rediscovering the joy of being in the company of loved ones and living in the absolute moment. The food – and wine – are merely accessories after the fact.

Opposite: Vineyards and the town of Elciego, Alava, Basque Country.

Above: Fishing boats and the harbour of Marbella, Andalucia.

Jamón, Jamón

Paella aside, the other food that defines and delights Spain is *jamón*. Never before has one race become so obsessive about pork meat. Spaniards feed their best purebred pigs a lavish diet of acorns and spring pasture. The meat is then cured for a couple of years in the dry mountain breezes to produce the finest ham known to mankind. To taste a tissue-thin slice of *jamón ibérico de bellota* is to take part in an almost sacred national rite.

Sausages, too, are a countrywide obsession, from Majorca's spreadable and spicy *sobrasada* to León's *botillo* sausage of pigs' tails, ribs and other offcuts, smoked and seasoned with paprika, oregano and garlic.

The fruits of freedom

The 20th century was one of the most difficult Spain has faced in its history. A devastating civil war, a decade-long depression and 36 years of dictatorship depleted the nation beyond recognition, condemning a generation to poverty. Basic peasant dishes such as *migas* – fried breadcrumbs – and the Spanish nose-to-tail philosophy of butchery hark back to days when food was scarce, starvation was common, and the people of the Iberian Peninsula had to eat what they could get.

When it finally emerged from dictatorship in 1975, Spain was shell-shocked but wasted no time finding its feet and forging ahead. In some ways it seems as if those regions most oppressed during General Francisco Franco's 36-year reign are the ones who have found the fullest expression in their freedom since then. The Basque Country and Catalonia, in particular, have distinguished themselves to the world as dynamic, exciting corners of Spain where the imagination seemingly knows no bounds. Gehry's Guggenheim is the futuristic symbol of new Spain and the Basque Country, while Catalonia overcame great obstacles to shine at the 1992 Barcelona Olympics and the gloss still hasn't worn off.

The world's best restaurants are found here at *elBulli* and *El Celler de Can Roca* in Catalonia and the Basque Country's *Arzak* and *Mugaritz*, and the standard of cuisine and the sheer exuberance of degustation in these two Spanish states is unmatched anywhere. The Basque are so passionate about cooking they established the world's first private members' clubs devoted solely to the pleasures of gastronomy. These cultured folk beside the Bay of Biscay also created the elaborate *pintxo*, like a *tapas* that's been to finishing school. Such is the ingenuity and effort that Basque chefs put into these bar snacks that they are known collectively as '*alta cocina en miniatura*', 'haute cuisine in miniature'.

Looking at Spain today it almost feels as if their newfound freedom, democracy and economic success have allowed Spaniards to indulge again in their first love – eating. Closely followed by their second love, which is wine. It is almost impossible to discuss Spanish food in the absence of wine, because that would never happen in real life. Spain's wines do not have the gravitas of some of the French and even Italian grand vintages, but their winemaking is more experimental, more fun and produces regional drops that are ideally matched to the local cuisine. Think of fried fish in Andalucia washed down with a chilled glass of fino sherry, or *pintxos* in San Sebastian with a *txakoli* chaser, and it is difficult to imagine a more perfect match in either instance.

Despite the great heights to which Spanish cuisine has risen in recent years, *Gourmet Pilgrim Spain* is about the food of Spanish homes, not its Michelin-starred restaurants. And while the preparation is decidedly simpler, its inspirations are undeniably the same. Food. Passion. Life.

Above: Outdoor dining in the old town of Ibiza, Balearic Islands.

Opposite: View over Parc Güell, Barcelona, Catalonia – an architectural garden park designed by the famed Catalan architect Antoni Gaudi, now a UNESCO World Heritage site.

gourmet
pilgrim

Ensaladas
Salads

In Spain, a salad
is a lot more than
a side dish – it's a
celebration of an
abundance of high
quality fresh produce.

Ensaladas (Salads)

Made with quality ingredients, a Spanish salad can be a meal in itself.

There's a beauty to Spanish salads that goes beyond tossing together some greens in a bowl. Spanish salads vary from the super-light to the downright hearty. The unifying factor is the Spanish flavour, whether it's due to the use of *jamón*, extra virgin olive oil, *pimentón* or the combination of ingredients.

A salad for all seasons

A Spanish salad could be as traditional as *zarangollo extremeño* – a salad from Extremadura made with roasted tomatoes and red peppers, dressed with paprika and extra virgin olive oil. It's garnished with chopped parsley; the green flecks contrasting beautifully with the shimmering red of the roasted vegetables.

It could also be a meal in itself like a *salpicón de mariscos* – a mix of cucumber, green peppers, onion and poached seafood that's dressed in a light sherry vinegar vinaigrette. This is a summery dish from Andalucia that could be served as part of a larger meal or as a small *tapas* with a glass of sherry.

The use of slightly bitter leaves, such as a salad made with endive *escarola*, could be matched with some meaty pieces of hazelnut and the sweetness of raisins.

A light meal before bed

An *ensalada* may be consumed after a night walking the streets enjoying the ambiance of the *tapeo*, the *tapas* promenade. Such socialising is hard work, so a light snack is often the perfect way to finish the night.

A salad may be dressed with some beautifully conserved tuna, a handful pickled olives, a small amount of cheese and even boiled hen eggs or quail eggs. These are used sparingly, more as a light hit of protein than one would find in a full meal.

Whatever the case, Spanish salads tend to change as the seasons progress, using whatever is at its peak at the time, with robust seasonings, and only the best and freshest produce.

Ensalada de atún, anchoas e hinojo
Romaine lettuce, tuna & anchovy salad

serves 4

Ingredients

12 x 150g pieces fresh tuna
(about 1cm thick)

2 teaspoons olive oil

2 baby romaine (cos) lettuces,
leaves washed

1 small fennel bulb, very thinly sliced

6 anchovy fillets*, drained and sliced

200g cherry tomatoes, quartered

2 pieces peeled, roasted* red pepper
(capsicum)*, thinly sliced

2 spring onions*, very thinly sliced

Dressing:

50ml extra virgin olive oil

1 tablespoon egg mayonnaise*

1 tablespoon lemon juice

Flaked salt

Freshly cracked black pepper

This is a great salad entrée. The lightness of the lettuce and tuna is matched by the richness of the olive oil and anchovies. Using really good extra virgin olive oil and quality anchovies will make the world of difference. Spanish anchovies from the Cantabric sea are perfect for this salad; they cost more but are worth it.

Method

Pat tuna dry with kitchen paper towel and lightly rub both sides with olive oil. Cook in a large non-stick frying pan (or char-grill over high heat) for 2 minutes each side. Remove from pan and allow to rest for a few minutes before slicing.

Place lettuce leaves onto a serving platter, tearing any large leaves into 2-3 pieces. Add fennel, anchovies, tomatoes and pepper, then gently toss to combine.

Lay tuna onto the salad and scatter with spring onions.

To make the dressing, place oil, mayonnaise and lemon juice into a small bowl and mix well with a fork or whisk. Season to taste.

Drizzle dressing over salad and serve.

Tip: When in a hurry, try this salad with canned tuna (ideally in olive oil).

* Refer to Glossary – Page 482

Ensalada Valenciana
Valencian orange & manchego cheese salad

serves 4

Ingredients

6 large oranges, peeled, segmented and juiced (see Note)

2 large avocados, deseeded, peeled and chopped

250g cherry tomatoes, halved

1 medium red onion, halved and very thinly sliced

120g manchego cheese*, crumbled

40g roasted* pine nuts

100g pitted black olives

Dressing:

60ml extra virgin olive oil

2 tablespoons red wine vinegar

2 tablespoons orange juice (see Note)

1 tablespoon finely chopped fresh mint leaves

Flaked salt

Freshly cracked black pepper

There are naturally occurring compounds in the ripe avocados, tomatoes, onions and manchego cheese that make this a deliciously rich salad. For balance, it's lightened and refreshed with juicy oranges and a hint of mint. The Spanish have an innate understanding of the pleasant mouth-filling sensation that the Japanese call umami. We call it 'savoury'.

Method

Decoratively arrange oranges, avocados, tomatoes, onion, cheese, pine nuts and olives onto a serving platter.

To make the dressing, place oil, vinegar, orange juice and mint into a small bowl and mix well with a fork or whisk. Season to taste.

Drizzle dressing over salad and serve.

Note – To segment the oranges, hold a peeled orange (which has had as much white pith removed as possible) in one hand over a bowl (to catch the juice for the dressing). Identify the membranes (white lines) between the individual segments, then take a sharp knife and cut either side of each membrane to release the membrane-free orange segments. Once segmented, squeeze the remaining orange flesh to obtain 2 tablespoons juice for the dressing.

* Refer to Glossary – Page 482

Ensalada Asturiana de arroz
Asturian rice & seafood salad

serves 4

Ingredients

400g long grain rice
12 anchovy fillets*
60g pitted black olives, chopped
425g can tuna in olive oil, drained
400g small-medium cooked shrimp
(prawns)*, peeled
250g cherry tomatoes, halved
1 small red onion, finely chopped
2 tablespoons chopped fresh flat-leaf
(Italian) parsley

Dressing:

1 tablespoon red wine vinegar
80ml extra virgin olive oil
1 tablespoon Dijon mustard
2 teaspoons freshly picked thyme leaves
Flaked salt
Freshly cracked black pepper

The Cantabric Sea off Asturias produce some of the finest anchovies in the world. The tiny fish are cured in huge barrels of very salty brine for nearly a year in nearby Cantabria, and then hand-filleted and canned. This delicious salad, rich with tuna, olives and shrimp, will benefit from using a tin of quality Spanish anchovies.

Method

Cook rice in boiling salted water for about 20 minutes or until tender. Drain in a colander and run under cold water to stop cooking. Drain well and allow to cool.

Drain anchovy fillets on kitchen paper towel and cut each into three pieces.

Place rice, anchovies, olives, tuna, shrimp, tomatoes, onion and parsley into a large bowl and mix well to combine.

To make the dressing, place vinegar, oil, mustard and thyme into a small bowl and mix well with a fork or whisk. Season to taste.

Pour dressing over salad 30 minutes before serving, then toss well to combine.

Tip: Use cooked, sliced tuna steaks as an alternative to canned tuna.

* Refer to Glossary – Page 482

Ensalada de judías con huevos
Green bean salad with quail eggs

serves 4

Ingredients

500g fresh green beans, trimmed

10 hard-boiled* quail eggs*, halved

1 small red onion, thinly sliced

8 cherry tomatoes, halved

30g sunflower seeds, roasted*

Dressing:

60g thick natural yoghurt

2 tablespoons extra virgin olive oil

1 tablespoon water

1 tablespoon chopped fresh flat-leaf (Italian) parsley

1 teaspoon chopped fresh oregano leaves

1 teaspoon lemon juice

Flaked salt

Freshly cracked black pepper

Method

Cook beans in a medium saucepan of lightly salted boiling water for 4-5 minutes or until tender. Drain in a colander and refresh under cold running water.

Place beans on a serving platter and top with eggs, onion, tomatoes and sunflower seeds.

To make the dressing, place yoghurt, oil, water, herbs and lemon juice into a small bowl and mix well with a fork or whisk. Season to taste.

Drizzle dressing over salad and serve.

* Refer to Glossary – Page 482

Ensalada de tomate
Tomato, goat's cheese & pine nut salad

serves 4

Ingredients

3 large ripe tomatoes, washed
250g firm goat's cheese*
40g roasted* pine nuts
Freshly picked oregano leaves, to serve
Flaked salt
Freshly cracked black pepper
1 ½ tablespoons extra virgin olive oil

Method

Cut tomatoes into slices 5mm thick. Cut cheese into slices 5mm thick, and in half again through the middle if they are a little big.

Decoratively arrange tomatoes and cheese on a serving platter, beginning with two slices of tomato and one cheese, continuing along the platter.

Sprinkle with pine nuts and oregano, then season to taste.

Drizzle oil over salad and serve at room temperature for the best flavour.

* Refer to Glossary – Page 482

Ensalada de remolacha con manzana
Beetroot, apple & pomegranate salad

serves 4

Ingredients

400g fresh beetroot bulbs (see Tip)
2 medium green apples
½ pomegranate*, seeds removed
½ lemon, juiced

Dressing:
70g thick natural yoghurt
2 tablespoons egg mayonnaise*
2 teaspoons lemon juice
1 teaspoon caster (superfine) sugar
Flaked salt
Freshly cracked black pepper
1 spring onion*, thinly sliced, to serve

Method

Preheat oven to 180°C.

Wash beetroot, wrap individual bulbs in foil and place on a baking tray. Bake in preheated oven for 45-60 minutes or until tender (test with a skewer, which should insert easily into the cooked beetroot).

Allow beetroot to cool slightly before peeling (wear disposable kitchen gloves to prevent staining your hands), then thinly slice.

Quarter apples and remove core, then thinly slice lengthways and drizzle with lemon juice to prevent browning.

Place alternate beetroot and apple slices onto a serving platter.

To make the dressing, place yoghurt, mayonnaise, lemon juice and sugar into a small bowl and mix well with a fork or whisk. Season to taste.

Drizzle dressing over salad, sprinkle with pomegranate seeds and spring onion and serve.

Tip: If possible, buy young beetroot in a bunch and reserve some of the small beetroot leaves to add to the salad.

* Refer to Glossary – Page 482

Ensaladilla Rusa
Russian salad

Ingredients

500g washed baby new potatoes
2 large carrots, peeled
120g fresh or frozen peas
8 hard-boiled* quail eggs*, halved
Sliced jamon*, to serve
Salad leaves, to serve

Dressing:

300g home-made egg mayonnaise*
(see recipe, page 148)
60ml extra virgin olive oil
2 tablespoons lemon juice
Flaked salt
Freshly cracked black pepper

When the late afternoon summer sun pours into the narrow streets that cut through the heart of Madrid, people take solace in the cool of the bars. They'll enjoy a refreshing caña of ice-cold beer and a small plate of Russian Salad. It's a dish of rich egg mayonnaise that's folded through new potatoes dotted with carrots and peas. It's sometimes draped with roasted peppers, and is a lovely pick-me-up on a hot day.

Method

Boil whole unpeeled potatoes until just cooked when tested with a skewer. Drain and cool, then cut into small pieces.

Cut carrots in half lengthways, then slice. Cook peas in boiling salted water and refresh under cold running water. Drain well.

Place potato, carrots and peas into a large bowl.

To make the dressing, place mayonnaise, oil and lemon juice into a small bowl and mix well with a fork or whisk. Season to taste. Pour dressing over salad and toss well to combine.

Serve topped with quail eggs, sliced jamon and salad leaves.

Tip: If quail eggs are unavailable, use 4 hard-boiled quartered chicken eggs; a quality store-bought egg mayonnaise can be used here, if desired.*

* Refer to Glossary – Page 482

Ensalada Mediterránea de marisco
Mediterranean seafood salad

Ingredients

11 bunch green or white asparagus, trimmed

2 lamb's lettuce (mâche)* or soft green lettuce leaves

½ bunch endive*

½ yellow pepper (capsicum)*, seeded and thinly sliced

4 radishes, thinly sliced

1 small cucumber, shaved (with vegetable peeler)

60g button mushrooms, thinly sliced

½ small red onion, very thinly sliced

200g baby cherry tomatoes

500g whole medium cooked shrimp (prawns)*, peeled and de-veined

200g sliced smoked salmon

1 tablespoon baby capers*, drained

Dressing:

2 tablespoons extra virgin olive oil

1 tablespoon red wine vinegar

1 teaspoon Dijon mustard

Flaked salt

Freshly cracked black pepper

Method

Steam asparagus until just tender, then refresh under cold running water and cut into pieces.

Wash and gently dry salad leaves (or use a salad spinner) and place onto a large platter.

Decoratively arrange asparagus, pepper, radishes, cucumber, mushrooms, onion and tomatoes onto salad leaves. Top with shrimp, salmon and capers.

To make the dressing, place oil, vinegar and mustard into a covered container and shake well. Season to taste.

Drizzle dressing over salad and serve.

* Refer to Glossary – Page 482

Canónigos con jamon y queso
Jamon, cheese & date salad

serves 4

Ingredients

2 lamb's lettuce (mâche)* or soft green lettuce leaves

250g cherry tomatoes, halved

200g sliced jamon* or prosciutto

200g sliced mortadella*

100g Emmental cheese*, cut into small cubes

2 large oranges, peeled and thinly sliced (or segmented – see Note on 'Valencian orange and manchego cheese salad' recipe, page 18)

4 fresh dates, pitted and quartered

Nasturtium flowers* (optional)

Dressing:

Aged balsamic vinegar

Extra virgin olive oil

Flaked salt

Freshly cracked black pepper

Method

Wash and gently dry salad leaves (or use a salad spinner) and place onto a large platter.

Decoratively arrange tomatoes, jamon, mortadella, cheese, oranges and dates onto salad leaves. Sprinkle with flower petals, if desired.

Serve dressing ingredients separately, so that each person can dress their own salad.

Tip: As an alternative to orange slices, enjoy this salad with fresh mango or nectarine slices when in season.

* Refer to Glossary – Page 482

Ensalada de patata y achicoria
Potato, chicory & tuna salad

Ingredients

1kg medium washed new potatoes

6 stalks chicory*

2 x 95g cans tuna in olive oil, drained

125g can sweet corn kernels, drained

1 tablespoon snipped fresh chives

2 pieces roasted* red pepper (capsicum)*, peeled and cut into strips, to serve

Dressing:

75g egg mayonnaise*

1 tablespoon lemon juice

1 tablespoon extra virgin olive oil

1 teaspoon Dijon mustard

Flaked salt

Freshly cracked pepper

Method

Boil whole unpeeled potatoes until just cooked when tested with a skewer. Drain and cool, then cut into large pieces.

Cut the white stem from the chicory and discard; wash, dry and thinly slice the leaves.

Place cooled potatoes into a large bowl and add chicory, tuna, corn and chives, then gently toss to combine.

To make the dressing, place mayonnaise, lemon juice, oil and mustard into a small bowl and mix well with a fork or whisk. Season to taste.

Pour dressing over salad and gently toss to coat. Serve chilled with roasted red pepper strips.

Tip: This salad is the perfect accompaniment to fried sardines or seafood.

* Refer to Glossary – Page 482

Ensalada Catalana
Catalan salad

Ingredients

1 cooked Spanish chorizo sausage*
1 mignonette lettuce
½ bunch endive*
2 large ripe tomatoes, cut into segments
¼ red pepper (capsicum)*, seeded and thinly sliced
1 small carrot, cut into julienne*
1 small cucumber, thinly sliced
¼ red onion, very thinly sliced
200g thinly sliced leg ham

Dressing:

60ml extra virgin olive oil
1 tablespoon lemon juice
Flaked salt
Freshly cracked black pepper

The Catalan kitchen isn't an elaborate affair. The dishes are simple collections of the seasonal harvest; perhaps fruit, vegetables or nuts, made richer with the addition of some preserved meat and perhaps a splash of beautiful Arbequina extra virgin olive oil. It's always a careful balance of seasonal bounty and a hint of richness.

Method

Cut chorizo sausage in half lengthways and thinly slice.

Wash and gently dry salad leaves (or use a salad spinner) and place onto a large platter.

Arrange tomatoes, pepper, carrot, cucumber and onion over salad leaves and gently toss to combine. Top with sliced chorizo and ham.

To make the dressing, place oil and lemon juice into a covered container and shake well. Season to taste.

Drizzle dressing over salad and serve.

Tip: If cooked Spanish chorizo sausage is unavailable, buy an uncooked chorizo, thinly slice and pan fry.

36
gourmetpilgrim Spain

* Refer to Glossary – Page 482

Las Conservas (Preserves)

An Iberian culinary tradition – preserving nature's bounty.

In a small village in Extremadura, on the edge of the great *dehesa*, the massive oak forest that covers much of southern Spain and Portugal, is a church, a bar, a few cottages and a factory that makes rich flavoursome *caldillo* - a kind of pâté from the livers of the Iberico pigs that dine on the acorns of the *dehesa*.

Across Spain there are thousands of like-minded, small artisanal food manufacturers who preserve the very best of the seasonal bounty from the wild, the land and the sea. This is the art of *las conservas*. Taking something at its prime and conserving it in a jar or in a tin so that it lasts for at least one or, perhaps, a few seasons more.

This is a Spanish culinary tradition. Only the best of the catch or the season makes the grade, and, therefore, into a tin or a bottle.

Presentation counts

Some *conservas* are artfully presented in jars in such a considered manner that they take centre stage in the showroom and the retailer thereafter. Top retailers may charge the same for a jar of prime preserved fresh fava beans as they do for a vintage bottle of wine.

From the white asparagus of Navarra to the anchovies of the Cantabric Sea, the art of *conservas* is national phenomenon.

Scuba divers delve into difficult waters to find *navajas*, little pen knife-shaped shellfish. Some are sent to the city markets. Others are kept, cleaned, scooped from the fingernail-like shells, then laid out in olive oil and preserved under a lid and a sanitising scald of steam.

Spanish tuna loin preserved under glass is perhaps one of the most delicious products that flies under the radar. Yes, it's pricier than its other Mediterranean brothers but it's a very fine and sumptuous addition to a salad. Look out for this costly but exquisite product.

Spanish *conservas* are now available around the globe.

Naranjas y cítrícos
(Oranges & citrus fruit)

With the name Valencia practically synonymous with oranges, Spain takes its citrus fruit very seriously.

Below: Citrus fruit for sale; Saranjassa, Mallorca, Balearic Islands.

The streets of southern Spain are perfumed with the heady scent of orange blossom in summertime, heralding a winter citrus harvest that has sustained the Mediterranean coastline for centuries. Vast plantations of oranges, tangerines, clementines and lemons concentrated in Valencia, Murcia and Andalusia have earned these regions a reputation as the orchard of Europe.

Originally from China and the subcontinent, oranges were a delicacy during the Roman Empire but it was the Arabs who first cultivated them in Spain in the 12th century. These were the bitter Seville oranges, used for conserves, perfumes and flavourings. The sweet Valencia variety, now the most popular in the world, is thought to have arrived from India in the 15th century.

The conquistadors planted citrus trees along their routes of discovery so sailors would have a constant source of vitamin C to ward off scurvy. Columbus took orange and lemon seeds to the Caribbean on his second voyage in 1493; Juan Ponce de León introduced oranges to Florida, now one of the world's foremost orange-growing regions.

Despite lending its cities' names to two famous varieties of the fruit, Spain is not the world's largest producer of oranges. That title goes to Brazil though Spain remains the top exporter of fresh citrus fruit – around 70 per cent of which comes from Valencia.

The importance of citrus fruit to the Spanish economy is evident from Valencia's *Mercado de Futuros y Opciones sobre Cítricos*, an exchange whose sole purpose is to trade options and futures in fresh fruit.

Murcia

Overshadowed by its more famous neighbours Valencia and Andalucía, the Mediterranean-meets-mountains province of Murcia harbours a rich historical heritage and fertile plains that feed Europe.

The remnants of its Roman heyday are strewn throughout the region but none is more evocative than the tiered stone amphitheatre at Cartagena, the settlement the Romans called New Carthage. The legacy of early Phoenician occupation lives on in ancient shipwrecks preserved at Cartagena's Naval Museum, while elaborate palaces and fortresses dotted throughout the province recall its prosperity as part of the Moorish Granada Empire.

The Arabs brought sophisticated irrigation systems to arid Murcia – their waterwheels and canals still define the area – fuelling a flourishing trade in vegetables, fruit and flowers that thrives today.

Water – lifeline of the *huerta*

The lifeline of the province is the Segura River, which bisects the capital city Murcia and nourishes the abundant crops of the river basin. The market gardens or *huerta* grow an abundance of lettuces, lemons, peaches, artichokes and tomatoes, but the most valued crop is *Calasparra* rice. Especially the *bomba* variety, prized for *paella-making* because it absorbs more broth than any other rice grain.

The region's cuisine is proudly Mediterranean, combining the freshness of seafood with vegetables and fruits from the *huerta*.

There are three distinctively characteristic Murcian preparations: *chanquetes* are whitebait deep-fried in olive oil and consumed, ideally, with a cold beer; grey mullet roe which is served as a salad with olive oil, peppers and onion; and *mojama,* tuna loin that's been salted and air-cured before it's served sliced with olive oil.

Another distinctive taste is the *Mar Menor* shrimp, fished from the salty, sandbarred lagoon beside the Mediterranean, grilled simply and seasoned with lemon. *Mar Menor,* or 'little sea', is a favourite holiday destination for Murcia locals and has supplied salt to the region since Roman occupation. The surrounding wetlands are a favourite transit point for flamingos en route to Africa.

Ancient irrigation systems transformed this once arid land into a fertile producer of fresh fruit, vegetables and rice.

Opposite: Moratalla and the 15th century Castillo Fortaleza, Murcia.

Right: Idyllic coastline, fishing village of La Manga del Mar Menor, Murcia.

Caldero – cooked on the waves

The fame of Valencian *paella* eclipses Murcia's own *caldero*, a soupy rice casserole of peppers and catch of the day, traditionally cooked on fishing boats in an iron cauldron (hence *caldero*) and finished with garlic mayonnaise. The province also has its own *paella*, a vegetarian version known as *paella huertana*. Murcia's favourite meat dish is *pastel de cierva* or doe pie, but it contains no deer meat, instead a mix of veal or chicken, spiced sausage, hard-boiled eggs and sometimes rabbit, wrapped in puff pastry and baked.

Wines from Jumilla, in the foothills north of Murcia city, have been produced since Roman times when legionnaires were pensioned off here with villa-and-land packages. The main grape varieties are the deep purple Monastrell that is transformed into elegant rosés and robust crianzas, and the white grapes Macabeo and Arién. Jumilla wines are protected by a *Denominación de Origen* dating to 1966, one of Spain's oldest wine classifications.

Like all of southern Spain, the region is piping hot in summer. Murcia city recorded Spain's highest temperature of the 20th Century with 47.2 degrees in July 1994. The best antidote to the searing heat besides a swim is a sorbet made from *higo chumbo*, the prickly pears that flourish in this parched province.

gourmet
pilgrim

Sopas

Soups

From simple
peasant-style to rich
and multi-layered,
soups in Spain are
steeped in tradition
and ritual.

Sopas (Soups)

From refreshing to hearty, there is a delicious soup for every Spanish season.

It's a brisk winter's day in Aranjuez, the old royal summer palace just south of Madrid. Outside a bar near the train station hangs a rough black board with the words "Hay caldo!" scrawled on it. This means soup is on the menu, or more accurately, a thin broth that's flavoured with chicken and jamon bones. A quick hit of delicious hot consommé – taken with a brandy, if necessary – warms the men who wander in before they walk home from the station.

One soup, two courses

Some dishes, such as Madrid's *cocido*, produce a soup as a side dish as the main protein, or meat, slowly cooks in the soup pot to make a rich stock. In the case of *cocido*, pasta is cooked in the stock as a first course of chicken and noodle soup, followed by the vegetables and meat.

In another example, a consommé is drawn from the pot in which a duck is cooked for Catalonian *canelones*. The duck flesh is then mixed with béchamel and stuffed into *canelones*, or pasta tubes, and baked. While this is happening, the stock is seasoned and served as a first course.

Every last drop

Thicker soups are simple, one-pot dishes into which some meat or sausage is cooked with vegetables and pulses, such as chickpeas. So many flavour compounds and nutrients are released into the stock it's absolutely necessary to finish it all. That's why so much bread is served with soup – to sop up the *'sopa'*.

Spanish soups are very regional and reflect the climate of the products of the region.

Andalusia, in the south, is famous for its chilled soups, while the seafaring people from regions on the Bay of Biscay produce rich and multi-layered seafood soups.

Some soups are only made when a certain vegetable is ripe, others only eaten at Christmas time or for Holy Week. The Spanish love and respect their soups and consume them with abandon.

Sopa marinera
Sailor's seafood soup

Ingredients

1kg mussels*, cleaned and debearded

1 litre water

500g cockles, soaked if necessary (see Note)

150g scallops, deveined if necessary (see Note)

2 tablespoons olive oil

1 large brown onion, finely chopped

2 garlic cloves, finely chopped

1 teaspoon smoked paprika*

400g can chopped tomatoes

Freshly cracked black pepper

1 lemon, juiced

1 tablespoon chopped fresh flat-leaf (Italian) parsley, to serve

Fried bread croutons*, to serve

Such a simple dish but so delicious. By cooking the shellfish separately you apply just enough heat to open them and collect their beautiful juices without overcooking them. The flesh is added back to the juice with the simplest of seasonings and the fresh sourness of lemon. This is one of Spain's great little treasures.

Method

Place mussels and half the water into a large saucepan, then cover and cook for 4-5 minutes or until they begin to open. As each mussel opens and is cooked, remove it with tongs to a side bowl – this will result in plump, rather than overcooked, mussels. Remove all cooked mussel meat from shells; discard shells, including any unopened ones.

Strain the mussel-cooking liquid into a large bowl through a double layer of kitchen paper towel or muslin; discard the paper and sediment. Reserve strained liquid.

Add cockles to saucepan with remaining water and cook in the same way as the mussels. (Sometimes the cockles need a little prompting to open so rattle them in the pan or tap them with tongs.) Remove cooked meat and again strain liquid through kitchen paper towel or muslin into the bowl of reserved mussel liquid. Set aside.

Wipe the saucepan clean with kitchen paper towel. Heat oil in saucepan over medium heat and cook onion and garlic for 3 to 5 minutes, stirring. Add paprika and cook for 1 minute.

Add tomatoes and reserved mussel-and-cockle liquid to saucepan, then cook covered for a further 20 minutes over low heat. Season to taste with pepper.

Just before serving, add the mussel, cockle and scallop meat to soup and cook for 2 minutes. Add lemon juice to taste. Serve with parsley and croutons.

Note – If the cockles have sand in them, soak them in lightly salted water for 1 hour before using; if necessary, remove black vein along the side of each scallop and discard.

* Refer to Glossary – Page 482

Sopa de puerros
Leek & potato soup with croutons

serves 4

Ingredients

4 large leeks

800g floury potatoes, such as russet (Idaho) or King Edward, peeled

120g butter

2 tablespoons olive oil

750ml water

1 teaspoon mild Spanish paprika*

1 teaspoon flaked salt

Pinch of ground white pepper

Fresh flat-leaf parsley (Italian), to serve

Fried bread croutons*, to serve

Method

Cut off and discard the root end and about 8cm of the tough, dark green top of each leek. Cut remaining stalk in half lengthways and wash well between the layers; thickly slice.

Cut potatoes into large pieces.

Heat butter and oil in a large saucepan over low-medium heat and cook leeks and potatoes for 10-15 minutes or until leeks are soft, stirring occasionally. Add water, paprika, salt and pepper.

Simmer, partially covered, for 20 minutes or until potato is tender.

Blend soup until smooth with a stick blender or process in a blender or food processor. Adjust seasoning to taste. Serve with parsley and croutons.

* Refer to Glossary – Page 482

Sopa de tomate y jamón
Butter bean, tomato & jamon soup

serves 4

Ingredients

2 tablespoons olive oil

1 medium red onion, finely chopped

1 large garlic clove, finely chopped

500g smoked ham hock

2 x 400g cans chopped tomatoes

150g carrots, finely chopped

1 litre salt-reduced chicken stock

2 x 420g cans butter beans, drained and rinsed

2 tablespoons chopped fresh mint

Flaked salt

Freshly cracked black pepper

Method

Heat oil in a large saucepan over low-medium heat and cook onion and garlic for 5 minutes or until lightly golden brown, stirring occasionally. Add ham hock, tomatoes, carrots and stock and bring to a gentle boil; cover and simmer, stirring occasionally, for about 2 hours or until the meat falls off the bone.

Remove bone from soup and cool slightly before peeling away and discarding the outside skin (rind). Remove meat from the bone and roughly chop; discard bone. Return meat to the saucepan with beans and mint. Season to taste. Heat through and serve.

Tip: If soup is a little thick, thin with a little water. This soup is delicious made with fresh tomatoes when they are in season.

Sopa de castañas
Chestnut & mushroom soup

Ingredients

250g fresh chestnuts

400g mixed mushrooms (portobello, Swiss brown and chestnut)

1 leek

60ml olive oil

1 stick celery, finely chopped

100ml dry sherry

2 litres salt-reduced chicken stock

Flaked salt

Freshly cracked black pepper

Fresh flat-leaf (Italian) parsley, to serve

As the days shorten and the rains of autumn fall on the forests of Spain, natural bounties slowly emerge. From the forest floor come mushrooms: ceps, black trumpets, pine mushrooms and more than a hundred other edible versions. The chestnuts swell in the forest canopy and the shiny nuts fall from their hard, prickly shells. These foraged foods were once the food of the poor but here make a wonderfully rich soup.

Method

Preheat oven to 180°C.

Cut a small cross into the tough outer skin of each chestnut. Place onto a baking tray and roast in preheated oven for about 20 minutes or until the outer skin cracks. Place chestnuts onto a clean tea towel to keep them warm while you peel off the tough outer and thin inner skins from each chestnut. Discard the skins, reserving the inner chestnut meat.

Lightly brush the mushrooms, if required, with damp kitchen paper towel and thinly slice.

Cut off and discard the root end and about 8cm of the tough, dark green top of the leek. Cut remaining stalk in half lengthways and wash well between the layers; thinly slice to obtain 1 cup of leek.

Heat oil in a large saucepan over low-medium heat and cook the leek and celery for 5 minutes or until leek is tender, stirring occasionally. Add prepared chestnuts and mushrooms and cook, stirring, for a further 5 minutes. Pour in sherry and simmer until evaporated.

Add stock and simmer, partially covered, for 20 minutes or until leek and chestnuts are tender.

Blend soup until smooth with a stick blender or process in a food processor or blender. Season to taste, sprinkle with parsley and serve.

Gazpacho a la Andaluza
Andulacian chilled tomato & garlic soup

serves 4

Ingredients

800g very ripe tomatoes, chopped

1 small cucumber, peeled and chopped

1 small red onion, finely chopped

2-3 garlic cloves, finely chopped

200g rustic white bread (crusts removed)

125ml extra virgin olive oil

2 tablespoons sherry vinegar*

Flaked salt

Freshly cracked black pepper

Water

2 hard-boiled eggs*, peeled, to serve

30g thinly sliced leg ham, cut into strips, to serve

1 small tomato, seeded and finely chopped, to serve

1 tablespoon extra virgin olive oil, to serve

Perhaps the most famous chilled soup in the world, gazpacho comes from the hot heart of Andalucia.

While there are scores of different gazpachos, the one that is best known is made with bread, oil, garlic, tomatoes and cucumbers. The gazpacho we know today is a smooth, velvety blend of bread, oil, summer veg and chilled water. This is the result of the arrival of cheap and reliable food processors into Spain a decade or so after the end of World War II.

Before WWII gazpachos were made in mortar and pestles, with each new ingredient that's added to the stone bowl being slowly ground down. Some old-fashioned cooks prefer this rustic method but the food processor method is now the norm.

By making this soup you are joining the hundreds of generations of cooks who have made this dish since Roman times when it consisted of just bread, water, oil and vinegar. Today, modern chefs are experimenting with fruit gazpachos but there's an undying devotion to the original Andalucian classic.

This recipe relies on using sturdy rustic bread (sliced white bread from a plastic bag simply won't do) and good-quality extra virgin olive oil. The traditional way of keeping it cool is by serving it in a terracotta bowl.

Method

Place tomatoes, cucumber, onion and garlic into a blender or food processor and process until smooth. Strain the mixture through a coarse strainer into a glass bowl to collect juice. Discard pulp.

Cut bread into cubes and add to the tomato-juice mixture. Cover and soak for 4 hours in the refrigerator.

Return mixture to blender or processor and process until the consistency is creamy; at this point, and while the motor is running, add the oil in a thin, continuous stream. Add vinegar and season to taste. Add a little water to thin the soup, if necessary. Refrigerate.

To serve, finely chop or grate the eggs, keeping the whites separate from the yolks. Serve gazpacho chilled, with the egg, ham and tomato and drizzle with olive oil.

* Refer to Glossary – Page 482

Escudella Catalana
Catalan Escudella

serves 4-6

Ingredients

Meatballs:
200g minced lamb
1 egg yolk
15g fresh breadcrumbs*
Flaked salt
Freshly cracked black pepper

Broth:
2.5 litres water
200g shin bone of beef
2 chicken drumsticks
200g boneless pork spareribs
1 fresh bay leaf
150g dried chickpeas
1 medium parsnip, peeled and cut into julienne*
1 carrot, cut into julienne*
1 large all-purpose potato, peeled and cut into large pieces
200g Spanish white sausage* (or pork-style sausage)
8 spring onions*, cut into 5cm lengths
¼ cabbage, shredded
100g dried pasta (such as small shells)

If Catalonia were a dish then this would be it. A rich, hearty and flavoursome soup, some would even say a stew, made with the humblest of ingredients but transformed in the pot as it slowly cooks.

It was originally made over the hearth, which was the heart of the Catalan home, and then in cuina econòmica – small, coal-burning stoves that were common in 19th century industrial city apartments.

Foods that are not initially tantalising go into the pot: cabbage; chickpeas; bones and sausages. When cooked together the flavours meld to make a soup that has beautiful richness and texture.

Added to this soup is cooked fideus – Catalan-style noodles that were introduced to the region by Italian workers and merchants during the past 200 years. It's served as a two-part play, opening with noodles cooked in the rich soup followed by the final act of melt-in-the-mouth tender flesh and super-succulent chickpeas and vegetables.

Method

To make the meatballs, place lamb, egg yolk and breadcrumbs into a bowl and mix well. Season to taste and shape mixture into 4 meatballs. Cover and set aside in the refrigerator.

To make the broth, place water, beef, chicken, pork and bay leaf into a large saucepan and cook, covered, over low heat for 1½-2 hours or until meat is falling off the bones. Remove meat from bones and set aside; discard bones.

Meanwhile, soak chickpeas in boiling water for 1 hour, then drain. Place chickpeas into a medium saucepan, cover with plenty of water and bring to the boil, then reduce heat to low and simmer, uncovered, for 1 hour or until tender. Drain.

To the broth, add parsnip, carrot, potato, whole sausage, spring onions and prepared meatballs. Simmer, covered, over low heat for a further 25 minutes or until vegetables are tender. Add cooked chickpeas and meat and season to taste. Lastly, add cabbage, stir it through and cook for a further 5 minutes.

To serve, remove meatballs and sausage from the broth, then slice the sausage and place onto a serving platter with the other cooked meats and vegetables. Keep warm.

Add pasta to the broth and cook for about 8 minutes or until just tender.

Serve the broth in bowls, along with the platter of meat and vegetables.

* Refer to Glossary – Page 482

Sopa de tomate con calamar
Tomato & calamari soup

serves 4

Ingredients

800g whole squis (calamari), cleaned
and skinned

2 tablespoons olive oil

3 eschalots*, finely chopped

1 medium carrot, finely chopped

1 stick celery, finely chopped

400g can chopped tomatoes

1 tablespoon tomato paste*

125ml dry white wine

1 bouquet garni*

330g all-purpose potatoes, peeled and
cut into large cubes

Flaked salt

Freshly cracked black pepper

Garlicky bread, to serve (see Note)

Method

Wash squid and pat dry with kitchen paper towel. Cut the body into thin rings and the tentacles and side wings into pieces.

Heat oil in a large saucepan over low-medium heat and cook eschalots, carrot and celery for 10 minutes, stirring occasionally. Increase heat to high, add squid and cook for a further 2 minutes.

Add tomatoes and tomato paste, wine and bouquet garni. Bring to the boil, cover and simmer over low heat for 20 minutes. Add potatoes and cook for a further 15-20 minutes or until potatoes are tender. If the soup is a little thick, thin it with some water.

Season soup to taste, remove bouquet garni and discard. Serve with garlicky bread.

Note – To make the garlicky bread: take 4 slices of sourdough bread and brush both sides with 1-2 tablespoons olive oil. Cut a garlic clove in half and rub over the bread slices. Place bread on a baking tray and bake in the oven at 180°C for about 10 minutes or until lightly golden.

* Refer to Glossary – Page 482

Sopa de caballa
Mackerel, pasta & paprika soup

serves 4

A big, tasty dish that draws the flavour from a full-bodied fish to make a stock as the dish cooks – this is typical Spanish one-pot cooking. Potato and pasta are cooked in the stock and flavoured with garlic, paprika, oregano and a hint of chilli.

Ingredients

400g Spanish mackerel or swordfish fillet/ steak, skin removed

2 tablespoons olive oil

1 small red onion, finely chopped

1 garlic clove, finely chopped

½ green pepper (capsicum)*, seeded and finely chopped

2 teaspoons mild Spanish paprika*

¼ teaspoon chilli paste* or 1 small fresh red chilli*, finely chopped

1 tablespoon finely chopped fresh oregano leaves

1 litre fish or salt-reduced chicken stock

500ml water

Pinch saffron threads*

200g all-purpose potatoes, peeled and cubed

100g dried macaroni pasta

Flaked salt

1/3 cup chopped fresh flat-leaf (Italian) parsley, to serve

Method

Cut fish into 2cm cubes. Set aside.

Heat oil in a large saucepan over low-medium heat and cook onion, garlic and pepper for 8-10 minutes, stirring occasionally. Add paprika, chilli and oregano, then cook for a further 2 minutes. Add stock, water and saffron and bring to a gentle boil. Reduce heat to low and add potatoes, then simmer, partially covered, for 20 minutes or until potatoes are just tender.

Add pasta and cook for 10 minutes or until pasta is just cooked. Season to taste.

Add fish cubes to soup and simmer for only 2-3 minutes. Serve sprinkled with parsley.

Tip: For a little extra spice, serve soup with Romescu sauce (see recipe, page 150).

* Refer to Glossary – Page 482

Sopa de calabacín
Creamy zucchini soup

Ingredients

1.5 litres salt-reduced chicken or
vegetable stock

80ml olive oil

1 small brown onion, finely chopped

2 large garlic cloves, finely chopped

400g zucchini (courgettes)*, chopped

2 tablespoons chopped fresh flat-leaf
(Italian) parsley

220g floury potatoes, such as russet
(Idaho) or King Edward, peeled and
chopped

50g soft goat's cheese*, crumbled

Flaked salt

Freshly cracked black pepper

75g manchego cheese*, thinly shaved,
to serve

Fried bread croutons*, to serve

Fresh flat-leaf (Italian) parsley, extra,
to serve

Method

Heat stock in a small saucepan covered with a lid.

Meanwhile, heat oil in a larger saucepan over low-medium heat
and cook onion and garlic for 5 minutes, stirring occasionally. Add
zucchini and parsley and cook for a further 5 minutes.

Add hot stock and potato to zucchini mixture, then add the goat's
cheese. Simmer for 20 minutes, partially covered, until potato is
cooked. Season to taste.

Blend soup until smooth with a stick blender or process in a
blender or food processor.

Serve with cheese, croutons and parsley.

* Refer to Glossary – Page 482

Sopa de tomate con lentejas y jamón
Lentil, tomato & jamon soup

serves 4

Ingredients

2 tablespoons olive oil

1 small brown onion, finely chopped

1 stick celery, finely chopped

1 medium carrot, finely chopped

1 garlic clove, finely chopped

100g Serrano jamon* or prosciutto, chopped

260g dried red lentils, rinsed and drained

200g all-purpose potatoes, peeled and chopped

400g can chopped tomatoes

1 fresh bay leaf

½ teaspoon sweet paprika*

1 litre salt-reduced chicken stock

500ml water

1 tablespoon red wine vinegar

Flaked salt

Freshly cracked black pepper

Method

Heat oil in a large saucepan over low-medium heat and cook onion, celery, carrot and garlic for 10 minutes, stirring occasionally. Add jamon and cook for a further 2-3 minutes.

Add lentils, potatoes, tomatoes, bay leaf and paprika, stock and water and stir to combine. Cover and simmer for 30 minutes or until potato is tender and lentils are cooked.

Stir in vinegar, season to taste and serve.

* Refer to Glossary – Page 482

Ajoblanco
Chilled almond & garlic soup

Ingredients

150g blanched almonds

125ml milk

2 slices rustic bread, crusts removed
and lightly toasted

3 garlic cloves, roughly chopped

125ml extra virgin olive oil

250-375ml chilled water

2 tablespoons sherry vinegar

Flaked salt

Halved green grapes, to serve

Finely chopped fresh flat-leaf (Italian)
parsley, to serve

On a hot day in southern Spain a bowl of cool ajoblanco is the perfect pick-me-up. Fresh ground almonds, garlic and bread are blended with a little chilled water and, very gradually, some sweet, fruity extra virgin olive oil. The soup is enlivened with some nutty sherry vinegar and finished with chilled, peeled grapes. Spanish varieties of extra virgin olive oil, such as hojiblanca, are perfect for this dish.

Method

Place almonds and milk into a bowl and stand for 30 minutes, then drain almonds, discarding milk. Blend almonds and garlic in a food processor or blender until a paste begins to form.

With the motor running, slowly add oil. Then slowly begin to add just enough water until the mixture develops a thin, smooth soup-like texture. Lastly, add vinegar and season to taste.

Transfer to a large bowl or jug, then cover and chill until ready to serve.

Garnish with grapes and parsley and serve.

Sopa de tomate
Tomato soup

Ingredients

600g ripe tomatoes

80ml olive oil

1 large brown onion, finely chopped

1 stick celery, finely chopped

1 tablespoon tomato paste* (optional, see Tip)

1.5 litres boiling water

150g fresh breadcrumbs*

Flaked salt

Freshly cracked black pepper

Fresh oregano or flat-leaf (Italian) parsley

Method

Cut a small cross into the base of each tomato and place into a heatproof bowl; cover with boiling water and stand for about 3-4 minutes. Remove and cool under running water. Peel away the skins, starting from the cuts you made. Discard the skins and finely chop the tomato flesh.

Heat oil in a large saucepan over low-medium heat and cook onion and celery for 5 minutes, stirring occasionally. Add tomatoes and cook for a further 10 minutes. Add tomato paste, if you choose, boiling water and breadcrumbs. Season to taste.

Simmer, partially covered, for 30 minutes.

Blend soup until smooth with a stick blender or process in a food processor or blender. Taste and add more seasoning if desired.

Serve with oregano or parsley.

Tip: When tomatoes are in season and full of flavour, the tomato paste may not be required.

* Refer to Glossary – Page 482

Sopa de pimiento rojo y berenjena
Roasted red pepper & aubergine soup

serves 4

Ingredients

700g aubergine (eggplant)*
220g red peppers (capsicum)*
1 medium red onion, finely chopped
1 garlic clove, finely chopped
1 tablespoon olive oil
350g ripe tomatoes, chopped
1 teaspoon sweet paprika*
1 teaspoon ground cumin
1 litre salt-reduced chicken stock
60ml lemon juice

Red pepper cream:
1 small red onion, finely chopped
1 tablespoon water
125ml thickened cream*
Fresh marjoram leaves, to serve (optional)

Method

Preheat oven to 200°C.

Place whole aubergine and peppers onto a baking tray and bake in preheated oven for 45 minutes or until aubergine flesh is soft and the skin on the peppers blackens and blisters. Turn occasionally during cooking. Remove from oven and cool for about 15 minutes.

Peel skin from the aubergine and roughly chop flesh. Remove skin and seeds from peppers and roughly chop. Set aside one cooked pepper for the red pepper cream.

Heat oil in a large saucepan over low-medium heat and cook onion and garlic for 5 minutes, stirring occasionally. Add aubergine, remaining peppers, tomatoes, paprika and cumin and cook for a further 5 minutes. Add chicken stock and lemon juice, then cover and simmer for 30 minutes.

Meanwhile, to make the red pepper cream, place the reserved roasted pepper, onion and water in a blender or food processor and process until smooth. (For a very smooth result, you can strain through a sieve, too.) Stir in cream and set aside.

Blend soup until smooth with a stick blender or process in a blender or food processor. Season to taste and serve with a generous dollop of red pepper cream and fresh marjoram, if you choose.

Tip: For a smoother soup, strain through a sieve and discard remaining pulp.

* Refer to Glossary – Page 482

Almendras (Almonds)

Shortly before the beginning of spring, the almond trees along the eastern seaboard of Spain burst into the palest pink flowers, sweetening the sea breezes with a scent of roses and marzipan. The buzzing of countless bees can be heard almost as soon as you smell the blossom of the almond grove.

Over the coming months, nuts form in the place of the blossoms on the boughs of the almond trees, which are generally grown in the rougher, stony soils not suited to grazing or grape growing.

Come autumn, the nuts have formed inside a hairy covering and are shaken from the tree, traditionally by hand but now more often by mechanical harvester.

From soup to sauces

Almonds are integral to Spanish cuisine. They form the milky foundation of the refreshing summer soup *ajoblanco* (see page 66), are eaten roasted as a snack, are pounded with garlic and saffron to make a *picada*, can thicken a sauce and are used extensively in baking and the arts of confectionery.

Take a break at a truck stop in the almond-growing regions of Spain and there are great pyramids of candied roasted almonds – surprisingly delicious for a roadside offering.

There are several different varieties of almond grown in Spain, including the sweet, round *marcona* and the long *largueta*. Freshness is essential with almonds, as they're packed with delicate oils that can oxidise easily, leaving a taste of rancidity.

For the best Spanish produce, buy almonds from dedicated nut specialists if possible, otherwise many Middle Eastern and Mediterranean food stores will stock good almonds too.

Almonds get an extra lift when gently roasted. Lay the almonds flat on an oven tray and place into an oven that's preheated to 180°C. Roast for eight to 10 minutes until very lightly golden. Cool before using.

A handful of salted almonds (see page 86) is an excellent snack with a little glass of fino or even amontillado sherry.

This one little nut has so many delicious possibilities.

Above: Harvesting almonds, Malaga region, Andalucia.

Opposite: Almond orchard in bloom and Los Mallos de Riglos mountains, Huesca, Aragon.

Extremadura

Tucked away beside Portugal in Spain's wild west, Extremadura is landlocked by mountains, irrigated by the great rivers Tajo and Guadiana, and would be largely overlooked by the rest of the country if not for two vital elements – pork and paprika.

The region's vast groves of holm oak trees provide fodder for the acorn-fed Iberian pigs that produce the incomparable jamón ibérico de bellota. And from the Cáceres province comes *Pimentón de La Vera*, the prized smoky paprika first cultivated by monks at the Yuste Monastery in La Vera Valley and today used to season everything Iberian, from chorizo to eggs.

Despite its geographic isolation, Extremadura has a vibrant history. The capital, Mérida, was originally the capital of the Roman province of Lusitania and still boasts impressive relics of that era, including an aqueduct, amphitheatre and a Temple of Diana.

The Moorish period invested the land with fortresses or *alcazars*, and a treasury of Baroque art recalls the heyday of the Spanish Empire. Two of the most famous conquistadors, Hernan Cortés and Francisco Pizarro, hailed from Extremadura.From the New World these adventurers brought back potatoes, tomatoes and peppers to supplement the lamb and pork diet of the region's shepherds and farmers.

Cherries, cheese & thistles

The cuisine remains heavily traditional, simple and rural, but it has contributed four distinctive Denomination of Origin (DO) products to Spanish gastronomy. Aside from jamón and paprika, Extremadura is also renowned for its hand-picked *Cereza del Jerte*, cherries introduced by the Arabs and grown en masse in the Jerte Valley, Europe's largest cherry orchard. From the small municipality of Casar, with its flock of 20,000 Merino sheep, comes the DO *Torta del Casar* cheese. The sheep's milk is curdled using thistle (cardoon) flowers and then left to mature for at least two months, creating a creamy cheese with a distinctive aroma.

Humble but hearty fare

Migas, or breadcrumbs, is a dish that typifies the humbleness of Extremaduran cooking. Stale bread is broken into small pieces, softened with water and then fried with dried green peppers, paprika, garlic and bacon. Soups also tend to be simple, based on stale bread and flavoured with whatever is to hand; the popular *sopas engañadas* combines peppers, pickled spring onions, figs and grapes. During the hot summers chilled soups are common with the best known local *gazpacho* being *ajoblanco* (recipe page 66), a white soup of bread, almonds, garlic and olive oil.

Extremaduran cuisine is simple and traditional, but the gourmet specialties of this isolated region have a dedicated national following.

River trout and Portuguese cod (*bacalao*) provide balance to a diet that is typically carnivorous. Lamb dominates the distinctive regional dish *Chanfaina*, a rustic casserole seasoned with garlic, bay leaves and paprika. *Chanfaina* is central to the celebrations of the *Chanfaina Fiesta* in April, when villagers compete to prepare the finest stew of lamb loin and offal cooked with garlic, tomatoes, white wine, onion and bay leaves.

And in this land of the celebrated Iberian pig there is a well-known dish called *lagarto*, or lizard. While Extremadurans did once enjoy grilled lizards – they're protected now – this dish features pork, not reptile. Specifically, the juicy flesh from around the pig's backbone, simmered with potatoes, tomatoes, onion, garlic plus a little thyme and bay leaves for good taste.

Below: Iglesia de San Martin (Church of St Martin) and city of Trujillo, Caceres, Extremadura.

Opposite: The dehesa – pasturelands of holm oak, Monfrague National Park, Caceres, Extremadura.

Tapas

Tapas

Tapas are not simply
fancy canapés –these
tasty morsels shared
with friends and family
are a celebration of
Spanish life.

Tapas (Tapas)

Tapas may have become a global dining phenomenon, but in Spain it's about a lot more than simply eating.

La Venencia is a nicotine-stained tavern of faded posters and dusty wine barrels in central Madrid. Just a short walk from the theatre and bars quarter of *Santa Ana* square, the 80-year-old tavern serves only five drinks, all of them Andalucian white wines, and simple plates of olives, cheese or ham. Staff chalk cuneiform marks on the wooden bar to keep tab and then tally the cryptic scribbles when it is time to pay. Wine is poured straight from the barrel using antique-looking ladles. The novelty of the experience seems to make people drink faster, and eat more. And everyone talks endlessly.

This is the simplest expression of *tapas*. It is not just about the food – though that is almost always excellent. It is about the people and the positive energy that forms when random groups come together to have fun.

Tapas are not simply fancy canapés; rather a way of life, a celebration, and a byword for Iberian hospitality.

The art of *tapas*

The *tapas* ritual is now so entrenched in Spanish culture that an entire lingo has emerged to describe the phenomenon. But tapas are not always tapas – they become *pintxos* in Basque Country and parts of Navarra. If they are on a skewer they are *banderillas*, named after the barbed darts used in bullfights. *Cazuelas* are *tapas* that come in small earthenware dishes, like meatballs or sizzling garlic shrimp. A *montadito* can refer to a bread slice topped with something scrumptious – unless you are in Seville where it is a tiny toasted sandwich, but still *tapas*. If we sit down to a meal we *comemos*, eat, but if we snack on tapas we *picamos* – pick at, like a bird. And the performance of hopping from bar to bar grazing on food and wine is known as the *tapeo* – except in the Basque Country where it is *txikiteo*, or sometimes *poteo* after the type of glass (*pote*) used for drinking the regional wine, *txakoli*. It's all very confusing – but eminently enjoyable.

Tapas are eaten standing up at a bar or a high table, often facing barrels of wine and a curtain of crimson-coloured hams slung from the rafters. Prepared *tapas* are kept behind glass or in structural piles on a counter for ease of ordering, while a blackboard menu will list the hot dishes available from tiny rear kitchens. This is not sit-down food.

RACIONES RAC

JAMON IBERICO DE BELLOTA 21'0
LOMO IBERICO DE BELLOTA 22'0
SALCHICHON IBERICO DE BELLOTA 10'00
CHORIZO IBERICO DE BELLOTA 10'00
QUESO MANCHEGO CURADO 9'00
QUESO DE CABRA 8'00
CHORIZO PICANTE DE ZAMORA 8'60
MORCILLA CURADA 8'00
BOQUERONES EN VINAGRE 12'0
MOJAMA DE LA ALMADRABA 12'00
CECINA DE LEON 22'0
FUENTE DE IBERICOS 14'00 con piparras pan tostado
ANCHOAS EN SALAZON 3'00 €
EMPANADA GALLEGA DE ATUN O CARNE 15'60
TORTA DEL CASAR 13'00 €
MI-CUIT DE PATO

ENSALADAS

ENSALADA DE TOMATE, Ajo, ACEITE DE OLIVA 6'50 €
ENSALADA DE VENTRESCA CON PIMIENTOS DEL PIQUILLO 14'60 €

Above: *Raciones* – a portion from a shared plate – a 'serve' of tapas.

Opposite: *Casa Placido* Tapas Bar, Barrios Santa Cruz, Seville, Andalucia.

The nightly ritual of moving from bar to bar, grazing on food and sipping wine, is known as the *tapeo*.

A practical – and tasty – solution

There are several theories as to how the *tapas* tradition originated but the most plausible is the one that says it evolved as a means to keep flies out of patrons' drinks (hence *tapa*, 'lid' or 'cover'). In their most basic form, *tapas* are small tastes of Spanish delicacies on a disc of crusty bread that, in times past, doubled as a device to keep your drink safe. The bread might be topped with a glistening slice of silky *jamón Serrano*, some marinated white anchovies (*boquerones*), chunks of *manchego* or rough slices of *tortilla*.

Tapas are also a practical response to the Spaniards' extraordinary meal times and eating customs. When a nation rises to coffee and a meagre feed of *churros* or tomato on toast, and lunch is not until 2pm, snacking becomes a survival instinct. Even more so in the evenings, given the Spanish don't eat until late – anywhere between 9.30pm and midnight. So friends, colleagues and lovers sensibly gather after work at the local for a drink and something to tide them over till dinner-time.

The *tapas* experience

For the most uninhibited *tapeando* experiemce, head to Bar Pilar, a 70-year-old tavern in Valencia's old city where crowds jam in so tightly there is no room, no seating and definitely no quiet corner. Bar staff somehow manage to supply everyone with a plate of Pilar's signature mussels and a drink to wash them down. In full flight, the floor is carpeted in shells and discarded napkins while rowdy patrons spill onto the street.

Similar scenes are played out across Spain, most commonly in university cities where students are wooed into bars by the promise of free food. Along the buzzing boulevarde of Santiago de Compostela's Rua Franco, the taverns that have welcomed Christian pilgrims for centuries continue the age-old tradition of offering free tapas with drinks. In one bar it might be something as simple as a dish of olives and pickles or chips, or thin pork steaks called *cocodrilos* (crocodiles).

A national obsession

Every region of Spain would love to lay claim to inventing *tapas* but the consensus seems to be that it originated in Andalucia. That explains Seville's enduring obsession with bite-sized delights, though Madrid, with its myriad bars, could possibly lay claim to the country's most dynamic *tapas* scene. In both cities the passion for snacking is so intense an outsider can feel as if she or he has stumbled on some obscure cult dedicated to hedonistic consumption. The best response is to go with it.

Waiters in Seville are famed for their 'recital of the *tapas*', a well-rehearsed inventory of the day's tasty specials that will usually include excellent hams, some form of fried fish – probably anchovies (*boquerones*) with mayonnaise – and sizzling shrimp with garlic and chilli.

In Madrid, the choice of tapas is as big as the country. The capital famously absorbs the premier produce and ideas from around the nation and adopts them as its own. In the space of a city block you can go Galician with grilled octopus or the fried and salty green peppers *pimientos de Padrón*, grab a bowl of Andalucian *gazpacho*, or channel Asturias with some blue *Cabrales* cheese and a glass of cider. Madrid is also home to the legendary Sunday session in the neighbourhood of *La Latina*, whose cobbled, centuries-old laneways are lined with bars serving innovative tapas. But only until 4pm – it is Sunday, after all.

Each region has its preferred *tapas* tipple. In Andalucia it is often a crisp *fino* sherry; in Catalonia it has to be *cava* or a still wine from Penedès; in La Rioja a young *crianza* brings out the best in meaty tidbits, while the Basques prefer a glass of the lightly effervescent white wine *txakoli* with their *pintxos*. In apple-mad Asturias, *tapas* are mostly consumed with a freshly poured *sidra*, cider.

Bar interiors are not important. They can be festooned with religious icons, like *La Fresquita* bar in Seville, or drab and dusty, like *La Venencia*. *Tapas* are primarily about socialising; the setting is secondary.

Most important of all, *tapas* are class-free and democratic. Politicians might rub shoulders with house-painters, lawyers with landscape gardeners, barristers with baristas. Good food is all very well, but *"el buen rollo"* – great times, good vibes – are the heart of the *tapas* experience.

Basque *Pintxos*

The polar opposite to *La Venencia* is found in San Sebastian, the sophisticated beach resort of the Basque Country. Everyone knows San Sebastian (called Donostia in Basque) has more Michelin stars per capita than anywhere on Earth, but the culinary excellence of its celebrated restaurants has also filtered down to its bar food.

In the atmospheric taverns of the old city or *casco viejo*, the preparation of *tapas* – known as *Pintxos* here – has evolved into a high art where chefs channel their talents into displays of *la alta cocina en miniatura*, haute cuisine in miniature.

Renowned bars like *Aloña Berri* in the heart of the Baroque old city create visual and gastronomical delights such as *milhojas*, millefeuilles of potato layered with mushrooms, sliced apple and foie gras. Or 'sea foam', a designer dish of salt-cod brandade, purple potato, seaweed and trout roe. At nearby *A Fuego Negro*, a few dollars buys patrons a plate of *elBulli*-inspired ham and almond foam with sweetbreads.

A night of tapeo in San Sebastian will confirm that this is truly the home of the finest bar snacks in the world.

Opposite: Casa Vallés Pintxos Bar, San Sebastian, Basque Country.

Atún fresco con cebollitas
Fresh tuna with baby onions & olives

Ingredients

2 tablespoons red wine vinegar
4 sprigs fresh thyme
60ml olive oil
Flaked salt
Freshly cracked black pepper
250g fresh tuna steaks
2 tablespoons plain (all-purpose) flour
10 cocktail onions
2 garlic cloves, crushed
10 whole black olives, pitted
Thyme leaves, extra, to serve

Method

Place vinegar, thyme and only two tablespoons of oil into a shallow glass or ceramic dish. Season to taste. Add tuna and coat in the marinade. Cover and set aside to marinate for 30 minutes.

Place flour onto a plate and season lightly with salt and pepper. Drain tuna, reserving the marinade. Coat tuna in flour, shaking off the excess.

Heat remaining oil in a large non-stick frying pan over high heat and cook tuna for 2-3 minutes on each side or until well sealed. Transfer to a side plate and cover loosely with foil to keep warm.

Reduce heat to medium, add onions and cook for 5-8 minutes or until golden brown, stirring occasionally. Add garlic and cook, stirring for a further 2 minutes.

Add reserved marinade and olives to the pan. Simmer, uncovered, for 3 minutes or until sauce has thickened slightly. Return tuna to the frying pan, spoon the sauce over and allow to heat through.

Serve sprinkled with extra thyme leaves.

Deliciosos tomates cherry
Tasty cherry tomatoes

Ingredients

20 whole ripe cherry tomatoes

Filling:
1 garlic clove, crushed
120g smoked salmon, finely chopped
2 tablespoons finely chopped red onion
50g soft goat's cheese*
1 teaspoon finely chopped fresh oregano leaves
2 teaspoons finely chopped fresh flat-leaf (Italian) parsley
Flaked salt
Freshly cracked black pepper

Method

Cut a thin slice from the base of each tomato to make it stable. Cut a circle, 2cm in diameter, into the top of each tomato and scoop out the flesh with a small spoon; discard flesh. Place the tomatoes upside down on kitchen paper towel to drain for 5 minutes.

To make filling, place garlic, salmon, onion, cheese, oregano and parsley into a medium bowl. Mix well and season to taste.

Use a teaspoon to spoon the filling into the tomatoes. Serve.

* Refer to Glossary – Page 482

Almendras saladas
Salted almonds

Ingredients

2 tablespoons olive oil
1 egg white, lightly beaten
200g raw almond kernels
1 tablespoon coarse sea salt, finely ground
½ teaspoon smoked paprika*

Spanish fast food could be as simple as a bag of sunflower seeds or a handful of almonds, perhaps cooked with toffee or served freshly toasted. The Spanish are picky about their almonds, because they arguably grow the best in the world. The best can be found in large city markets and in shops that are popular with Middle Eastern customers.

Method

Preheat oven to 200°C.

Line a baking tray with kitchen baking paper. Drizzle oil over the paper.

Place egg whites and almonds into a medium bowl and mix well. Add salt and paprika and toss gently until almonds are well coated.

Spread nuts in a single layer onto the baking tray and bake in preheated oven for 6-8 minutes or until golden. Toss once during cooking.

Leave the nuts to cool on the tray. Serve.

Note – Salted almonds can be stored in an airtight container for up to 1 week.

Espárragos enrollados con jamón
Jamon-wrapped asparagus with fennel salad

Ingredients

12 fresh green asparagus spears
Flaked salt
Freshly cracked black pepper
6 slices jamon* or prosciutto
2 tablespoons olive oil
2 whole baby fennel
1 garlic clove, crushed
1 teaspoon olive oil, extra
1 lemon, juiced
1 tablespoon sliced pitted green olives
1 tablespoon sliced pitted black olives
Feathery fennel tips, to serve (optional)

Method

Preheat oven to 180°C.

Trim ends of asparagus, and season lightly with salt and pepper.

Cut jamon slices in half and wrap around each asparagus spear. Brush each spear well with oil.

Line a baking tray with kitchen baking paper, then place asparagus spears in a single layer onto the tray. Bake in preheated oven for 10-12 minutes or until tender.

Meanwhile, very thinly slice the fennel with a sharp knife or mandolin*. Place fennel into a large bowl and add garlic, oil, lemon juice and olives. Season to taste and toss gently to combine.

Garnish asparagus spears with fennel tips, if you choose, and serve with salad.

Tip: The jamon-wrapped asparagus could also be char-grilled or barbecued.

(See photo on previous page).

* Refer to Glossary – Page 482

Flores de calabacín rellenas
Manchego stuffed zucchini flowers

Ingredients

18 zucchini (courgette)* flowers

Pine nut sauce:
80g pine nuts
Pinch of saffron threads*
2 teaspoons flaked salt
80ml extra virgin olive oil
1 medium brown onion, finely chopped
1 teaspoon sweet paprika*
2 garlic cloves, crushed
15g fresh breadcrumbs*
400g can chopped tomatoes
250ml salt-reduced chicken stock

Filling:
8 whole black olives, pitted and finely chopped
2 anchovy fillets*, drained and finely chopped
120g manchego cheese*, finely grated
2 teaspoons finely chopped fresh oregano leaves
Flaked salt
Freshly cracked black pepper

Batter:
100g plain (all-purpose) flour
1 teaspoon flaked salt
1 tablespoon oil
150ml chilled beer
1 egg white
Vegetable or canola oil for deep frying
Lemon wedges, to serve

Tip: Don't overfill the flowers as the filling may fall out during frying.

Calabacín (zucchini or courgette) is a popular Spanish vegetable, its bright yellow and voluminous flowers make a natural receptacle for all manner of stuffing, before it's coated in batter and deep-fried. Some may consider putting a warm teaspoon of the bacalao al ajoarriero, see page 112. This filling of cheese and olives with a pine nut saffron sauce is just as delicious.

Method

Preheat oven to 180°C.

To prepare zucchini flowers, use your thumbs to gently open the flower petals and expose the stamens. Use fingertips to snap off and discard yellow stamens in centre of each flower.

To make the sauce, spread pine nuts onto a baking tray and toast in preheated oven for 10 minutes, stirring occasionally until fragrant and lightly golden. Transfer to a plate to cool.

Place saffron and salt into a mortar, then pound with the pestle until combined. Add half the toasted pine nuts and pound until finely ground.

In a medium frying pan, heat 2 tablespoons of oil over medium heat. Add onion and cook for 8 minutes, stirring occasionally. Add paprika, garlic, saffron mixture and breadcrumbs. Cook for 3 minutes, stirring. Add tomatoes and stock, bring to the boil and simmer uncovered for a further 5-8 minutes or until thickened slightly, stirring occasionally. Taste and season further, if you choose. Roughly chop remaining pine nuts and add to sauce. Set aside.

Reduce oven temperature to 140°C.

To make the filling, place olives, anchovies, cheese and oregano into a large bowl. Season to taste. Use a teaspoon to spoon 1-2 spoonfuls of mixture into the centre of each flower, then twist flower petal tips to enclose the filling.

To make the batter, place flour and salt in a medium bowl. Add oil and beer then whisk until a smooth batter forms. Whisk egg white in a small bowl until soft peaks form. Gently fold the beaten egg white into the batter.

Heat oil in a deep fryer or large heavy-based saucepan over medium-high heat. Dip stuffed flowers into the batter one at a time, and cook in batches or 3-4 at a time in hot oil until lightly golden. The flowers will float to the top as they cook.

Place cooked flowers onto a wire rack sitting on an oven tray (to collect oil drips) to drain. Keep warm in preheated oven until all the flowers are cooked. Serve immediately with prepared pine nut sauce and lemon wedges.

* Refer to Glossary – Page 482

Gambas al cava
Shrimp with cava

Ingredients

16 whole medium green shrimp
(king prawns)*

1 tablespoon olive oil

1 medium red onion, finely chopped

2 garlic cloves, crushed

2 vine-ripened tomatoes, deseeded
and finely chopped

250ml cava* or sparkling wine

1-2 teaspoons flaked salt

2 tablespoons chopped fresh flat-leaf
(Italian) parsley, to serve

Method

Peel and de-vein shrimp, leaving tails intact.

Heat oil in a large frying pan over medium heat and cook onion,
garlic and tomato, for 5-8 minutes, stirring occasionally.

Add cava and simmer uncovered over low heat for 5-8 minutes,
stirring occasionally. Add the shrimps and stir into the sauce. Cook
a further 3-4 minutes or until just cooked through. Season to taste
with salt.

Serve sprinkled with parsley.

Habas con jamón
Broad beans with jamon

Ingredients

1 tablespoon olive oil

20g butter

100g lean bacon, roughly chopped

100g jamon* or prosciutto, roughly
chopped

1 medium brown onion, finely chopped

2 garlic cloves, crushed

60ml white wine

125ml salt-reduced chicken stock

300g frozen or fresh broad beans,
blanched and peeled

Flaked salt

Freshly cracked black pepper

2 tablespoons chopped fresh flat-leaf
(Italian) parsley (optional)

Method

Heat oil and butter in a large frying pan over medium-high heat and
cook the bacon and jamon for 3-5 minutes or until lightly golden.

Add onion and garlic, cook a further 5 minutes, stirring
occasionally, until onion is soft but not coloured.

Add wine, stock and broad beans. Bring to the boil, simmer
uncovered for 10-15 minutes, or until beans are tender and sauce
has reduced and thickened. Season to taste.

Serve garnished with parsley.

* Refer to Glossary – Page 482

Pulpo a la Gallega
Slow-cooked Galician octopus

Ingredients

2kg whole medium-large octopus
4 whole cloves
1 medium brown onion, peeled
2 litres water
4 dried bay leaves
60ml extra virgin olive oil
2-3 teaspoons smoked paprika*
Flaked salt

When done properly, this is one of the most wonderful dishes in the world. Little disks of perfectly rich, salty octopus drizzled with sweet olive oil and finished with smoky paprika.

Naturally, this is washed down with a light red, but it's also good with a textural white wine, perhaps an Albariño from the Rías Baixas bayside vineyards of Galicia.

You'll find this dish across Spain, as the Galicians are the 'Irish of the Iberia' and are traditionally big emigrators. Unfortunately, the dish itself doesn't emigrate as well in the bars across Spain, as the rich flavours tend to be dulled down when refrigerated, as necessitated by health regulations. The best version of this dish is made at home or served fresh from the pot in a bar on Galicia's wet, green coast.

Method

Clean octopus and leave bodies whole. Wash well and place into a large saucepan. Press the cloves into the onion and place into saucepan with water and bay leaves.

Cover saucepan and bring to a gentle boil over medium-high heat. Reduce heat to low and simmer, covered, for 40-50 minutes or until octopus is tender (a skewer or the point of a sharp knife should be able to be inserted easily).

Remove cooked octopus from water and set aside to cool slightly for 15 minutes; use kitchen paper towel to rub off the purplish skin.

Cut tentacles into slices (about 1cm thick) and place into serving bowl. Drizzle with oil, sprinkle with paprika and season with salt to taste.

* Refer to Glossary – Page 482

Tostada con tomate y anchoas
Tostada with tomato & anchovies

Ingredients

6 slices white bread, crusts removed

1 large garlic clove, peeled and halved

2 tablespoons extra virgin olive oil

3 small vine-ripened tomatoes

6 anchovy fillets*, drained and finely chopped

2 tablespoons finely chopped fresh oregano leaves

Freshly cracked black pepper

Method

Preheat oven to 180°C.

Cut 2 circles from each bread slice with a 5cm cutter. Place onto a baking tray and rub bread slices with cut side of the garlic clove and drizzle with oil. Bake in preheated oven for 5-8 minutes or until golden.

Thinly slice only two of the tomatoes. Halve and deseed remaining tomato, then finely chop. Place tomato slices onto toasted bread.

Place chopped tomato, anchovies and only half the oregano into a bowl. Stir well and season to taste with pepper. Spoon the mixture on top of the tomato slices and sprinkle with remaining oregano.

Serve immediately.

Tip: You could also make this recipe with a spread of olive tapenade topped with smoked trout and sprinkled with chopped dill.

Calamares con mayonesa de ajo
Squid with garlic mayonnaise

Ingredients

600g whole squid (calamari), cleaned and rinsed

35g cornflour

90g fine semolina*

1 teaspoon smoked paprika*

½ teaspoon ground chilli

Flaked salt

Freshly cracked black pepper

Oil for deep frying

Garlic mayonnaise:

250g egg mayonnaise*

2 garlic cloves, crushed

1 lemon, juiced

Method

Cut squid in half lengthways down the middle and open out into one larger piece. Score shallow diagonal slashes in a criss-cross pattern on the inside surface of the flesh. Then cut into pieces about 2cm x 6cm. Pat dry with kitchen paper towel.

Place cornflour, semolina, paprika, chilli, salt and pepper into a large bowl or a plastic bag, then add squid and shake well to coat. Remove squid from bowl, shaking off the excess and transfer to a side plate until ready to cook.

To make the garlic mayonnaise, place egg mayonnaise, garlic and lemon juice into a small bowl and mix well.

Heat oil in a deep fryer or heavy-based deep saucepan over medium-high heat and cook squid in batches for 2-3 minutes or until golden. Drain on crumpled kitchen paper towel. Serve with garlic mayonnaise.

Tip: To test if oil is hot enough, drop a cube of bread in; if it sizzles the oil is ready.

* Refer to Glossary – Page 482

Huevos con pisto
Eggs on pisto

Ingredients

2 tablespoons olive oil

1 medium brown onion, finely chopped

2 garlic cloves, crushed

1 zucchini (courgette)*, finely chopped

1 small red pepper (capsicum)*, halved, deseeded and finely chopped

1 green banana pepper (capsicum)*, halved, deseeded and finely chopped

45g Serrano jamon* or prosciutto, chopped

1 medium ripe tomato, deseeded and finely chopped

½ teaspoon chilli powder

Flaked salt

Freshly cracked black pepper

4 eggs, preferably free-range

2 tablespoons chopped fresh flat-leaf (Italian) parsley, to serve

Method

Preheat oven to 190°C.

Heat oil in a large frying pan, over medium heat. Cook onion for 5-8 minutes or until soft but not coloured. Add garlic, zucchini and peppers and cook a further 5-8 minutes, stirring occasionally. Add jamon, tomato and chilli powder and cook for 5 minutes. Season to taste.

Divide the mixture between four small ovenproof dishes and bake in preheated oven for 15 minutes.

Remove from oven and crack an egg into each dish. Return to oven, cover and bake for a further 5-8 minutes or until eggs are cooked.

Sprinkle with parsley and serve hot.

Note – Pisto is a Spanish version of ratatouille, which is often served with egg and some bread or as an accompaniment to a main dish.

Pinchos de salmón ahumado y rábanos
Smoked salmon & radish pinchos

Ingredients

5 slices rustic white bread

40ml olive oil

5 radishes

70g sliced smoked salmon

60g egg mayonnaise*

1 tablespoon capers*, finely chopped

Extra virgin olive oil, to serve

Freshly cracked black pepper

Toothpicks

Method

Preheat oven to 180°C.

Use a 5cm round cutter to cut 2 circles out of each bread slice. Lightly brush both sides with oil and place onto a baking tray. Toast the bread in the preheated oven for 8 minutes or until lightly golden. Remove.

Cut the radish into very thin circles. Cut the salmon slices in half to obtain 2 pieces from each slice. Place the mayonnaise into a small bowl and add the capers, stir to combine.

To assemble, spread the toasted bread with about 1 teaspoon of mayonnaise, top with a radish slice then loosely fold/roll the salmon and secure it to the bread with a toothpick.

Serve drizzled with olive oil and seasoned with pepper.

* Refer to Glossary – Page 482

Palitos de hojaldre con manchego y anchoas
Pastry sticks with manchego & anchovies

makes 12

Ingredients

1 sheet pre-rolled puff pastry*
100g manchego cheese*
12 anchovy fillets*, drained
1 egg
2 tablespoons milk

Method

Preheat oven to 190°C.

Filling

Preheat oven to 200°C. Line a baking tray with kitchen baking paper.

Cut the sheet of pastry into 12 equal rectangular pieces (about 6cm x 4cm). Thinly slice cheese into similar size pieces.

Top each piece of pastry with a slice of cheese and an anchovy. Roll up from one corner to another to enclose filling and place onto prepared tray. Place egg and milk into a small bowl and whisk to combine; lightly brush mixture over pastry.

Bake in preheated oven for 10-15 minutes or until golden. Serve immediately.

Tiras de lenguado con mayonesa
Lemon sole strips with dill mayonnaise

makes 16

Ingredients

2 whole lemon sole, cleaned and filleted
75g plain (all-purpose) flour
Flaked salt
Freshly cracked black pepper
2 eggs, lightly beaten
75g dried breadcrumbs
Vegetable oil for shallow frying

Dill mayonnaise:
1 cup egg mayonnaise*
2 tablespoons finely chopped fresh dill
1 teaspoon finely grated lime rind
3 teaspoons lime juice
Flaked salt
Freshly cracked black pepper

Method

When filleted, each fish should result in four fillets (two from each side). Cut each fillet in half again to make bite-sized pieces.

Place flour into a medium bowl, and season lightly with salt and pepper. Place eggs into a second bowl and breadcrumbs into a third bowl.

Coat the fish by first putting into flour, shaking off the excess, then into egg mix and finally into breadcrumbs. Press the crumbs onto the fish.

Heat oil in a large frying pan over high heat. Cook fish in 2 batches for 2 minutes each side or until lightly golden and cooked through. Drain on crumpled kitchen paper towel. Serve immediately with dill mayonnaise.

To make the dill mayonnaise, place egg mayonnaise, dill, rind and juice into a medium bowl and mix well. Season to taste. Cover and set aside.

* Refer to Glossary – Page 482

Aceitunas negras maceradas con ajo y chili
Chilli & garlic marinated black olives

Ingredients

500g whole black Spanish olives, drained with brine reserved

4 garlic cloves, thinly sliced

2 dried whole red chillies

8 black peppercorns

1 slice lemon

4 sprigs fresh flat-leaf (Italian) parsley

4 fresh bay leaves

2 teaspoons flaked salt

300ml red wine vinegar

Method

Place olives, garlic, chillies, peppercorns, lemon, parsley, bay leaves and salt into a large bowl and mix well. Transfer to a jar with a non-corrosive (plastic or plastic-coated) lid, large enough to fit the olives. Pour the vinegar over the olives and enough of the reserved brine to completely cover them.

Shake well and marinate at room temperature for 2 weeks.

Tip: The olives will keep for up to 1 month in the refrigerator; ideally, serve at room temperature for the best flavour.

Aceitunas verdes maceradas con especias
Herb-marinated green olives

Ingredients

500g whole green olives, drained with brine reserved

6 garlic cloves, thinly sliced

1 tablespoon crushed whole coriander seeds

1 tablespoon crushed whole fennel seeds

6 sprigs fresh thyme

4 sprigs fresh rosemary

1 orange, rind finely grated, then juiced

200ml good quality extra virgin olive oil

Method

Place the olives, garlic, coriander, fennel, thyme, rosemary, rind and juice into a large bowl. Mix well to combine then transfer to a jar with a non-corrosive (plastic or plastic-coated) lid, large enough to fit the olives. Pour the oil over the olives and enough of the reserved brine to completely cover.

Shake well and marinate at room temperature for 6 days.

Tip: The olives will keep for up to 1 month in the refrigerator; ideally, serve at room temperature for the best flavour.

Tortilla de patatas
Potato tortilla

Ingredients

100ml olive oil

750g medium waxy potatoes
(e.g, Desiree), peeled
and thinly sliced

1 medium brown onion, finely chopped

Flaked salt

Freshly cracked black pepper

6 eggs, preferably free-range*

2 tablespoons finely chopped fresh
flat-leaf (Italian) parsley, to serve

Method

Heat oil in a heavy-based, 24-25cm frying pan with deep sides over medium heat. Add the potatoes and onion and season with salt and pepper. Reduce heat to low and cook for 20-25 minutes. Stir frequently so vegetables cook evenly.

Meanwhile, place eggs into a medium bowl, season well with salt and pepper and lightly whisk.

When potato and onions are cooked, use a slotted spoon to transfer them from the frying pan to a side plate; reserve any remaining oil.

Wipe frying pan with kitchen paper towel, then return 60ml of the reserved oil to the pan. Return potatoes and onion to the pan and spread out to form an even layer.

Pour egg mixture evenly over vegetables. Cook for 10 minutes over low heat or until the tortilla is still a little soft in the centre.

Position a large plate over the pan and quickly invert the tortilla on to it. Carefully slide the tortilla back into the pan and cook for a further 2-3 minutes, which will cook and set the base.

Slide out onto a serving plate, top with parsley and serve warm or cold.

Tip: For variety, add different fresh herbs, such as basil or oregano.

* Refer to Glossary – Page 482

Pastel de carne de cordero
Lamb & red pepper meatloaf

Ingredients

500g lean minced lamb

45g quick-cooking oats or dried breadcrumbs

1 medium brown onion, finely grated

2 garlic cloves, crushed

2 roasted* red peppers (capsicum)*, finely chopped

1 tablespoon finely chopped fresh oregano leaves

1 egg, lightly beaten

1 tablespoon tomato paste*

1 teaspoon Dijon mustard

1 tablespoon Worcestershire sauce

Flaked salt

Freshly cracked black pepper

50g manchego* cheese, finely grated

4-6 ripe cherry tomatoes, halved

Method

Preheat oven to 180°C.

Lightly grease a large loaf ovenproof dish or pan about 20cm x 15cm.

Place the mince, oats, onion, garlic, peppers, oregano, egg, tomato paste, mustard and Worcestershire sauce into a large bowl and mix well with a clean hand to combine. Season with salt and pepper.

Place the mixture into the prepared loaf dish, pressing firmly to compact the meat into the dish. Top with cheese then tomato halves.

Bake in preheated oven for 20-30 minutes or until firm and cooked through.

Serve.

Pinchos de salmón y aceitunas
Green olive, artichoke & salmon pinchos

Ingredients

120g jar stuffed Spanish green olives*, drained

200g sliced smoked salmon

10 artichoke halves

Good quality extra virgin olive oil, to serve

Picked fresh lemon thyme leaves, to serve

Wooden skewers

Method

To assemble, thread an olive, a loosely folded piece of salmon, artichoke half and two more olives onto a skewer.

Serve drizzled with olive oil and sprinkle with lemon thyme.

Tip: These are easy to assemble, however if you think the artichoke halves you have are a little big, simply cut in half. Cut the salmon slices in half to get two pieces from each slice.

Note – Spanish green stuffed olives are readily available and varieties include stuffed with peppers, or lemon or anchovies.

* Refer to Glossary – Page 482

Patatas con chorizo
Chorizo & potatoes

Ingredients

500g chat (new) potatoes, cut into
2cm chunks

60ml olive oil

300g Spanish chorizo sausage*, cut into
2cm chunks

100ml dry sherry

Flaked salt

Freshly cracked black pepper

¼ cup chopped fresh flat-leaf (Italian)
parsley, to serve

Packed with smoky Spanish paprika, herbs and garlic, a chorizo isn't just a little pack of protein but also a powerful flavouring agent. The spice-laden fat renders out as it cooks, which is essential in flavoursome Spanish cooking. Here, we're cooking new potatoes in this fat, which gives them a punchy flavour.

Method

Cook potatoes in a large saucepan of lightly salted boiling water for 5 minutes or until slightly softened. Drain.

Heat only half the oil in a large frying pan over medium-high heat and gently fry the potatoes, stirring frequently, for 8-10 minutes or until they are lightly golden. Transfer the potatoes with a slotted spoon to a side plate.

Add remaining oil to the frying pan and cook the chorizo for a further 5 minutes until lightly browned. Remove the pan from the heat and stir in the sherry. Return to heat and cook gently, stirring frequently, until the sherry has almost evaporated.

Return potatoes to the pan, season to taste and heat through for 2 minutes before serving with parsley.

* Refer to Glossary – Page 482

Patatas bravas
Pan fried potatoes with tomato sauce

Ingredients

1kg all-purpose potatoes
60ml vegetable oil for frying
2 tablespoons freshly chopped coriander
leaves, to serve

Sauce:
1 tablespoon olive oil
2 medium garlic cloves, chopped
1 teaspoon smoked paprika*
¼ teaspoon ground cumin
¼ teaspoon chilli* powder
250ml tomato passata
1 tablespoon red wine vinegar
Flaked salt

Method

Peel potatoes and cut into 3cm cubes. Pat dry with kitchen paper towel. Heat the oil for frying in a large heavy-based frying pan over medium heat. Add only half the potatoes and cook for 8-10 minutes until lightly golden and tender. Drain on kitchen paper towel and cook the remaining potatoes.

Make the sauce by heating the oil in a medium frying pan over low-medium heat. Add garlic, paprika, cumin and chilli and cook for 1 minute or until aromatic, stirring continuously. Add the passata, stir and bring to a gentle simmer. Cook for a further 2 minutes. Stir in vinegar and season with salt to taste.

Serve potatoes drizzled with sauce and sprinkled with chopped coriander.

Tip: Preheat oven to 100°C to keep the first cooked potatoes warm while cooking the second batch.

* Refer to Glossary – Page 482

Boquerones en vinagre
Marinated anchovies

Little marinated fish, boquerones are the cornerstone of many tapas and pintxos (Basque bar snacks) across the country. When skewered on a toothpick with an olive and a pickled onion they become a banderilla. On their own they're a salty little hit, perfect with a little beer or sherry.

Ingredients

250g fresh whole anchovies, butterflied*
100ml white wine vinegar
200ml good quality extra virgin olive oil
3 garlic cloves, thinly sliced
1 tablespoon finely chopped fresh flat-leaf (Italian) parsley

Method

You will need to make this dish two days in advance to allow time for the anchovies to marinate.

Pat anchovies dry with kitchen paper towel and place into a glass bowl with the vinegar. Marinate in the refrigerator overnight.

Drain anchovies and discard vinegar. Lightly rinse anchovies under cold running water and pat dry with kitchen paper towel. Place into a serving dish or glass container and add oil, garlic and parsley.

Cover and chill overnight in the refrigerator. Allow anchovies to return to room temperature before serving with bread or as an accompaniment to another dish.

Salsa Mediterránea
Mediterranean dip

makes about 300ml

Method

Preheat oven to 200°C. Line a baking tray with kitchen baking paper. Place pepper halves and the whole eggplant onto a tray and bake for 30 minutes or until skin blisters and they are tender. Remove and cover with foil and allow to cool for as long as possible. Remove the skin from the peppers and eggplant and chop. Discard the skins.

Make a crisscross cut into the base of the tomato and place into a heatproof bowl, cover with boiling water and stand for 1-2 minutes. Drain and remove skin. Chop flesh into chunks.

Heat the oil in a large frying pan over medium heat. Add the peppers, eggplant and tomatoes, cook for 5 minutes, stirring constantly. Add garlic, sugar, paprika, cumin and coriander and cook for 1-2 minutes or until aromatic.

Place into the bowl of a food processor or blender and process until smooth. Garnish with fresh coriander and serve hot or cold with toasted bread.

(See photo on previous page).

Ingredients

1 large red pepper (capsicum)*, halved and deseeded
1 medium eggplant (aubergine)*
1 large vine-ripened tomato
40ml olive oil
2 garlic cloves, thinly sliced
½ teaspoon granulated sugar
¼ teaspoon paprika*
¼ teaspoon ground cumin
¼ teaspoon ground coriander
1 tablespoon chopped fresh coriander leaves, to serve (optional)
Toasted bread, to serve

* Refer to Glossary – Page 482

Bacalao al ajoarriero
Salt cod potato cakes with roasted red pepper

Ingredients

500g salted cod*

300g all-purpose potatoes, peeled and cut into chunks

2 garlic cloves, crushed

2 egg yolks

2 tablespoons plain (all-purpose) flour

½ teaspoon white pepper

Oil for shallow frying

2 roasted* medium red peppers (capsicums)*

2 teaspoons fish sauce

100g crème fraiche*, to serve

Tiny sprigs of fresh thyme leaves, to serve

Salt cod can be found in every nook and cranny of Spain; from the highest peaks in Pyrenees to the most remote valleys of Extremadura, many hundreds of kilometres from the nearest coastline. It's the foundation for countless scores of dishes.

Over the centuries bacalao made its way into every kitchen, and, therefore, the heart of every Spaniard along the vein-thin network of sheep tracks and mule paths that have intersected the Iberian Peninsula since time immemorial.

Shepherds and mule drivers took garlic and salt cod with them as they worked away from the towns. Mixed with vegetables or bread it became a hearty staple. The words ajo and arriero are 'garlic' and 'mule driver'. This is mule drivers' cod – a centuries-old recipe that's still served smeared on bread in bars across Spain.

Rich, slightly salty and extremely delicious, it's a lovely way to start a meal or to enjoy at a picnic with a loaf of rustic bread.

Method

First, soak the salted cod; begin preparation the day before (36 hours before if possible). Brush any excess salt off the cod and place cod into a large bowl and cover with cold water. Refrigerate for 12 hours. Drain water and repeat soaking step twice. Cut cod into large pieces.

Place cod and potatoes into a large saucepan. Add enough cold water to just cover and bring to the boil over medium heat. Reduce heat to low and simmer gently for 10-15 minutes or until potatoes are tender. Drain water, return potatoes to the pan and transfer cod to a side plate; when cool enough to handle, flake cod into small pieces, discarding skin and bones.

To the potatoes, add garlic, egg yolks, flour and pepper and mash together. Add the flaked cod and mix well to combine. Take a dessertspoonful of the mixture in your hands, shape it into balls and flatten into little cakes. Place onto a tray lined with kitchen baking paper.

Heat oil in a large frying pan over medium-high heat and cook the potato cakes in batches for 3-4 minutes each side or until golden. Place on crumpled kitchen paper towel to drain.

Meanwhile, deseed and finely chop the peppers. Place peppers and fish sauce into a small bowl and stir; set aside until ready to serve.

To serve, spoon a little crème fraiche on top of each potato cake, top with pepper mixture and thyme leaves. Serve immediately.

* Refer to Glossary – Page 482

Bocados de manchego
Manchego bites

Ingredients

250g manchego cheese*

35g plain (all-purpose) flour

1 teaspoon smoked paprika*

1 teaspoon flaked salt

1 teaspoon ground white pepper

1 egg

1 teaspoon water

70g lightly toasted fresh breadcrumbs*

Olive oil for shallow frying

Membrillo (quince paste)*, to serve

Method

Slice cheese into even pieces, about 2cm thick, then cut into triangles or thick strips.

Place flour, paprika, salt and pepper into a small bowl and mix well. Place egg and water into another small bowl and whisk with a fork to combine. In a third bowl, place the breadcrumbs.

Coat the cheese pieces first in the seasoned flour, shaking off the excess, then into egg mix and, finally, into breadcrumbs. Press breadcrumbs onto the cheese and set aside on a plate.

Heat oil in a large heavy-based frying pan and cook the cheese in 2-3 batches for about 30 seconds or until lightly golden on both sides. Drain on crumpled kitchen paper towel.

Serve immediately with membrillo.

Tip: If, after a few batches, the oil contains many small burnt breadcrumbs, discard the oil, wipe out the frying pan with kitchen paper towel and replace with fresh oil. Heat and continue cooking.

Huevos a la Navarra
Navarra-style eggs

Ingredients

60ml olive oil

1 small brown onion, finely chopped

1 garlic clove, crushed

60g jamon*, Serrano jamon* or prosciutto, chopped

100g Pamplona* cured sausage (or Spanish chorizo sausage*), chopped

125ml tomato puree*

½ teaspoon hot paprika*

Flaked salt

Fleshly cracked black pepper

4 free-range eggs*

20g butter, at room temperature

1 Pamplona* sausage (or Spanish chorizo sausage*), sliced, extra

Fried bread strips, to serve

Method

Preheat oven to 190°C.

Heat oil in a large frying pan over medium heat and cook the onion, garlic, jamon and Pamplona sausage for 5 minutes, stirring occasionally. Add tomato puree, paprika, salt and pepper and cook for a further 2 minutes.

Divide sauce between 4 lightly greased ovenproof ramekins and break an egg into each dish. Top each egg with a dollop of butter and place extra sausage slices around the edge of the egg.

Bake in preheated oven for 8-10 minutes or until whites are set and yolks are still a little runny.

Serve with strips of fried bread.

* Refer to Glossary – Page 482

Empanadilla de aceitunas y jamón
Empanadilla of olives & jamon

makes 27

Ingredients

2 tablespoons olive oil
1 large red onion, finely chopped
2 garlic cloves, crushed
4 slices jamon* or prosciutto, chopped
4 slices hot salami, chopped
400g can chopped tomatoes
2 hard-boiled* eggs, chopped
40g green olives, pitted and finely chopped
25g finely grated manchego cheese*
Flaked salt
Freshly cracked black pepper
3 sheets pre-rolled puff pastry*
1 egg, lightly beaten

It would seem every culture in the world has a little hand-held dish of pastry filled with meat and vegetables – from India's samosa to Cornwall's pasty. Spain's version is a deep-fried (or baked) morsel that's finished in a few bites. Found in bars and cafés, it can be filled with salt cod or a creamy sauce. These empanadillas are also filled with eggs and garlic, making them perfect with a glass of chilled dry sherry.

Method

Preheat oven to 180°C.

Heat oil in a medium frying pan over medium heat and cook onion and garlic for 5-8 minutes, stirring occasionally. Add jamon and salami and cook for a further 3 minutes.

Add tomatoes and simmer, uncovered, for 5-8 minutes or until tomato juice has evaporated and mixture has thickened a little. Remove from heat and cool completely.

Fold in eggs, olives and cheese. Season to taste.

Then line two baking trays with kitchen baking paper.

From each pastry sheet, cut out 9 circles using a 7cm cutter. Place a spoonful of cooled mixture into the centre of each round. Fold over, pressing the edges together with a fork to seal them.

Place the empanadillas onto the prepared trays, leaving a 2cm gap between each one. Brush with egg and bake in preheated oven for 15-20 minutes or until golden.

Serve hot or warm with *Mojo colorado* (Red sauce), see page 156.

* Refer to Glossary – Page 482

Pescadito frito con aliolí
Whitebait with alioli

Ingredients

75g plain (all-purpose) flour
1 teaspoon ground cumin
1 teaspoon Spanish smoked paprika*
2 teaspoons smoked sea salt*
1 teaspoon finely grated lime rind
300g fresh whole whitebait
Vegetable or canola oil for deep-frying
Extra smoked sea salt*, to serve (optional)
Alioli (see sauce chapter), to serve
Lime wedges, to serve (optional)

Method

Place the flour, cumin, paprika, salt and lime rind into a large bowl or a plastic bag and shake well to combine.

Pat whitebait dry with kitchen paper towel then coat in the seasoned flour, shaking off excess flour.

Heat oil in a large heavy-based saucepan or deep fryer over medium-high heat. Fry whitebait in batches for 5 minutes or until crisp and golden. Drain on crumpled kitchen paper towel.

Serve immediately with extra smoked salt, alioli and lime wedges.

Note – Whitebait are very small fish, usually about 4-5cm in length, which are generally cooked and served whole and uncleaned.

Champiñones rellenos
Chorizo & herb-stuffed mushrooms

Ingredients

12 medium-sized mushrooms
60ml olive oil
60g butter
1 medium brown onion, grated
3 garlic cloves, crushed
45g finely chopped jamon* or prosciutto
1 Spanish chorizo* sausage, skin removed, meat crumbled
15g fresh breadcrumbs*, toasted
2 tablespoons finely chopped fresh flat-leaf (Italian) parsley
1 tablespoon finely chopped fresh marjoram leaves
Flaked salt
Freshly cracked black pepper
25g manchego* cheese, grated

Method

Preheat oven to 200°C.

Wipe mushrooms tops over with slightly damp kitchen paper towel. Remove the stems then finely chop stems and reserve.

Heat the oil and butter in a large frying pan over medium heat. Add whole mushrooms and cook for 2-3 minutes or until browned on each side. Transfer to a baking dish.

Reheat frying pan over medium-high heat and add mushroom stems, onion, garlic, jamon and chorizo. Cook for 5 minutes stirring occasionally. Add breadcrumbs, parsley and marjoram. Season to taste.

Spoon and divide the mixture between the mushroom caps, sprinkle with cheese and bake in preheated oven for 10-15 minutes or until cheese is melted.

Serve straight from baking dish or transfer to a platter.

Pollo con especias y páprika
Paprika & herb-coated chicken

Ingredients

2 skinless chicken breast fillets

2 lemons

1 tablespoon sweet paprika*

Flaked salt

Freshly cracked black pepper

75g plain (all-purpose) flour

2 eggs, lightly beaten

35g dried breadcrumbs

1 teaspoon finely chopped fresh oregano

2 teaspoons finely chopped fresh coriander

Vegetable oil for deep frying

Lemon wedges, to serve

Mojo verde (see recipe, page 152), to serve

Method

Cut chicken into strips (about 1cm wide). Finely grate the rind of only one lemon and set aside; juice both lemons.

Place lemon juice and paprika into a large glass or ceramic bowl, season to taste and mix well. Add chicken and stir to coat. Cover and marinate in the fridge for 1 hour.

Place flour into a shallow bowl. Place eggs into another small bowl, then into a third bowl, place breadcrumbs, oregano, coriander and season with salt and pepper.

Coat chicken strips by first putting into the flour and shaking off the excess, then into egg mixture and finally into herbed breadcrumbs. Press the crumbs onto the chicken.

Heat oil in a deep fryer or large heavy-based saucepan. Cook the chicken in 2-3 batches for 6-8 minutes or until lightly golden and cooked through. Drain on crumpled kitchen paper towel.

Serve with lemon wedges and Mojo verde (Green salsa).

Setas fritas picantes
Spicy fried mushrooms

Ingredients

2 tablespoons olive oil

100g butter

250g button mushrooms

250g Swiss brown mushrooms

6 garlic cloves, finely chopped

1 small fresh red chilli*, finely chopped

45g Serrano jamon* or prosciutto, finely chopped

125ml white wine or dry fino or Manzanilla sherry*

¼ cup chopped fresh flat-leaf (Italian) parsley

Flaked salt

Freshly cracked black pepper

4 slices sourdough bread, char-grilled (optional)

Method

Heat oil and butter in a large frying pan, over high heat. Add mushrooms and cook for 8-10 minutes or until mushrooms are tender, stirring occasionally.

Reduce heat to medium and add the garlic, chilli and jamon. Cook for a further 2 minutes. Add wine or sherry and simmer, uncovered, for about 2 minutes or until the liquid has evaporated.

Add the parsley, stir well and season to taste.

Serve with char-grilled sourdough, if desired.

Canapés de tortilla y pimento verde
Green pepper & tortilla canapés

Ingredients

1 potato tortilla (see recipe, page 102)

6 slices white bread, crusts removed

2 tablespoons olive oil

1 small green pepper (capsicum)*, deseeded and thinly sliced

Flaked salt

Freshly cracked black pepper

2 tablespoons finely chopped roasted* red pepper (capsicum)*

2 tablespoons finely chopped pitted Spanish black olives

Method

From the cooked potato tortilla, cut 12 circles using a 6cm cutter; set aside.

Using the same cutter, cut two circles from each slice of bread.

Heat oil in a large frying pan over medium-high heat and cook bread pieces for 2 minutes each side or until lightly golden. Remove and drain on crumpled kitchen paper towel. Add green pepper slices to the frying pan and cook for 2-3 minutes to soften. Season to taste.

To serve, place a piece of potato tortilla on top of a bread round, add green pepper slices and garnish with roasted red pepper and olives.

Serve immediately.

Canapés de jamón y huevo
Jamon & egg canapés

Ingredients

4 slices white bread, crusts removed

2 tablespoons extra virgin olive oil

2 slices jamon* or prosciutto

4 hard-boiled* quail eggs*, halved

Finely chopped chives, to serve

Method

Preheat oven to 180°C.

Cut 2 circles from each bread slice with a 5cm cutter. Place onto a baking tray and drizzle with oil. Bake in preheated oven for 5-8 minutes or until golden.

Cut jamon into 8 thick strips and place a piece onto each bread round. Top with half an egg and secure with a toothpick, if required.

Sprinkle with chives and serve immediately.

Tip: Bread rounds could also be pan fried in olive oil until lightly golden.

Pa amb tomàquet
Catalan tomato bread

Ingredients

1 small baguette (or small rounds of white bread)

2 garlic cloves, halved

3 small vine-ripened tomatoes, halved

60ml extra virgin olive oil

Flaked salt

Freshly cracked black pepper

Albert the Barman at Bar Pinotxo, situated at Barcelona's famous La Boqueria market, plates up little snacks of tomato bread and glasses of cava. The pa amb tomàquet is always good, little pieces of sliced bread, perhaps a baguette, lightly toasted, seasoned with garlic, dressed with extra virgin olive oil and smeared with ripe tomato.

It's the food of the vineyard worker who will tear off some bread, toast it over his fire and prepare it as above, washed down with a bottle of wine that he shares with his co-workers. It's so entrenched in Catalan culture that they have even developed a special variety of juicy, thick-skinned tomato to smear on the bread.

It's also a familiar flavour with the wealthy city dwellers, who will snack on it in train station bars and cafés across the region. They may even celebrate a little moment in life by pausing to order a freshly made pa amb tomàquet with a glass of bubbles.

Albert's cook at Bar Pinotxo never peels his garlic before he rubs it over the bread; he leaves the skin on so he doesn't get the odour of garlic on his fingers.

Method

Slice bread thinly on the diagonal and toast the slices until lightly golden on both sides.

Rub one side of each of the toasted bread slices with the cut side of a garlic clove, then with a tomato half, squeezing the juice from the tomatoes onto the bread.

Drizzle with olive oil and season to taste.

Serve immediately.

Tip: If you can't find juicy tomatoes, grate them instead so that you can coat the bread well, and drizzle with olive oil. For variety, top with crisp jamon* or thinly sliced manchego cheese*.

* Refer to Glossary – Page 482

Pollo al ajillo con un toque de cava
Garlic chicken with a touch of cava

Ingredients

500g chicken thigh fillets, cut into 3cm cubes

1 tablespoon sweet paprika*

Flaked salt

Freshly cracked black pepper

80ml olive oil

6 garlic cloves, halved

3 sprigs fresh thyme

150ml cava* or Manzanilla sherry*

125ml salt-reduced chicken stock

2 tablespoons finely chopped fresh flat-leaf (Italian) parsley

Tip: If the juices in the casserole look too thin after the chicken is cooked transfer the juices to a saucepan and cook over medium to high heat until reduced.

Method

Preheat oven to 200°C. Place chicken and paprika into a large bowl, season with salt and pepper and mix well to combine. Cover and chill for 20 minutes.

Heat oil in a large frying pan over medium heat and cook garlic for 2 minutes or until slightly tender and lightly golden; remove garlic from pan and set aside.

Return pan to high heat and cook chicken for 2 minutes each side or until golden. Remove and arrange chicken in a single layer in a baking dish or ovenproof casserole dish. Sprinkle with the cooked garlic.

Return frying pan to medium heat and add thyme, cava and stock, then increase to high heat and bring to a gentle boil. Pour liquid over the chicken in the baking dish.

Bake chicken, uncovered, in preheated oven for 20-25 minutes or until cooked through. Sprinkle with parsley and serve.

Croquetas de jamón
Jamon croquettes

Ingredients

2 tablespoons olive oil

1 medium brown onion, finely chopped

100g Serrano jamon* or prosciutto, finely chopped

60g butter

150g plain (all-purpose) flour

500ml milk

2 egg yolks

100g dried breadcrumbs

Vegetable oil for deep frying

Lemon wedges, to serve

Method

Heat oil in a large frying pan over medium heat and cook onion for 4 minutes. Add jamon and cook for a further 2-3 minutes. Add butter and allow to melt, then add flour and cook, stirring, for about 2 minutes or until mixture bubbles and changes colour. Gradually pour in milk; cook, stirring, until sauce thickens.

Remove from heat, add egg yolks and stir vigorously to combine with sauce. Season to taste. Transfer to a bowl, cover and allow mixture to cool.

To make croquettes, take a large tablespoon of mixture and roll it into a log or round shape. Roll all the croquettes in breadcrumbs, shaking off excess crumbs, and set aside.

Preheat oven to 150°C. Heat oil in a deep fryer or heavy-based saucepan and cook croquettes a few at a time for 2-3 minutes or until golden. Drain on crumpled kitchen paper towel. Keep warm in preheated oven until ready to serve. Serve with lemon wedges.

* Refer to Glossary – Page 482

Pinchos de higos con jamón
Figs & jamon pinchos with balsamic glaze

makes 10

Ingredients

5 small slices jamon
1 tablespoon olive oil
5 fresh figs (not too soft), halved
½ cup fresh watercress sprigs
60ml balsamic vinegar
10 wooden skewers

Method

Cut each slice of jamon in half then roll up to form a small, tight roll and thread each roll onto its own skewer. Lightly brush with oil and char-grill or pan fry until lightly browned.

To assemble, place the fig halves onto a serving platter then top with 1-2 small sprigs of watercress and then skewer the jamon roll into the fig.

Place the balsamic vinegar into a small saucepan over medium heat and simmer for 5 minutes or until slightly syrupy. Serve pinchos drizzled with balsamic glaze.

Tip: After cooking the jamon skewers, kept them warm in the oven and then skewer into the figs just prior to serving. Cover with foil to prevent drying out.

Pinchos de manzana y queso azul
Cabrales & apple pinchos

makes 7

Ingredients

7 slices rustic white bread
40ml olive oil
1 small green apple
1 lemon, juiced
100g Cabrales cheese
Toothpicks

Method

Preheat oven to 180°C.

Using an 8cm round cutter, cut out a circle from each bread slice. Lightly brush both sides with oil and place onto a baking tray. Toast in the preheated oven for 8 minutes or until lightly golden. Remove.

Meanwhile, slice the apple very thinly. Do this by leaving it unpeeled and placing onto a chopping board with the stem lying horizontally. Next, using a sharp knife cut the apple into thin, round slices. Pull out seeds rather than cut them (it's all about presentation). Cut each apple slice in half then place into a bowl and drizzle with lemon juice to prevent browning.

Place the cheese into a small bowl and use a fork to soften slightly – don't over mix as the cheese will become a grey colour, which is not ideal.

To assemble, spread an even layer of the cheese onto the toasted bread. Try to achieve an even, smooth edge and a thickness of about 1-2mm. Next, top with two apple halves, slightly overlapping. Secure with a toothpick (optional) and serve.

Note – Cabrales is a Spanish blue cheese*; if unavailable, Gorgonzola could be used.

* Refer to Glossary – Page 482

Sardinas con pan tostado
Sardines on toast

Ingredients

12 fresh sardines, butterflied*

2 garlic cloves, thinly sliced

1 tablespoon extra virgin olive oil, to serve

Toasted bread, to serve

2 teaspoons fresh lemon thyme leaves, to serve

Marinade:

2 lemons, juiced

1 teaspoon smoked paprika*

1 teaspoon flaked salt

375ml white wine vinegar

Red pepper sauce:

100g roasted* red peppers* (capsicum), skin removed

1 garlic clove, chopped

1½ tablespoons red wine vinegar

60ml extra virgin olive oil

Method

Pat sardines dry with kitchen paper towel and place into a large glass or ceramic bowl. Add the sliced garlic.

To make the marinade, whisk the lemon juice, paprika, salt and vinegar in a medium jug. Pour marinade over the sardines, cover and refrigerate for 8 hours or until the sardine flesh looks like it is cooked (this will occur due to the acid in the marinade giving the flesh a "cooked look").

When ready, carefully transfer the sardines from the marinade to a serving platter and drizzle with olive oil. Cover and refrigerate until ready to serve.

To make the sauce, place the red peppers, garlic, vinegar and olive oil into the bowl of a food processor and process until slightly coarse.

Place sardines onto the toast and drizzle with red pepper sauce. Finish with lemon thyme leaves and serve with bread.

Serve immediately.

Note – Ensure the sardines aren't too cold from the fridge. Ideally, serve them at room temperature.

Pan frito con chorizo y aceitunas
Fried bread, chorizo & black olives

Ingredients

5 slices rustic white bread (a day old is best)

300g Spanish chorizo sausage*

2 tablespoons olive oil

4 garlic cloves, thinly sliced

30g pitted black olives

2 tablespoons chopped fresh flat-leaf (Italian) parsley

Flaked salt

Freshly cracked black pepper

Method

Cut bread into 2cm cubes. Cut chorizo into slices about 2mm thick.

Heat oil in a large frying pan over medium heat, add the garlic and fry for 1-2 minutes or until lightly golden. Remove with a slotted spoon and set aside. Return pan to heat and add the bread, stirring until crispy and lightly golden.

Add the chorizo and cook for 3-5 minutes. Add olives, parsley and the garlic, stir to combine and cook a further 2 minutes.

Season to taste and serve hot.

* Refer to Glossary – Page 482

Caracoles
Garlic snails

The French don't have a monopoly on snails. The Spanish are probably even more passionate about their caracoles. They appear in paellas cooked in the hills, in restaurant dishes and, when snail season is at its peak, served in bowls with a flavoursome stock in bars. In this case it's cooked in a white wine, garlic and tomato sauce, so serve them with toothpicks to pick out the flesh and some bread to mop up the juices.

Ingredients

100g prepared snails (see Note)
60ml extra virgin olive oil
2 garlic cloves, thinly sliced
1 large ripe tomato, finely chopped
100ml white wine
Flaked salt
Freshly cracked black pepper

Note – Prepared snails (that have been removed from their shells) can be sourced in the warmer months when they are in season. Try using the web to source a supplier in your area.

Method

Pat snails dry with kitchen paper towel and set aside.

Heat oil in a large frying pan over medium heat and cook garlic for 1 minute. Add tomato and white wine and cook for a further 2 minutes.

Add snails and stir well to combine with sauce.

Cover and cook over a low heat for 30-45 minutes or until snails are tender. Add a little water if the sauce begins to dry out before cooking time is complete.

The snails must be tender when ready, not rubbery. If rubbery, continue to cook for a further 10-20 minutes, tasting and testing occasionally. Season to taste and serve with garlicky sauce, which will be slightly thick.

(See photo on next page).

Salchichas de ternera al vino
Beef sausages in white wine

Ingredients

2 teaspoons olive oil
8 beef chipolatas*
2 garlic cloves, crushed
125ml dry white wine
60ml salt-reduced chicken stock
1 fresh bay leaf
2 teaspoons finely chopped fresh flat-leaf (Italian) parsley
Flaked salt
Freshly cracked black pepper
Toasted sourdough bread, to serve

Method

Heat oil in a medium frying pan over medium-high heat and cook chipolatas for 3-4 minutes each side, browning on all sides. Remove and drain on crumpled kitchen paper towel.

Return frying pan to low-medium heat and cook garlic, stirring continuously for 1 minute. Increase heat to medium-high, add wine, stock and bay leaf and bring to the boil. Reduce heat and simmer, uncovered, until the liquid has reduced by two-thirds. Add browned chipolatas and cook for 2 minutes or until heated through. Remove from heat add parsley and season to taste.

Serve with toasted sourdough.

(See photo on following page).

* Refer to Glossary – Page 482

Canapés de pescadito y pimientos del piquillo
Piquillo pepper & whitebait canapés

Ingredients

20 fresh whole whitebait (see Note)
1 large roasted* red pepper (capsicum)*, seeded
75g plain (all-purpose) flour
Flaked salt
Freshly cracked black pepper
1 egg
Olive oil for shallow frying

Method

Pat whitebait dry with kitchen paper towel.

Cut the roasted pepper into thick strips. Place a strip of pepper onto a chopping board and place one whole whitebait at one end. Roll the whitebait up in the pepper. Repeat with remaining peppers and whitebait and set aside on a large plate.

Place flour into a shallow bowl and season with salt and pepper. Place egg into a second bowl and lightly beat.

Heat oil in a heavy-based frying pan.

Dip wrapped whitebait into beaten egg, draining the excess, then into the seasoned flour, shaking off the excess flour.

Cook whitebait in 2 batches for 5 minutes or until lightly golden. Remove with a slotted spoon and drain on crumpled kitchen paper towel. Serve immediately.

Note – Whitebait are very small fish, usually about 4-5cm in length, and are generally always served whole and uncleaned.

Canapés de cebolleta
Spring onion canapés

Ingredients

6 medium all-purpose potatoes, peeled
60ml olive oil
6 spring onions*, thinly sliced
1 garlic clove, crushed
1 tablespoon white (granulated) sugar
60ml balsamic vinegar
Flaked salt
Freshly cracked black pepper
1 small ripe tomato, deseeded and finely diced
Spring onion* slices, extra

Method

Thinly slice potatoes (about 1-2 mm thick) and pat dry with kitchen paper towel.

Heat only half the oil in a large frying pan over medium heat. Cook half the potato slices until golden on both sides. Remove and drain on crumpled kitchen paper towel. Heat remaining oil and cook remaining potato slices.

Reduce heat to low, add spring onions and garlic to frying pan and cook for 2-3 minutes. Add sugar and vinegar and cook until the liquid has evaporated. Remove from heat and season to taste.

Place only half the potato slices onto a serving platter, top each with a small spoonful of cooked spring onion mixture then top with a second potato slice. Garnish with diced tomato and spring onion slices.

* Refer to Glossary – Page 482

Pincho de sardinas marinadas y olivas
Pincho of marinated sardines with olives

makes 12

Ingredients

12 whole fresh sardines, butterflied*

1 small red onion, very finely chopped

½ green pepper (capsicum), very finely chopped

Good quality extra virgin olive oil, to serve

12 wooden skewers

Marinade:

200ml white wine

60ml lemon juice

1½ teaspoon flaked salt

Method

Remove the tails from the sardines, if necessary. Cut the butterflied sardine into two halves, lengthways. Thread and weave two sardine halves (fillets) onto each skewer.

Lay the skewered sardines flat into a large glass or ceramic dish (not metal, as it can react with the acid in the marinade). Try to arrange skewers in a single layer.

To make the marinade, pour the wine, lemon juice and salt into a jug and stir to combine.

Pour the marinade over the sardines, cover, refrigerate and allow to marinate for 4-5 hours. Turn every hour to ensure that all the flesh has the chance to be in contact with the marinade.

To serve, remove sardines from the marinade. Gently shake the skewers to remove excess marinade. Place onto a serving platter and top with onion and pepper. Drizzle generously with olive oil.

Tip: If the skewers are too long to fit into a (non-metal) dish, cut the length of the skewers with kitchen scissors.

Aceitunas y aceite de oliva (Olives & olive oil)

With the offering of olives seen as a sign of hospitality and olive oil used as the basis of so many national dishes, it's fortunate that Spain is a prolific producer of some of the best olives and olive oils in the world.

Which oil for what?

The Spanish home cook, depending on their budget, will more likely use 'olive oil'. This is refined olive oil to which some high quality extra virgin olive oil has been added for flavour and mouth-feel.

Extra virgin olive oil is best to cook with at lower temperatures as it has great body and flavour. It's not suited to deep-frying, as the flavour compounds tend to burn. Instead the Spanish often use sunflower oil.

Some varieties of extra virgin olive oil are better suited to some uses than others – *hojiblanca* is a sweeter, more delicate, variety, while *picual* is great for dressing salads as it has a lovely sharpness that catches the back of the throat.

Buy small amounts of extra virgin olive oil and use them often. Store in a cool, dark place when you're not cooking with them. Some cooks pour their oil into a small plastic squeeze bottle and have this next to them while they're cooking.

Travel south of Córdoba, towards Jaén, and the hills are covered in olive trees, hundreds of thousands of them. Giant processing plants stand on the outskirts of every town. The old stone mills, once used to crush the oil from the olive, decorate the streetscapes as a memorial to a simpler time. Some of the best olive oil in the world is produced here and exported around the globe.

Olive oil is the bedrock of Spanish cuisine – it is the start of every *sofrito* and is used in a popular dessert, *pan con chocolate*, which is bread and chocolate sprinkled with salt and drizzled with some sweet *hojiblanca* olive oil.

With modern technology, the quality of olive oil has increased over the years with a much greater proportion of extra virgin olive oil being produced than in the past. This is olive oil that has less than 0.8 % acid.

Olive offering

Walk into a bar anywhere in Spain and a little plate of pickled olives will be placed in front of you as soon as you order your drink. The barman will ladle the olives out of a big terracotta pot or jar filled with olive oil, flavoured with herbs and perhaps some citrus skin, and covered with a plate for a lid. Salty, sharp and flavoursome, they're the classic bar snack.

It's just as likely that you'll be served olives in someone's home. The Spanish are great preservers and they love harvesting table olives at the end of autumn. They soak them in water for weeks, changing the water daily, then bottle them in brine with a few aromatic herbs. Months later they will open the jar, rinse the olives and then cover them with olive oil and more herbs.

In the north of the country factories preserve olives in savoury brine and then stuff them with pieces of *pimientos* red pepper, or *anchoas* (anchovies). Whatever the case, a small plate of pickled olives offered to a guest is a sign of hospitality.

Opposite: Olives at the market of Alcala de Henares, Madrid.

País Vasco
(Basque Country)

The world barely registered the Basque Country's existence before Frank Gehry's stunning titanium Guggenheim Museum debuted in Bilbao in 1997. Now the twin narratives of Bilbao, the heavily industrial city that reinvented itself as a centre of architecture and design, and an avant-garde cuisine boasting more Michelin stars per capita than any other region, have put the *País Vasco* firmly on the global radar.

A unique people with no known connection to the Hispanic bloodline, the roots of the Basque are so ancient that the origins of their unique and complex language have been lost over time. This makes it difficult to say precisely where these proud and industrious people hailed from. Some theories suggest they are the oldest remnant European population, inhabiting this green patch of the Iberian Peninsula for at least 4000 years.

A new lease of life

By the 14th century Bilbao had become one of Spain's principal ports. By the late 20th century it was one of the country's most contaminated cities, its mining and shipbuilding industries were crippled and it desperately needed a new lease of life.

Enter some of the luminaries of world design – Zaha Hadid, Norman Foster, Arata Isozaki, Philippe Starck, Gehry, of course – and local heroes like Santiago Calatrava and Rafael Moneo. Together, they transformed this city of steelworkers and stevedores into a wonderland of architectural whimsy.

While it is a gastronomic epicenter of modern Spain, the traditional Basque respect for food, freshness and provenance lies at the foundation of the extraordinary cuisine for which *País Vasco* has become world famous.

Right: Basque farm in the hills of Valle de Onate, Guipuzcoa, Basque Country.

Opposite: *Casa Urola* Restaruant and Pintxos Bar, San Sebastian, Basque Country.

Over pages: Fishing port of Pasajes, Guipuzcoa, Basque Country.

TXOKOS – the Basque gastronomic club.

Txoko – the word means nook or cosy corner – is the name given to the private gastronomic societies found throughout the Basque Country, including the Basque-speaking areas of Navarra. Men have been gathering in these underground epicurean clubs to cook for each other and share companionship since the 1870s.

Some suggest the matriarchal Basque society drove them to it. The theory goes that women often banished their meddlesome husbands from the home and, rather than simply hang around the streets, the men got busy in their custom-built kitchens. Often run like fine restaurants, *txokos* are an opportunity for men to gather and gossip over great meals. It's the ultimate expression of civilisation in the Basque culture – superb cuisine and wines enjoyed in the leisurely company of your people.

Txokos became more popular under Franco's dictatorship (1939-1975) when harsh regulations outlawing Basque culture meant there were few places where people could legally gather to be themselves. In the *txokos*, they could speak their language, fly their flag, sing their songs and celebrate without fear of punishment. These underground (and they are often in the basement) cooking clubs also helped to preserve and, following Franco's efforts to smother their heritage, to revive Basque gastronomy.

While men's clubs in other countries are devoted to business networking or affairs of state, here they're dedicated simply to food. Members shop at markets, taking turns to cook for each other in what almost amounts to a competitive sport.

Freshness is paramount to local taste buds so *txoko* dishes tend to be strictly seasonal, perhaps delicacies such as young eels, or mushrooms in the lightest omelettes in the springtime.

Wine is also important – it must be high quality and there should be plenty of it. When the Basque entertain they do it with pleasure, because otherwise they can't see the point.

In keeping with changing social mores, most *txokos* now permit women as guests. They are welcome to eat, but not to cook.

"The best place to eat in Spain, in Europe, in the West."

Ferran Adrià, chef at the fabled elBulli restaurant in Catalonia, describing the city of San Sebastian.

Royal acknowledgement

Meanwhile, the coastal city of San Sebastian – a fashionable resort since 1845 when Queen Isabel II started spending her summers there – was gaining a formidable reputation for its food.

The Basque people have always been fastidious about the freshness and provenance of their produce, and about preserving *el patrimonio del sabor*, the traditional recipes and cuisine. There are even societies dedicated to the protection of such esteemed Basque ingredients as anchovies, Tolosa black beans and *Txakoli de Getaria* wine. Other standout products and dishes from the region include chestnuts, broadbeans, corn, fish and seafood from the Bay of Biscay, small squid called *chipirones* cooked in their own ink, the tuna and vegetable stew *marmitako*, and *angulas*, baby eels, simply dropped into a sizzling pot of olive oil, garlic and dried chilli and then served immediately with wooden spoons.

The progressive ideas of French *nouvelle cuisine* in the 1970s influenced a new generation of Basque chefs and sparked what has become known as *la nueva cocina vasca*, the new Basque cuisine. Its champion is Juan Mari Arzak who runs a three-star Michelin restaurant, self-titled, in a 100-year-old apartment building in San Sebastian. Arzak is consistently ranked in the world's top 10 restaurants. While some of the cooking techniques may be considered avant-garde, the sentiment and philosophy behind the food is 100 per cent traditional.

Provenance & *pintxos*

Basques are fanatically obsessed with food. *La Bretxa* in San Sebastian is the model of a fresh produce market. Its displays look like art installations, using only the best quality raw materials, from line-caught hake and bream to mountains of mushrooms in all shapes and sizes. Along with mushrooms, Basque people are also passionate about the local ewe's milk cheese, *Idiazabal* that comes in myriad forms.

This food obsession explains why the region's *pintxos* or *tapas* bars have evolved into purveyors of what is commonly known as 'miniature haute cuisine'. Snacking in San Sebastian's *pintxos* bars is like a progressive degustation at a top restaurant. The Basque custom of *txikiteo*, bar-hopping between establishments, is rewarded with such delicacies as crunchy pig's ears in romesco sauce, cannelloni stuffed with *morcilla* (blood sausage), always superb plates of *jamón* and excellent winelists.

The ideal alcoholic accompaniment to *txikiteo* is *txakoli*, the Basque Country's DOC, slightly sparkling white wine. Cider is another preferred tipple, traditionally consumed straight from the barrel in a cider house with a three-course meal of salt cod omelette, steak, and *Idiazabal* cheese.

Whether eating at its world-renowned restaurants or a *pintxos* bar, Basque cuisine is a refined expression of taste.

Salsas
Sauces

Whether created in the cooking process or as a seperate dish, salsas are an essential part of Spanish cuisine.

Salsas (Sauces)

A defining and essential accompaniment – salsa is exuberant, and must be fresh.

Many great Spanish dishes create their own sauce as they cook, with the juices from the meat cooking in tomatoes, for example, slowly reducing to make a thick sweet sauce that's sopped up with bread or vegetables.

Whole fresh fish, cooked over coals in the Basque Country, are soused with brine as they cook. When served on the plate, the flesh releases its juice along with a little of the brine. The chef may then drizzle over a little extra virgin olive oil and, as it cools, the juices, brine and oil come together to make a rich, sweet sauce that complements the fish's delicate flesh perfectly.

Make your own

Some ingredients, however, don't produce juices that can be used for a sauce, but they benefit wonderfully from the addition of a little extra flavour and moisture.

Enter such Spanish culinary favourites as *mayonesa, alioli, romesco* and *mojo*. These are either olive oil emulsion sauces or purées of herbs, nuts and/or vegetables. As these sauces have such predominant flavours, it's essential that only the very best eggs, extra virgin olive oil, herbs, nuts and vegetables are used.

When seasoning these sauces it's permissible to be a little heavy handed with the salt, as just a few tablespoons sit to one side as a condiment, justifying a little extra 'oomph'.

These sauces are not really for keeping – they are all vibrant and powerfully fresh – capturing the exuberance of Spanish cuisine at its best.

Salsa mayonesa
Mayonnaise

Ingredients

3 free-range* egg yolks, at room temperature

150ml extra virgin olive oil

150ml light olive oil or vegetable oil

Flaked salt

Ground white pepper

1-2 tablespoons lemon juice

Mayonnaise is an everyday miracle of kitchen science. Olive oil is emulsified with lemon juice by egg yolk to make a thick, rich yellow sauce that complements potatoes, seafood and almost anything served with it. The fact that it's supposedly named after the town of Mahon makes this a very important Spanish addition to the culinary world.

Food scholars, however, believe that mayonnaise-type sauces were invented spontaneously all around the Mediterranean many, many years ago.

It's a sauce best prepared slowly. A lot of people put a moist folded dishcloth under the bowl to prevent it from slipping. Others, before adding any more salt, dissolve it in a little lemon juice to prevent white spots developing in the mayonnaise. Some swear by finishing it off by whisking in a few tablespoons of hot water to stabilise it. Whatever the case, a great mayonnaise can't be made without the best eggs and the freshest extra virgin olive oil.

Method

In a tall narrow container or bowl whisk egg yolks until they are an even consistency. Combine the oils and begin to add to the eggs in a slow thin stream, whisking continuously until all the oil has been added and is incorporated. (The amount of oil can be increased from a thin stream to a faster drizzle once the sauce begins to develop and thicken, but ensure that each addition of oil is emulsified before adding more.)

Season to taste and, lastly, slowly add the lemon juice, again in a thin stream, to taste and to cut through the richness. While you are making this sauce, make sure the consistency is continually thick and creamy.

Tip: Mayonnaise can be refrigerated for about 1 week – place a piece of plastic wrap directly onto the surface to prevent it drying out and forming a skin.

Note – Mayonnaise can also be made in a food processor, however purists believe the best is handmade.

Salsa romescu
Romescu sauce

makes about 180ml

Ingredients

1 tablespoon olive oil

1-2 small whole fresh red chillies*

1 thick slice of rustic white bread, crust on

2 garlic cloves, crushed

1 teaspoon sweet paprika*

6 blanched almonds, roasted*

6 hazelnuts, roasted*

2 small very ripe tomatoes, skinned, seeded and chopped

1 tablespoon red wine vinegar

60-80ml extra virgin olive oil

Flaked salt

In the hills behind Tarragona, one of the great old Roman cities of Catalonia, is a little restaurant where the heart of the kitchen is a charred hardwood burning char-grill. During service it's covered in cuts of lamb and pork, but after the diners have left the chef, a matronly woman called Victoria, chars baskets of ripe peppers over the dying embers.

This is the beginning of her romescu sauce for the next day. The peeled peppers are ground with roasted hazelnuts, garlic and olive oil. She then pours this over the tomatoes, black olives and soft shreds of moist salt cod that have been layered in a terracotta bowl. Romescu or romesco also goes wonderfully over jacket potatoes, grilled meats, fish, chicken and over a variety of salads. It will keep fresh in the fridge for several days if stored in an airtight jar.

Method

Heat only half the olive oil in a small frying pan over medium heat and lightly fry the chillies for about 2 minutes or until soft. Remove and place into a large mortar.

Cut bread into small cubes and add to the frying pan with the remaining oil and cook until lightly golden then add to chilli in mortar. Add garlic, paprika, almonds, hazelnuts and tomatoes. Pound with the pestle and mix until it looks smooth.

Add vinegar and enough of the extra virgin olive oil to form a soft paste or preferred consistency (depending on how the sauce is being used). Season to taste with salt.

* Refer to Glossary – Page 482

Mojo verde
Green dipping sauce

Ingredients

1 bunch fresh flat-leaf (Italian) parsley
2 hard-boiled* free-range eggs*, peeled
1 small brown onion, finely chopped
½ teaspoon ground cumin
Flaked salt
Ground white pepper
60ml extra virgin olive oil
vinegar

Pronounced mo-ho, this vibrant sauce from the Canary Islands is the perfect accompaniment to fish dishes. Some versions of mojo verde use fresh coriander; one of the few times you'll see coriander in Spanish cooking. The power of this sauce is in its fresh flavours, so it's best to make it just prior to serving.

Method

Wash parsley, pat dry and roughly chop leaves; discard stalks.

Remove yolks from the cooled eggs (keep whites for another use, such as a sandwich) and place into a mortar with parsley, onion and cumin. Pound with the pestle and mix until it looks smooth. Season to taste.

Continue to mix while you add oil and vinegar (to taste) until it forms a smooth paste of a sauce consistency.

Note – Serve this sauce with fish, chicken or virtually any other dish. It's also perfect served over steamed beans or potatoes.

* Refer to Glossary – Page 482

Alioli
Garlic sauce

Ingredients

2 free-range* egg yolks, at room temperature

2-3 large garlic cloves, crushed

150ml extra virgin olive oil

150ml light olive oil or vegetable oil

Flaked salt

1-2 tablespoons lemon juice

Warm water, if required

Alioli is mayonnaise's garlicky twin. Made with garlic that's crushed to a pulp and blended with fresh extra virgin olive oil, it's best known as allioli, which is Catalan, although it's sometimes called ajiaceite in the rest of the country. Purists would argue that true allioli is made with just garlic and olive oil, and perhaps a pinch of salt. But it's hard sauce to make and the addition of egg yolks allows the oil to emulsify and thicken much more easily. It's perfect accompaniment to new season's asparagus and barbecued fish.

Method

In a tall narrow container or bowl whisk egg yolks until they are an even consistency, then add garlic. Combine the oils and begin to add to the eggs in a slow thin stream, whisking continuously until all the oil has been added and is incorporated. (The amount of oil can be increased from a thin stream to a faster drizzle once the sauce begins to develop and thicken, ensure that each addition of oil is emulsified before adding more.)

Season to taste with salt and, lastly, slowly add the lemon juice, again in a thin stream, to taste and to cut through the richness. While you are making this sauce, make sure the consistency is continually thick and creamy. If it is a little thick, add a very small amount of warm water.

Tip: Allioli can be refrigerated for about 1 week – place a piece of plastic wrap directly onto the surface to prevent it drying out and forming a skin.

Note – This sauce is delicious served with fried whitebait, char-grilled shrimp (prawn) and vegetables, such as asparagus, fennel and snow peas.

* Refer to Glossary – Page 482

Mojo colorado
Spicy red dipping sauce

makes about 350ml

Ingredients

6 garlic cloves, chopped

2 roasted* red banana peppers*
(capsicums), seeded and chopped

15g fresh breadcrumbs*

1 tablespoon hot paprika*

½ teaspoon flaked salt

1 teaspoon ground cumin

150ml extra virgin olive oil

60ml red wine vinegar

1-2 tablespoons water, optional

The Canary Islands are famous throughout Spain for their potatoes. Perched in the Atlantic Ocean off the coast of Morocco, the islands are basked in sunshine and produce little papas or potatoes.

They're delicious when baked in salt and served with this spicy red pepper sauce and perhaps a few dollops of alioli.

Method

Place garlic, peppers and breadcrumbs into a food processor bowl and process until smooth. Add paprika, salt and cumin and pulse to combine.

Transfer to a large bowl and whisk in the oil and vinegar. If the sauce is too thick, whisk in water as necessary.

* Refer to Glossary – Page 482

Islas Canarias (Canary Islands)

The Canary Islands are an enigmatic archipelago, closer to Africa than Europe, with landscapes that range from sand dunes and lava fields to rainforests and snow-capped Mount Teide, Spain's highest peak. The seven major islands –La Palma, El Hierro, Tenerife, La Gomera, Gran Canaria, Lanzarote and Fuerteventura – lure more than 10 million holidaymakers each year with their unique promise of African sun, European civilisation and 1500 kilometres of coastline.

The islands' fortunes were dictated by their mid-Atlantic location, just 100 kilometres off the coast of Morocco. Conquered by the Castilians in the 15th century, they formed a critical link in the ocean passage of the Conquistadors from the Iberian Peninsula to the New World. La Palma's capital city Santa Cruz became the third most important port in the Spanish Empire after Seville and Antwerp, and Columbus stopped for provisions at La Gomera on his famed 1492 voyage.

Las Palmas de
Gran Canaria

Below: Puerto Morgan, Gran Canaria,
Canary Islands.

Closer to Africa than Europe, the Islas Canarias have a culinary output that defies their size.

Fish and dips

The Spanish introduced sugar and wine and, in later centuries, the islands were known for cochineal, tobacco and banana cultivation. Being at the oceanic crossroads of Europe, America and Africa has lent a distinctive flavour to Canarian cuisine. Fish is a mainstay, especially *cherne*, a type of grouper, *sama* or gold sea-bream, *morena* (moray) and the popular *vieja* or parrot fish with its fine white flesh.

At the heart of island gastronomy are the spicy dips and sauces known as *mojos*, served with everything from meat and fish to potatoes and bread. *Mojo verde* is prepared from olive oil, garlic, coriander, vinegar, salt and cumin, while *mojo rojo* is flavoured with oregano, sweet paprika and sun-dried red peppers or chilli. They are the standard accompaniment to the *papas arrugadas* (literally, wrinkled potatoes), a colonial staple of potatoes boiled in sea salt then baked.

Protected produce

This farthest-flung outpost of the European Union has a surprising number of protected *Denominación de Origen* (DO) produce peculiar to *Las Islas Canarias*. The islands produce more goat's cheese than any other region of Spain, including three DO cheeses made from the milk of the *majorera*, *palmera* and *tinerfeña* goat breeds.

Majorero cheese, often cured in moulds made from palm-tree leaves and not unlike *Manchego*, is a specialty of Fuerteventura; the soft Palmero goat's cheese from La Palma is often smoked using almond shells or pinewood. Gran Canaria's DO *Flor de Guía* is a blend of goat's with sheep's or cow's milk, sweetened with blue thistle flowers. Cheeses are used widely as a base for cakes, *quesadillas* and *almogrote*, a spicy pâté of Palmero, tomato and olive oil.

Wine is still a mainstay of island agriculture, with 11 DO varieties dominated by the vineyards of Lanzarote and Tenerife. Lanzarote is famous for its *Malvasía* vines planted in a topsoil of volcanic ash and sheltered from harsh trade winds by ingenious half-moon shaped mounds called *zocos*. Tenerife has five DO wines, ranging from the distinctive red Tacoronte-Acentejo to the Ycoden-Daute-Isora white grapes grown on the slopes of the extinct Teide volcano.

And while canaries do hail from here, the islands were named after canines, not birds. The early inhabitants were a heathen race called the Guanches, famed for worshipping dogs.

Islas Baleares
(Balearic Islands)

There's far more to the Balearics than the famed clubs of Europe's party capital Ibiza and the beaches of Formentera. The three main islands of Majorca, Menorca and Ibiza are as different as they are similar, each shaped distinctly by its history.

Majorca was a stronghold of the Romans and their influence is evident in the amphitheatre at Pollença; Menorca is enduringly British – the local language features such pukka English words as gravy and mug; Ibiza's character was molded by the Carthaginians and the Moors.

Located in the western Mediterranean, between the Iberian Peninsula and North Africa, this small archipelago is renowned for its picturesque bays and secluded beaches but its geography ranges from the Tramuntana mountains to one of the world's largest subterranean lakes, Lake Martel, found inside Majorca's Dragon Caves.

Beyond the tourist resorts of the coast, the life of the interior continues much as it has for centuries. Windmills lazily draw water from the interior while prehistoric mausoleums and lookouts, or *talayots*, still define the Menorcan landscape.

A cuisine of many origins

History is also a vital ingredient in the islands' gastronomy. From the Romans came capers and olives, the latter commonly dressed with fennel and chilli as an appetiser, or pressed to release a distinctively aromatic oil. Arabic food traditions persist in pastries and the use of dried fruits, raisins and nuts mainly, that lend Balearic cuisine its distinctive sweet-salty flavours.

The British brought with them gin and puddings and are credited with introducing dairy farming and meat roasting to the region.

The most contentious menu item of the Balearics is mayonnaise, said to have originated in the Menorcan capital Mahon, hence the name, but the French also lay claim to its invention. Regardless of it origins, mayonnaise is a staple of the Balearic diet, alongside seafood, hearty soups of vegetables and bread, and stews.

The best-known stew and a favourite of King Juan Carlos is *caldereta de langosta*, a bouillabaisse made with lobsters from the channel between Mallorca and Menorca. It's said the best place to taste it is in Fornells, a small fishing port in northern Menorca. The Ibizan specialty *burrida de ratjada* is boiled ray, seasoned with chopped almonds and saffron.

This archipelago boasts a cuisine rich in the natural spoils of each island's diverse environment.

Chicken stuffed with pomegranate shows clear Moorish roots but the Balearic appetite for pork is a more contemporary taste. The islands' staple *sobrasada* is a sausage made from various parts of the pig minced and then seasoned with paprika and black pepper. It is air-cured and emerges soft enough to be spread on bread, preferably with fried eggs and a sauce of milk and vegetables. Majorcan pork lard is essential to island cooking, especially the *rostida* of roasted pig stuffed with liver, eggs, bread, apples, plums and a mixture of rosemary and thyme.

Gin came to Menorca in the 18th century and, thanks to the British introduction of juniper bushes, remains the drink of choice on this island. Served with lemon and sodas it is called a *pellofa*, with lemonade a *pomada*, and both are popular thirst-quenchers during fiestas on Menorca.

Opposite: Mending nets after the day's catch, Port de Soller, Mallorca, Balearic Islands.

Above: Farming in centuries old traditions, Mallorca, Balearic Islands.

Frutas y verduras
Fruit & vegetables

Spain's vast array of home-grown produce is proof of both a fertile land and a rich culinary heritage.

Frutas y verduras
(Fruit & vegetables)

For such an industrialised nation, Spain has its culinary roots deeply planted in the soil. The fruits of the land are highly regarded and revered. The city markets are almost temples to the seasonal bounty of the countryside, with great cornucopias of fruit and vegetables beautifully presented to tempt the shopper.

The home garden

Many Spaniards still keep a *huerto*, a kitchen garden, particularly those living in the country, and in small towns there might be a common gardening area located by the banks of nearby stream.

The urge to grow beautiful food is strong even in the cities, with sections of railway easements or an abandoned block of land often seconded to growing vegetables.

In a small *huerto*, as many as 50 different fruit trees and vegetables may be growing over the seasons. Fat chickpeas, sweet apricots, tiny strawberries, slender asparagus grown from wild stock, a handful of different lettuces, zucchinis (courgettes), various tomatoes types and sprawling pumpkin vines. Picked fresh from the garden, the fruit and vegetables might be prepared as simply as a sliced tomato sprinkled with salt and drizzled with extra virgin olive oil. Carrots might be cooked in a light stock and seasoned with a few spices.

Behind closed doors

It's interesting to note that the fruit and vegetables eaten by modern Spaniards are more often than not consumed in the home. A visitor to Spain, eating only at restaurants, could easily be misled into thinking this is a nation of meat eaters.

Vegetables, and even chicken, have traditionally been considered food of the home, so restaurants generally offer richer fare. There have always been exceptions, the arrival of the new season's asparagus will create a flurry of activity in the kitchen where the chef will change the menu to create space for this delicious and highly praised veg.

However, with a return to tougher economic times, some progressive restaurants are re-embracing vegetables, as they cost less to buy.

> From the garden straight to the plate… fresh is best.

New world influences

It wasn't until the discovery of the Americas in the 15th century that the foundations for what we now consider to be traditional Spanish cuisine were laid down. Tomatoes, peppers, potatoes, pumpkins, zucchinis (courgettes) and cucumbers – discovered in the conquest of Central and Southern America – were planted and harvested for the first time in the soils of Spain.

Focus on quality

Some vegetables are so highly regarded that they have their own *Denominación de Origen* (DO) – equivalent to the DOC used in other regions of Europe – to designate and protect both the provenance and quality of the produce. Highly regarded baby lettuces from Tudela are known as *Cogollos de Tudela* DO, and must therefore be grown in the designated area using defined practices so no other lettuce can claim that title.

The focus of the meal is shared between the meat and the vegetables in a Spanish home, with equal care and attention being given to all dishes in the preparation of a meal.

There's no simple steamed 'three veg with meat' here; every vegetable has the correct sauce or dressing or is made into a traditional dish. Vegetables dishes often include meat, usually chorizo or jamon, for a complementary layer of flavour.

Sweet discoveries

Prior to the Moorish invasion, the fruit and vegetable scene of the Iberian Peninsula was a very different landscape. After grains, native acorns and chestnuts were the mainstay carbohydrates. Root vegetables, such as carrot, were available and apples and pears were the main fruits. With the arrival of the Moors in the 8th century came not only sugar and spices, but also almonds, dates, pomegranates, oranges, rice and apricots.

Right: An abundance of fruit offered to shoppers at the famous La Boqueria market in Barcelona, Catalonia.

Opposite: A vegetable farmer works in the shadow of the ruins of the Aqueduct of Los Milagros, outside the city of Merida, Extremadura.

Samfaína
Samfaina bake

Ingredients

2 medium aubergine (eggplant)*
2 small red peppers (capsicums)*
2 small zucchini (courgettes)*
125ml olive oil
1 large red onion, roughly chopped
2 garlic cloves, finely chopped
400g can chopped tomatoes
3 sprigs freshly picked thyme
1 teaspoon flaked salt
Freshly cracked black pepper
150g manchego cheese*, grated

Across Spain, at the end of summer when tomatoes are plentiful, cooks take a basket into their huerto (kitchen garden) and pick the ripest, heaviest tomatoes, the ones that seem to be close to bursting. They take these to the kitchen and make a sauce with other ripe, abundant vegetables, such as zucchini (courgette) and aubergine, to make a slow-cooked dish rich with extra virgin olive oil and herbs.

The French have something similar called ratatouille, the Castilians make pisto, while the Basques produce a version with their fat peppers in which they cook salt cod to make bacalao a la vizcaína. Samfaina is the Catalan version. It can be served as a side with fish, chicken and pork but is also eaten on its own.

Method

Preheat oven to 180°C.

Thickly slice aubergine, then cut into large cubes. Halve peppers and deseed, then cut into large cubes. Halve zucchini lengthways and cut into thick slices.

Heat only half the oil in a large frying pan over medium-high heat and cook aubergine for 5 minutes or until lightly browned, tossing occasionally. Remove and set aside.

Heat remaining oil in frying pan over low heat and cook onion and garlic for 5 minutes. Add peppers and zucchini and cook for a further 5 minutes. Add tomatoes, thyme and aubergine and stir well to combine. Season to taste.

Transfer vegetables to an ovenproof dish and bake, uncovered, in preheated oven for 40 minutes.

Remove and sprinkle vegetables with cheese. Place under a grill until the cheese melts and is lightly golden.

* Refer to Glossary – Page 482

Esparrágos blancos con avellanas
White asparagus with hazelnuts & manchego

serves 4

Big, fat, white asparagus are your constant companions in Spanish bars where they sit on plates waiting to be scorched on la plancha or the flat grill. They sit in tall glass jars in grocers and markets and are preserved in artisan factories.

In this dish we're steaming them until just soft and marrying them with sharp manchego and the nutty crunch from roasted hazelnuts.

Ingredients

2 bunches white asparagus, ends trimmed

35g roasted hazelnuts, roughly chopped

1 tablespoon extra virgin olive oil

80g manchego cheese*, finely grated

1 tablespoon chopped flat-leaf (Italian) parsley

Flaked salt

Freshly cracked black pepper

Method

If necessary, lightly peel each asparagus stalk with a vegetable peeler to remove any slightly fibrous flesh. Wash and drain.

Steam asparagus for 8-10 minutes or until tender. Drain.

Place asparagus onto a serving plate or dish, sprinkle with hazelnuts then drizzle with oil. Sprinkle over cheese and parsley. Season with salt and pepper and serve.

Tip: When white asparagus is not available, use green; either is delicious when steamed and served with Alioli (see recipe, page 154).

Garbanzos con chorizo
Chickpeas with chorizo

Ingredients

180g dried chickpeas
750ml salt-reduced chicken stock
250ml water
260g cooked Spanish chorizo sausage*
2 tablespoons olive oil
1 medium red onion, finely chopped
1 garlic clove, finely chopped
250g baby (English) spinach leaves, washed
1 tablespoon chopped flat-leaf (Italian) parsley
Freshly cracked black pepper

The garbanzo, or chickpea, makes its way into so many Spanish dishes. From stews with tripe to Madrid's great cocido – a three-course hotpot – you'll find garbanzos.

Here, it's a rustic dish with spinach and some chorizo. Soaking and then cooking chickpeas is worth the effort as you get the best of their earthy, nutty flavour.

Method

Place chickpeas in a medium bowl and cover with boiling water. Stand for 1 hour then drain. Place chickpeas, stock and water into a saucepan. Cover and cook over a low-medium heat for 1-1½ hours or until tender. Drain.

Cut chorizo in half lengthways, then thinly slice and cook in a large non-stick frying pan over medium-high heat for 3-4 minutes or until lightly browned. Remove from frying pan and set aside.

Heat oil in the same frying pan over a low-medium heat. Add onion and garlic and cook for 3-4 minutes.

Place chorizo and chickpeas into the frying pan and cook for 5 minutes. Stir through spinach and parsley, cooking until the spinach begins to wilt.

Season with pepper and serve.

Tip: When in a hurry, canned chickpeas (1 x 400g can), which have been washed and drained, could be used instead of dried (soaked) chickpeas.

* Refer to Glossary – Page 482

Cebollas rellenas
Stuffed onions

Ingredients

8 small-medium brown onions

Filling:

2 tablespoons olive oil

150g lean minced beef

1 teaspoon chilli paste*

2 teaspoons finely chopped flat-leaf
(Italian) parsley

1 egg, lightly beaten

Flaked salt

Freshly cracked black pepper

20g butter

4 slices jamon* or prosciutto, to serve

Method

Preheat oven to 180°C.

Peel the onions, leaving the root end intact enough to hold the onion together; use a sharp knife to trim any hairy roots. Using a sharp paring knife, cut a 3cm-deep hole, 2-3cm in diameter, into the top of each onion. Reserve and freeze the onion flesh for later use.

To make the filling, heat only half the oil in a large frying pan over medium-high heat, add the mince and cook for 5-7 minutes or until lightly browned. Transfer to a bowl, cool slightly and add the chilli, parsley and egg. Season with salt and pepper.

Fill the onions with the mince mixture. Wipe the pan out with kitchen paper towel. To the pan add remaining oil and butter, then lightly brown the onions on all sides over medium-high heat. Remove to a small ovenproof dish that will hold the onions upright and close together in a single layer. Cover with a lid or foil and bake in preheated oven for 1 hour.

Meanwhile, on a separate baking tray, bake the jamon (alternatively, lightly pan fry until crisp), then serve with stuffed onions.

* Refer to Glossary – Page 482

Pimientos rellenos
Savoury filled peppers with tomato sauce

serves 4

Ingredients

4 medium red, green or yellow peppers
(capsicums)*

Filling:

2 tablespoons olive oil

1 small brown onion, finely chopped

100g minced pork

100g minced beef

1 egg, lightly beaten

Flaked salt

Freshly cracked black pepper

Tomato sauce:

2 tablespoons olive oil, extra

1 garlic clove, finely chopped

400g can chopped tomatoes

2 tablespoons tomato paste*

1 teaspoon white (granulated) sugar

2 tablespoons chopped flat-leaf
(Italian) parsley

Method

Preheat oven to 160°C.

Wash peppers and using a large knife, evenly slice off the tops
(leave stalks intact) and set aside. Remove seeds and membranes
from inside the peppers and discard.

To make the filling, heat oil in a large frying pan over low-medium
heat and cook onion for 5 minutes. Increase heat to high and add
minced meat. Cook, stirring, for 5 minutes until lightly browned.
Remove to a bowl and cool slightly. Add egg, mix well and season
with salt and pepper.

Place peppers side by side into an ovenproof dish and divide the
mince mixture between them.

To make the tomato sauce, wipe out the frying pan with kitchen
paper towel. Heat the extra oil in the frying pan over low heat and
cook garlic for 2 minutes without browning. Add tomatoes, tomato
paste and sugar; mix well. Cook over low heat for 5 minutes.
Season to taste and add parsley. If sauce is too thick, thin with
a little water.

Pour the tomato sauce evenly over the mince within the peppers.
Position the reserved tops onto each pepper and bake, uncovered,
in preheated oven for 40–50 minutes.

*Tip: Ideally, use an ovenproof dish that will hold the peppers upright
and close together in a single layer.*

* Refer to Glossary – Page 482

Colifor con puerros y ajos
Roast cauliflower with leek & garlic

serves 4

Ingredients

1kg white cauliflower

1 leek

6 garlic cloves, whole in skin

2 tablespoons olive oil

1 teaspoon flaked salt

Method

Preheat oven to 200°C.

Wash and drain cauliflower and cut into small florets. Cut off and discard the root end and about 8cm of the tough, dark green top of each leek; cut remaining stalk in half lengthways and wash well between the layers, then cut into 4cm lengths.

Place cauliflower, leek and whole garlic cloves into a baking dish. Drizzle with oil, season with salt and toss to combine.

Bake uncovered in preheated oven, for about 30 minutes or until cauliflower is tender and lightly golden, tossing occasionally.

When serving, squeeze the roasted garlic out of its skin and over the cauliflower.

Tomates rellenos
Stuffed tomatoes

Ingredients

8 medium ripe tomatoes

Filling:

1 large ripe avocado

1 garlic clove, crushed

4 anchovy fillets*, finely chopped

50g black olives, pitted and finely chopped

3 teaspoons lemon juice

Flaked salt

Freshly cracked black pepper

1 tablespoon chopped fresh chives

Method

Cut a thin slice from the base of each tomato to make it stable. Cut a circle, 2cm in diameter, into the top of each tomato and scoop out the flesh with a small spoon (see Tip). Place the tomatoes upside down on kitchen paper towel to drain for 5 minutes.

To make the filling, peel avocado and place flesh in a medium bowl; discard seed. Add garlic, anchovies, olives and lemon juice, then mash with a fork to combine. Season to taste.

Fill tomatoes with the filling and sprinkle with chives.

Tip: The removed tomato flesh could be used in a vegetable sauce.

* Refer to Glossary – Page 482

Alcachofas con pinones y aceitunas
Artichokes with pine nuts, olives & thyme

serves 4

Ingredients

4 fresh whole globe artichokes, prepared
1 lemon, juiced

Topping:
35g fresh breadcrumbs*, lightly toasted
40g roasted* pine nuts
50g green olives, pitted and finely chopped
1 tablespoon extra virgin olive oil
1 teaspoon freshly picked thyme leaves
Flaked salt
Freshly cracked black pepper
Chopped flat-leaf (Italian) parsley to serve
Extra virgin olive oil, extra

Method

To prepare the artichokes, cut off the stems, leaving about 4cm of stem directly below the artichoke head intact. Lightly peel the stem with a vegetable peeler (as if you were peeling a carrot). Remove and discard the tougher outer leaves, leaving the lighter green-coloured leaves. Cut about 2cm from the top of each artichoke and discard. Immediately rub all cut surfaces with the lemon juice to prevent discolouration.

Bring to the boil a large saucepan of lightly salted water. Place prepared artichokes into the boiling water and carefully cover with a plate that will sit inside the saucepan directly on top of the artichokes to keep them submerged. Cover with a lid and cook over medium heat for 15 minutes or until the flesh is tender (when a skewer can be easily inserted into the thickest part, usually where the stem meets the head).

Remove artichokes and stand upside down on a plate to drain. When cool enough to handle, cut in half lengthways. Use a teaspoon to scoop out the furry choke from the centre of each artichoke and discard.

Meanwhile, to make the topping, place the breadcrumbs, pine nuts, olives, oil and thyme into a bowl. Season to taste.

Place artichokes cut side up into a baking dish and divide the topping evenly over each half. Place under a medium-high grill and cook for 5 minutes or until the topping is lightly golden. To serve, sprinkle with parsley and drizzle with extra virgin olive oil and any remaining lemon juice.

Tip: Cooked artichokes are delicious served warm or at room temperature, with a vinaigrette dressing.

* Refer to Glossary – Page 482

Patatas asadas con alcachofas y tomillo
Roast potatoes with artichokes & thyme

serves 4

Ingredients

400g small-medium washed potatoes
60ml olive oil
Flaked salt
300g Jerusalem artichokes
2 teaspoons lemon juice
1 tablespoon butter
2 teaspoons freshly picked thyme leaves
Freshly cracked black pepper

Tomillo, or thyme, is used extensively in Spanish cooking. A native Mediterranean herb, the most flavoursome grows wild in the shallow soils and is short, squat and stunted. Growing slowly, it develops so much flavour that just a few tiny leaves can turn a dish into something spectacular. This is what it doing here – simple ingredients, potatoes and nutty Jerusalem artichokes are transformed into an incredibly moreish dish that's perfect served with chicken or fish.

Method

Preheat oven to 200°C.

Cut unpeeled potatoes into quarters. Place into a baking dish, drizzle with only half the oil and sprinkle with salt and bake, uncovered, in preheated oven for 20-25 minutes or until golden and tender, tossing occasionally.

Meanwhile, peel the artichokes and cut into cubes of about 2cm; immediately place into cold water with the lemon juice added (to prevent discolouration).

Heat remaining oil in a large frying pan over medium-high heat and add the butter. Pat the artichokes dry with kitchen paper towel, then pan fry for 5 minutes or until just tender and lightly golden. Remove from the pan and cover to keep warm.

When potatoes are cooked, add artichokes and thyme to dish and gently toss to combine. Season to taste and serve.

Escalivada de verduras (Catalana)
Catalan-style roast vegetables with herbs

serves 4

Ingredients

1 medium aubergine (eggplant)*

2 medium red peppers (capsicum)*, seeded

2 medium red onions, peeled

300g cherry tomatoes on the stem

6 whole garlic cloves, unpeeled

1 teaspoon flaked salt

60ml extra virgin olive oil

2 sprigs fresh rosemary

¼ cup chopped flat-leaf (Italian) parsley, to serve

While the origin of Catalan's flag is historically disputed, legend has it that when the great Catalan hero and Count of Barcelona, Wilfred the Hairy, lay wounded in battle, King Charles the Bald dipped his fingers into Wilfred's blood and ran it over his gold shield, thus creating the Catalan flag. This dish, with its red and gold colours, is sometimes laid out in strips to represent the flag. Rich and delicious, escalivada is great with meats and fish or on its own with bread

Method

Preheat oven to 200°C.

Thickly slice aubergine, then cut into cubes of about 2cm. Cut peppers into similar sized cubes. Cut each onion into eight wedges.

Place the cut vegetables, tomatoes and garlic into a baking dish. Sprinkle with salt, add oil and rosemary and gently toss to combine.

Bake uncovered in preheated oven for 30-40 minutes or until lightly golden, tossing 2-3 times during cooking.

Serve with chopped parsley.

Tip: For variety, add a little sliced, cooked Spanish chorizo sausage.

* Refer to Glossary – Page 482

Los mercados
(The markets)

The modern renaissance of *los mercados* – the food markets – has produced a lively meeting place surrounded by fresh produce as a daily fixture of Spanish life.

Fresh food markets are a window into their host culture and Spain's are vibrant, warmhearted and irresistible, much like the Spanish themselves. Few countries can boast such beautiful displays of agricultural abundance, proof of both a fertile land and a sophisticated culinary heritage.

The poster-child for Iberian bazaars is Barcelona's *La Boqueria*, whose Art Nouveau exterior is simply the latest incarnation of a market tradition that dates back many centuries. The original market was an open-air affair on La Rambla, the city's main boulevard, whose site is marked today with a mosaic plaque created by the Catalan artist Joan Miró. The 'new' market opened on the site of a former convent in 1837 and today is one of the most dynamic social hubs of the city, the place where housewives, city workers, top chefs and tourists converge to shop, drink or pick up some takeaway *bacalao frito* (fried cod).

Further along the Mediterranean coast at Valencia, the Modernist *Mercat Central* dates from 1928 but traders have gathered on the same spot for thousands of years to peddle their goods. Its 959 stalls sell everything from oranges (of course) to ostrich meat, as well as acquired local tastes like fresh snails that are sold bundled up in mesh sacks.

The best of the best

Perhaps the ultimate expression of Iberian market culture is *La Bretxa* in San Sebastian, the wealthiest city in the wealthiest region of Spain. Behind its 1870 neoclassical façade, this exquisite produce emporium abounds with immaculate stalls of fruits and vegetables, seafood and meats and a dizzying array of mushrooms including *setas, morels* and the harbinger of spring, *xixas*. There are myriad varieties of the raw sheep's milk cheese *Idiazabal*, each one's flavour subtly calibrated by the mountain where the sheep grazed and the process used to cure the cheese. Some Basques

Above: The famous La Boqueria markets in Las Ramblas, Barcelona, Catalonia.

Opposite top: Santa Caterina Market, Barcelona's original covered marketplace, Catalonia.

Opposite bottom: Jamon merchant in Mercat Central, Valencia City, one of the largest covered markets in Europe and a trading post since ancient times.

maintain that even the shepherds who tend the flock can have a bearing on the quality and taste of the end product.

During the turmoil of the 20th century some of the country's foremost markets were neglected and, in the case of Madrid's *Mercado de San Miguel*, even closed. But the cultural renaissance that has swept the country since 1975 has rescued them from oblivion. Barcelona's *Santa Caterina* market in the heart of the Old City has been given a striking architectural makeover along with a thriving *tapas* bar and restaurant which have helped restore the popularity of the city's first covered market.

The glass-and-iron *Mercado de San Miguel* is the pride of Madrid. After an extensive restoration it has reopened as a gourmet fresh-food hall. Stalls offer all the fundamentals of fine dining including breads and premium olive oils, freshly shucked French oysters, air-freighted seafood from Galicia's Atlantic coast and *jamón ibérico de bellota* from Guijuelo, Spain's ham capital. With typical Iberian inspiration, around half the stalls are bars so *Madrileños* can stop to sip on a *cava* or a *rioja* while doing the weekly shop.

Hongos y trufa
(Mushrooms & truffles)

When one of the top-rating TV shows in Catalonia is called 'The Mushroom Hunters', you know you're in a nation frantic about fungus.

As soon as the rains start to fall on the warm soil during autumn and spring, families drive to the hills around their city or town and head into the forest armed with a special mushroom knives and wicker baskets, often perched over Mother's arm.

They will spend the whole day searching for *chantarelas, trompetas de la muerte* ('death trumpets' that are tasty, not deadly), morels and other delectable fungus.

If they're lucky they'll come home with enough to make some super-soft and moist *revueltos de setas*, soft eggs with cooked mushrooms. If they have been out into the fields and found a patch of large, flat mushrooms they may cook these with thyme and sherry vinegar.

From famine to feast

Mushrooms are again finding favour after a few decades of neglect. Some older people have associated eating mushrooms with the years of famine during the Spanish Civil War, when people evacuated towns to survive in the forest on berries and mushrooms.

Truffles, however, are just as desired here as they are in France and Italy. Black truffles are native to Spain and grow in the oak and hazelnut forests. While the wild harvest may be in decline, propagated truffles are now the norm and Spanish truffles are sold across Europe. Large swathes of countryside have been set aside for raising the particular hazelnut trees under which truffles are grown.

Although Spanish chefs do tip their cap at the great fragrant truffle, it's the *boletus* which the Spanish go crazy for. Similar to the *porcini*, it's a big, meaty mushroom with a delicious flavour and is often served sliced, brushed with olive oil and a little garlic, seasoned and grilled over the smoky grill of a hardwood fire.

Such is the nature of Spaniards – they prefer the earthy flavours of the people to the fungus of the rich.

Wild harvested fungus delicacies are being rediscovered in modern Spain.

Opposite: Harvest of Saffron Milkcap mushrooms, Sierra Madrona, Castilla-La Mancha.

Alcachofas (Artichokes)

While peppers, tomatoes, rice and saffron are all pillars of the Spanish culinary canon, they are relatively recent imports from either the New World or introduced by the Moors. The native Mediterranean foodstuffs are vegetables such as carrots and artichokes.

Artichokes are closely related to the thistle. The artichoke is actually the immature flower bud. Artichokes, if they're let go to seed, look just like massive thistles. The outer petals of the artichoke are tough and need to be stripped away to reveal the soft heart within. This is generally boiled in acidulated water and can be served straightaway with vinaigrette.

Some places, such as the famous *Cova Fumada* bar in the Barcelona suburb of Barceloneta, deep fry the artichoke and serve it with a little oil and *pimentón* (paprika). There is a huge business across Spain of harvesting tight little artichokes and preserving them under glass, to be served as *tapas* throughout the year.

Some chefs are growing their own artichokes, harvesting them just before service then serving them very finely sliced with a lemon juice dressing witha very fine layer of translucent jamon fat to enrich the flavour.

Artichokes have a distinctive taste and the stalks of younger leaves make a delicious treat. Trimmed and boiled for a few minutes, dusted with semolina, deep-fried and served with almonds, lemon zest and toasted and crumbled jamon. Artichokes take a little time to prepare but are one of the true and original flavours of Spain.

Peel away the layers and this favourite Spanish vegetable is a real treat, either served with a simple dressing or deep-fried.

Pimentón (Paprika)

Smoky, hot or mild, this powdered red pepper adds flavour to myriad Spanish dishes.

Out in the west of Spain, where the rugged Extremadura hills meet the mountains to the north, the weather is too unpredictable to dry peppers under the sun as they do in Murcia in the south.

Instead, the people in the villages near Plasencia dry their peppers for hours and hours over smoky fires of slow burning oak logs. The peppers are then ground down on stone mills half a dozen times or more into a fine red powder. This is *pimentón ahumado* or smoky Spanish paprika.

The ever-present pepper

It's the background note to countless dishes, the cornerstone flavour of chorizo sausage and the final touch to Galician octopus. It's generally not spicy hot, but more of an earthy note that carries the flavour of the deep red peppers from which it's made.

Smoky Spanish paprika is excellent for slow-cooked dishes, meats and recipes that include peppers and tomato. Naturally occurring compounds in the peppers plus compounds in the smoke make *pimentón ahumado*, which is considered to be a natural preservative and is used extensively in the manufacture of smallgoods across Spain. There are three types of *pimentón* grown and produced in Extremadura – *pimentón* (plain), *agridulce* (bittersweet) and *picante* (slightly hot).

In the hot and dry south, the peppers are sun-dried and produce a brighter, fresher-tasting *pimentón*. They are identified by their colourful tins depicting saints and newlyweds. *Pimentón* from Murcia adds a lovely red blush to a dish and is particularly good for seafood and salads.

Pimentón added at the beginning of the cooking process cooks down to make a well-rounded background note, while a little sprinkled over food just prior to serving stands out and is the true highlight of the dish.

Opposite: Harvesting artichokes.

Above: Drying peppers, rural Mallorca, Balearic Islands.

La paella y su historia
(The story of paella)

> The *socarrat* – a crust of gently toasted grains at the edges of the pan – denotes a good *paella* cook.

In summer, the marshes fringing the Albufera lagoon just south of Valencia city are a ribbon of vibrant green punctuated by whitewashed farmhouses with thatched roofs. This picturesque stretch of Mediterranean coastline, extending west to Alicante and Murcia, has been the ricebowl of Spain for a thousand years and the birthplace of its most famous dish.

Paella is not one preparation but an endless variety of rice-based casseroles embellished with the harvest of sea and land. Traditionally, it features chicken or rabbit or both – often with snails, though they are expensive these days – plus wide green beans and fat dried limabeans known as *garrofón*. The open-air restaurants that sprang up along Valencia's Malvarrosa beach in the late 19th century popularised seafood *paellas*, and today versions with lobster, shrimp and calamari are common. During Lent, Valencianos feast on a simple *paella* of *bacalao* (salt cod) and cauliflower.

The art of cooking *paella*

With the correct rice and pan, the rest is up to the cook, who controls the order of ingredients – the browning of the meats with oil and salt, the sofrito of tomato and garlic, the measures of saffron (or paprika in cheaper versions) and stock – as well as the heat of the fire and even the type of wood used to fuel it. When cooked, the saffron-coloured rice grains should still be separate, never sticky or gluggy.

Spaniards refer to talented *paella* chefs as having a good 'touch' with rice. The unmistakable evidence of this is the *socarrat*, the irresistible crust, slightly caramelised and crunchy, that forms at the edges of the pan as the fire's heat gently burns the grains.

Just as there is an art to cooking *paella*, so is there an art to eating it. Diners traditionally gather around the *paella* pan and attack it with small wooden spoons, scooping succulent mouthfuls, savouring the *socarrat*, and then debating its quality relative to other *paellas* they have tasted. Eating *paella* is often a celebration and always a feast, so it is eaten at lunchtimes, not in the evenings.

Paella aside, Valencia is also known for its *caldosos*, or rice stews, and for dishes such as *arroz al horno* (*arrós al forn* in Valenciano), where the rice is baked in the oven in an earthenware dish, usually with blood sausage, beans and potatoes. And when Valencianos tire of *paella* there is always *fideuà*, which smells and tastes very like a seafood *paella* but uses vermicelli-like noodles instead of rice.

Opposite: Cooking *paella*, Nerja, Andalucia

Valencia

Sun-drenched Valencia is a postcard Mediterranean city that in recent years has reinvented itself as a dynamic and captivating European capital. Once dismissed as the pretty but dull little sister of Madrid and Barcelona, Valencia established itself as one of Spain's most visited cities by investing in landmark architecture and showcasing its compelling assets.

Paella is its most famous dish but this region is also known as orange orchard and rice bowl of Spain. The vast patchwork of the *huerta,* the market gardens that radiate out from the city, sustains the province, the nation and much of Europe with its bounty.

Valencia was founded in 2BC by retired Roman soldiers who named their settlement Valentia (valour). Under the flourishing ule of the Moorish empire it became *Balansiya*. Remnants of both eras can still be seen in Valencia's old neighbourhoods such as El Carmen, which forms part of the largest old city in Europe.

Trading hub of the Middle Ages

The Middle Ages were a golden era for the Kingdom of Valencia, by then a powerhouse of Mediterranean trade. Rich echoes of that era can still be found at the world heritage-listed *Lonja de la Seda,* a 15th century stock exchange for the silk industry. Valencia's business community was so prosperous at that time that it helped fund Columbus's exploration of the New World.

Valencia's history is written all over its streets, but so is its future. Santiago Calatrava's fantastically futuristic City of Arts and Sciences complex is only a few years old but already it has dramatically altered perceptions of a once sleepy city.

The celebration of food

Valencia is now associated with design and architecture, global sporting events, cutting-edge culture and progressive cuisine. It is also home to *Las Fallas*, an astonishing annual celebration when giant effigies are paraded through the streets before being torched in a massive night of fire. The famous tomato-throwing festival, *La Tomatina*, hails from this province too.

Its festivals might be madcap but Valencia is serious when it comes to food and wine. The myriad versions of *paella* are evidence of the local passion for culinary heritage. *Paella's* celebrity stems from the simple seaside shacks that began serving rice and seafood dishes on Malvarrosa Beach in the 19th century. But *paella* is just one of more than 100 proudly regional rice dishes including *arroz a banda* – rice cooked in a fish broth with seafood – and black squid ink rice with calamari. Crayfish, *merluza* (hake), sea urchins and swordfish are other specialties from the sea.

Valencia, custodian of Spain's most famous dish, *paella*, is focused on its future as a dynamic European city.

Above: *La Tomatina* – the annual tomato throwing festival in the streets of Bunol, Valencia.

Opposite: *El Palau de les Arts Reina Sofia* – the opera house and performing arts centre at Santiago Calatrava's futuristic City of Arts & Sciences, Valencia city, Valencia.

Legacy of the ancients

The Romans introduced the technique of preserving fish and roe with salt; the resulting Valencian *salmueras* and *salazones* include such delicacies as *mojama*, filleted and salt-cured tuna. Meats can also be preserved – as the blood sausage, *botifarras*, fiery chorizos and the spreadable red sausage, *sobrasada*. The Romans introduced salt but the Moors are responsible for the spices, such as cinnamon and nutmeg, that lend such delicate seasoning to the local cuisine.

From Valencia's mountain villages come the one-pot stews called *ollas*, *olletas* or *putxeros* made from meat and pulse stock. *Olla churra* mixes pork pieces, black pudding and oats while *olla de recapte* combines vegetables, beans and dried beef.

Almost anything grows in Valencia's agreeable Mediterranean climate but certain villages are known for the quality of their particular product. Gourmets covet artichokes from Benicarló, mountain cherries from Alicante, cheeses from La Nucía and Dénia shrimp. Blocks of almond and honey nougat known as *turrones* have denomination of origin protection, both for the hard version produced in Alicante and the soft, chewy one from Xixona (Jijona).

Well-rounded winemaking

Wines from the Valencia region are not as celebrated as those from other parts of Spain but there are more than 80 *bodegas* and three officially recognised winemaking regions. DO Utiel-Requena is known for its reds and roses, DO Valencia makes Alto Turia whites, roses and reds and DO Alicante does fruity reds and whites, both dry and sweet.

Rivalling wine as the region's most popular drink, and certainly its most refreshing during the scorching Mediterranean summers, is *horchata*. This chilled, creamy concoction, made from the tubers of the tigernut, was introduced by the Moors and has been quenching local thirsts ever since. Typically drunk in the beautifully tiled *horchaterías* of the old town, in recent years dozens of mobile kiosks have sprung up across the city hawking this sugary drink.

The region is also famed for *gazpacho*, but not as most people would know it. In Valencia, *gazpacho* refers to a heavy stew originating from mountain districts such as Vinalopó, La Plana and Requena-Utiel. A world away from Andalusian-style chilled soups, this version is made with shredded game meat, usually rabbit, partridge or quail, and thickened with bread.

Above: Lettuce farming at La Albufera, outside Valencia city, Valencia.

Opposite: Huge crowds wait for the opening salvo of the San Fermin festival – famous for 'the running of the bulls' – Pamplona, Navarra.

Navarra

The fiercely independent Kingdom of Navarra resisted the Romans and the Moors and, as a result, has been able to preserve its culture and language reasonably intact. Much of the region is Basque at heart – the language is still spoken in the northwest and centre – but the south is exclusively Spanish-speaking.

Set in the foothills of the Pyrenees, on the border with France, Navarra is a fairytale land of palaces and monasteries, medieval towns and towers along the famous pilgrimage route the Way of St James. The countryside ranges from snow-dusted peaks to forests and canyons with elegant hillsides ribbed with grapevines.

It is a part of Spain that takes its history and culture seriously. As well as a packed calendar of festivals, Navarra hosts a series of historical markets in ancient villages where dress and customs from the Middle Ages – complete with frolicking minstrels and troubadours – keep the past alive.

Running with bulls and eating beef

While most people couldn't locate it on a map, Navarra is famous for its annual display of madness that erupts in the streets of the capital, Pamplona. The gory Running of the Bulls spectacle during July's Festival of San Fermín has fascinated the world since author Ernest Hemingway immortalised the ritual in *The Sun Also Rises*. The other compelling attraction of Pamplona are its *tapas*, called *pintxos* here which, as in neighbouring Basque Country, have evolved into expressions of culinary art.

Like its neighbours La Rioja and Aragón, Navarra is watered by the Ebro River. Its flourishing valleys produce wheat, wine, olive trees (and DO Navarran olive oil) plus vegetables of all persuasions. The good people of Tudela, a riverside town famed for its tender artichokes and baby lettuce, give thanks for this profusion of produce at their annual Vegetable Week.

Given the local penchant for bull-running it's no surprise beef is a staple of the Navarran diet. Called *ternera*, it is usually served as a T-bone (*chuletón*) and barbecued. Denomination of Origin (DO) laws stipulate exactly how Pyrenean cows should be raised, right down to the number of months they must be milk-fed. Beef stews are understandably popular and the finest steaks in the kingdom are said to come from Baztan-Bidasoa.

Cordero, or lamb, is another key link in the Navarran food chain, often stewed with potatoes in a hearty *estofado*. As in La Rioja, lamb chops are barbecued over aromatic fires of vine prunings. Ram's fat is used to sauté *migas*, or breadcrumbs, with chorizo and melón to provide sustenance to the countless shepherds.

Not surprisingly, this region – famous for the 'running of the bulls' – is said to produce Spain's finest steaks.

Pig's trotters are popular, as are lamb's feet, which are served with tripe and blood in a dish called *menudicos*. Baby goat is often barbecued over a beechwood fire. Navarrans are keen hunters so their tables feature venison, wild boar and an aviary of birds from quail to partridge, the latter cooked in stock with white wine and bitter chocolate.

The kingdom has no coastline but, like most of Spain, its subjects have a craving for cod. Salt cod or *bacalao* is commonly cooked *ajoarriero* (mule-driver) style, in an earthenware dish with garlic, onions, tomatoes, potatoes, peppers, chilli and sometimes egg. The Pyrenees rivers and Navarra's extensive fish farms supply plentiful trout, preferably stuffed with, or wrapped in, *jamón*.

Navarrans are keen on the summery herb, borage, simmered with potatoes but really they appreciate any stew or soup containing vegetables, including one rather thin soup made from the boiled vegetable broth. They are passionate mycologists, especially where the hard-to-find, jealously guarded and meaty *perretxiko* mushroom is concerned. Truffles surface around December, when Navarra puts the culture into agriculture with a week-long celebration of this remarkable fungus.

The raw sheep's milk *roncal*, the 'son of the Pyrenees', is Navarra's DO cheese – a stout, nutty number produced in the northeast. The bluish rind contains a pressed cheese paste that is hard and creamy at the same time. Dairy and animal products also feature in the popular desserts, *leche frita*, a type of fried custard, and the sweet soup *sopa cana* made with sugared milk, cinnamon and chicken lard.

Spanish soil, French-style wines

Navarran earth shares similar DNA to its neighbours, La Rioja and Bordeaux, and is equally capable of nurturing outstanding wines. Like most Spanish regions, it has been making wine since Roman times, only these days the popularity of Navarra's traditional grape *garnacha* is being challenged by upstarts like tempranillo, cabernet sauvignon and merlot. French varieties, such as chardonnay and sauvignon blanc, also do well in the Bordeaux-like soils. The highest and one of the larger wine-growing areas is Baja Montaña, which produces one fifth of the region's wines and the finest rosados. Despite their low international profile, pilgrims traipsing across the Pyrenees in search of St James have treasured Navarran wines for centuries.

Opposite: Sunflowers and the monastery of Santa Maria la Real de la Oliva, thought to have been founded in 1150AD, Carcastillo, Navarra.

Below: Breakfast in the streets of Pamplona following the running of the bulls.

gourmet
pılgrım

Pescado y marisco

Fish & seafood

Spain's enormous appetite for the bounty of the sea is a joyful confluence of geography and religion.

Pescado y marisco
Fish & seafood

The one word that best sums up the Spanish relationship to fish is *bacalao* – the humble cod. This adaptable Atlantic Ocean fish has been a fixture in Spain since Basque fishermen first discovered it off Newfoundland in the Middle Ages. The fish was able to be transported long distances, thanks to the ancient Phoenician innovation of preserving it in salt – a practice further developed by the Romans into full-scale factories.

Cod soon became a staple food throughout the Iberian Peninsula, in the coast and landlocked interior. Each region has its favourite recipes but *bacalao* is commonly served shredded in a salad, with tomatoes, peppers, olives and fruits. The Andalucian version, *Remojón*, comes with citrus and smoked paprika, while *buñuelos*, a Basque dish of fried cod and potato dumplings, is also renowned.

Mule drivers who carried the salted fish across the vast interior are credited with inventing *bacalao al ajoarriero* ('mule-drivers cod'), a simple dish of cod, garlic and vegetables that's popular from Extremadura and the Castiles to Navarra and Andalucia. The cod-loving Basques are responsible for *bacalao a la vizcaina*, a basic preparation of fish, onion and dried peppers, and the more sophisticated *bacalao al pil-pil*, where the cod is fried with garlic and oil to release its natural gelatine and create a creamy emulsion.

Devoted to the daily catch

Spain's appetite for fish and seafood on the Iberian Peninsula is a happy coincidence of geography and religion. With the longest coastline in Europe, Spain is surrounded by sea on three sides. While living off the marine bounty has been a natural reflex of its people, the rise of Catholicism meant eating fish became a religious duty, particularly on holy days when the Vatican banned the consumption of meat. Miguel de Cervantes chronicled the custom 400 years ago in *Don Quixote:* "He said it must be Friday, the day he could not sell anything except servings of a fish known in Castile as pollock or in Andalusia as salt cod."

Spain is the biggest fish market in Europe, with annual seafood consumption at around 40 kilograms per person. Visit a portside market like *La Piedra* at Vigo on the Galician coast or *Palamós* on the Costa Brava and it is obvious this is a country with an uncommon passion for *los pescados*. The daily catch comprises shimmering mountains of bream, sea bass, tuna, snapper, swordfish, shark (*cazón*), sardines, hake, monkfish and dozens of other varieties. Mussels, squid, octopus, clams, oysters, shrimp and lobster head up the inventory of shellfish.

> Fish – possibly the defining ingredient of Spanish cuisine – is the natural bounty of a land surrounded by sea on three sides.

A fish dish for every region

Each region has its specialty, from the *vieiras* or scallops of Galicia whose shells have become the symbol of pilgrims on the *Santiago de Compostela*, to the freshwater salmon of Asturias commonly prepared *a la ribereña*, sautéed with Serrano ham and cider. Navarrese tastes tend to run to river trout, also paired with Serrano ham. In Murcia, *dorada* or gilthead bream from the *Mar Menor* is baked in a salt crust that cracks open to reveal sweet and meltingly moist flesh.

Cádiz and Huelva in Andalucia are famed for *mojama*, tuna loin hung in the wind and sun to dry naturally then served in paper-thin slices with a little olive oil. Tuna is also big business in the Basque Country, especially in *Ondarroa* whose *Ortíz* brand tuna belly in oil is widely regarded as the world's finest canned fish.

Spain's fishermen have contributed a wealth of hearty stews to the national diet. From the Costa Brava comes *suquet*, a casserole of rock fish and shellfish in a dense broth with an aromatic *sofrito* base of onions, garlic, peppers and spices. The Basques have *marmitako*, a tuna and potato casserole, while the Balearic Islands prefer lobster stews and *burrida de raya*, a soup of stingray cooked in fish stock and finished with a slick of garlicky *alioli*.

Opposite: Deep sea fishing vessels moored at Pasajes, San Sebastian, Basque Country.

Below: Drying fish on La Graciosa – a small, nature park island of 700 inhabitants and sand roads, sustained primarily by fishing, located just north of Lanzarote, Canary Islands.

Over left: Fisherman sort the catch of anchovies and sardines off the coast of Vigo, Galicia – the largest fishing port in Europe.

Over right: Fishing village of A Guarda, on the Atlantic coast of Galicia.

Delicacies of the deep

Seafood is regarded as a delicacy in many cultures but in Spain, with its abundance of species, the term 'delicacy' takes on extraordinary new meanings. Fishermen risk life and limb in heavy surf to collect bizarre looking goose barnacles called *percebes* from coastal rocks. Briefly steamed or boiled, the flesh from inside the barnacle's gooseneck-like stalk is said to taste like lobster. The Basques are mad for baby eels, creatures so delicate they disintegrate when cooked so they are typically just dropped into a pot of sizzling olive oil, garlic and dried chilli and eaten immediately. Basques also hanker for baby squid or *txipirones*, cooked in their own ink with a little onion.

On the Costa Brava, land of Salvador Dalí and some of the world's most extraordinary restaurants, seafood has even had the surrealist treatment. The landmark *Hotel Empandá*, where the late Josep Mercader pioneered new Catalan cuisine in the 1970s, greets diners with a jar of fish bones. Macerated in milk overnight, then rolled in a little flour and deep fried, they might appear at first glance to be something destined for the bin, rather than one's mouth. But they are crunchy, salty and wonderful – further proof the Spanish know their seafood inside and out.

Cantabrian anchovies

The fishing village of Santoña in Cantabria has two significant claims to fame. The first is that it was the birthplace of Juan de la Cosa, the marine cartographer who accompanied Columbus on his maiden voyage of discovery in 1492. Secondly, and far more importantly, it is home to the revered Cantabrian anchovy.

The anchovy is known as *bocarte* in the North but elsewhere in Spain it goes by the names of *boquerón, anchoa* or, in Catalonia, *anxova*. When cured in vinegar – to become a favourite *tapas* topping – they are called *boquerones*, which refers to their oversized mouth (*boquerón*).

Fishermen on the Atlantic coastline of northern Spain and neighbouring France have a long tradition of harvesting the plump, herring-like fish after they return from their feeding grounds in Norway to the Bay of Biscay. More than 200 ships on the coasts of the Basque Country and Cantabria hunt anchovies

with gusto but Santoña, where sales of anchovies contribute more than 80 per cent of its economy, is the epicenter of the annual catch.

During the 1960s Spanish and French fishing fleets hauled in 80,000 tonnes of the fish but that volume had plummeted to around 10,000 tonnes by the first decade of this century. The single biggest threat to the anchovy is overfishing by humans, which has forced the European Union to preserve the population by imposing strict quotas on the annual catch. Currently no more than 7,000 tonnes can be plucked from the seas each year – 90 per cent by Spanish ships and 10 per cent by the French.

Anchovies have an enthusiastic following on Spain's Mediterranean coast too, where a natural salt mountain in Catalonia has been used to preserve the fish since Roman times. They are most commonly seen in Catalan cuisine on top a piece of toasted bread and tomato. A commoner's snack, fit for a king.

Paella marinera
Seafood paella

Ingredients

800g whole medium green shrimp* (king prawns)

200g thick white fish fillets, skinned (monkfish, hake, Spanish mackerel or ling)

1 whole medium squid (calamari) or 2 cuttlefish, cleaned and skinned

80ml olive oil

1 large brown onion, finely chopped

2 garlic cloves, finely chopped

1 large ripe tomato, finely chopped

1 medium red pepper (capsicum)*, seeded and cut into strips

2 litres fish stock, approximately

¼ teaspoon saffron threads*

400g short grain 'paella' rice* (such as Calasparra)

2 teaspoons smoked paprika*

2 teaspoons flaked salt

300g mussels*, cleaned and debearded

200g clams, rinsed

8 langoustine (scampi)*

100g frozen peas, defrosted

Lemon wedges, to serve

Method

Leave 10 shrimp whole, then peel and devein the remaining shrimp. Pat fish dry with kitchen paper towel and cut into 2cm cubes. Cut squid into thin rings.

Heat oil in a 6-8 serve (base about 30cm in diameter) paella pan over a medium-high heat and cook the 10 whole shrimp for 1-2 minutes each side or until orange in colour; remove and set aside.

Reduce heat to low and add onion and garlic and cook for 8 minutes, stirring occasionally. Add tomato and pepper and cook, stirring, for a further 2 minutes.

Meanwhile, heat stock and saffron in a large saucepan over a medium-low heat, then cover and bring to a gentle simmer.

To the paella pan, add the remaining peeled shrimp, squid, rice, paprika and salt and cook, stirring, over a low heat for 5 minutes. Flatten out the surface of the rice with the back of a wooden spoon and begin to ladle hot stock into the paella, starting with about 500ml. Keep the stock hot and covered and add more stock to the paella as it is absorbed by the rice. Without stirring the paella, continue to ladle the hot stock onto the rice and cook, uncovered, for about 20 minutes.

When about 500ml of hot stock remains in the saucepan, add fish, mussels, clams and langoustine, pushing them into the hot rice. Scatter the peas and whole cooked shrimp over the rice. Continue to cook, uncovered, for a further 10 minutes or until seafood is cooked through. During the last 5 minutes, cover pan with a large piece of foil to assist in cooking the seafood.

When rice is cooked (see Note), remove pan from heat and cover with a clean tea towel and stand for 10 minutes. Open the mussel shells and place the open halves with the flesh intact around the outside edge.

Serve with lemon wedges.

Note – The amount of cooking stock may vary according to the rice quality. When cooked, the rice must appear a little moist, but this disappears during resting time. When testing the rice, the centre of the paella cooks faster so add extra stock to the outside edge of the pan, as this rice can remain a little crunchy during cooking.

Merluza y gambas a la sidra
Hake & shrimp in apple cider sauce

serves 4

Ingredients

300g thick white fish fillets, skinned (such as hake, monkfish, ling, Spanish mackerel)

8 whole medium green shrimp* (king prawns), peeled and deveined

8 large clams, rinsed (see Note, below)

Apple cider sauce:

60ml olive oil

1 small brown onion, finely chopped

2 garlic cloves, finely chopped

1 tablespoon plain (all-purpose) flour

250ml sparkling apple cider*

1 teaspoon freshly picked thyme leaves

Flaked salt

Freshly cracked black pepper

2 tablespoons chopped fresh flat-leaf (Italian) parsley

2 spring onions*, thinly sliced

Method

Pat fish dry with kitchen paper towel and cut into 2cm cubes. Set aside.

To make the apple cider sauce, heat oil in a large frying pan over a low-medium heat and cook the onion and garlic for 10 minutes, stirring constantly, or until soft but not brown. Add flour and cook, stirring, for a further 2 minutes. Remove from heat and gradually stir in apple cider and thyme until smooth. Return to medium heat and stir until sauce boils and thickens. Allow sauce to simmer for 1-2 minutes then season to taste.

Add fish, shrimp and clams to the sauce and stir to combine. Cook covered for 5 minutes or until the clams have opened and seafood is cooked.

Serve sprinkled with parsley and spring onions. Cooked rice makes the perfect accompaniment.

Note – If clams are unavailable try using mussels.

* Refer to Glossary – Page 482

Calamares rellenos
Calamari with anchovy, lemon & thyme stuffing

serves 2-4

Ingredients

8 whole small-medium (baby) squid (calamari)

Stuffing:

2 tablespoons olive oil

1 small red onion, finely chopped

1 garlic clove, finely chopped

35g fresh breadcrumbs*

2 tablespoons finely chopped fresh flat-leaf (Italian) parsley

1 teaspoon finely grated lemon rind

1 teaspoon freshly picked thyme leaves

2 anchovy fillets*, finely chopped

Flaked salt

Freshly cracked black pepper

1 tablespoon olive oil, extra

Rucola*/baby rocket leaves, to serve

Extra virgin olive oil, to serve

Lemon wedges, to serve

Method

Preheat oven to 200°C.

Clean and skin the squid and cut away the tentacles. Rinse squid body and tentacles well under cold water and pat dry with kitchen paper towel. Cut tentacles into small pieces and reserve for the stuffing.

To make the stuffing, heat oil in a medium frying pan over a medium heat and cook onion and garlic for 8 minutes or until lightly golden, stirring occasionally. Add the tentacles and cook, stirring, for a further 2 minutes. Add breadcrumbs, parsley, lemon rind, thyme and anchovies and stir well to combine. Season to taste. Allow to cool slightly before filling squid bodies with about 2 teaspoons of stuffing. Don't pack too firmly as the squid tubes will shrink a little when cooking. Secure the open end with a toothpick.

Rub squid with the extra oil and lightly season. Heat a char-grill pan over high heat until very hot. Add squid and cook for 2 minutes each side. Transfer char-grill pan to preheated oven and cook a further 6-8 minutes. Serve topped with rucola, drizzled with extra virgin olive oil and lemon wedges.

* Refer to Glossary – Page 482

Sardinas con salsa de tomate
Sardines with paprika tomato sauce

Ingredients

1kg whole fresh sardines, cleaned and butterflied*

75g plain (all-purpose) flour

2 garlic cloves, finely chopped

½ teaspoon ground nutmeg

1 tablespoon chopped fresh flat-leaf (Italian) parsley

Pinch of saffron threads*

2 tablespoons water

Flaked salt

Freshly cracked black pepper

60ml olive oil

1 medium brown onion, finely chopped

400g can chopped tomatoes

2 teaspoons sweet paprika*

2 tablespoons water, extra

Fresh flat-leaf (Italian) parsley to serve

Sardines are a true delicacy. Small, dense, sweet with a fresh tang of the sea, they're worth effort to source out – generally at markets and better fishmongers. Give a cloak of seasoned flour, a quick baptism in hot oil, they then sit in a saffron and spice-rich tomato sauce soaking up the flavoursome cooking liquor. Served with a salad, a loaf of crusty bread to mop up the sauce and a little glass of fino sherry, one could be on the Atlantic coast of Andalusia.

Method

Wipe over the sardines with damp kitchen paper towel. Dust lightly with flour, shaking off the excess.

Place the garlic, nutmeg, parsley, saffron and water in a mortar and pound with the pestle to form a paste. Season with salt and pepper. Set aside.

Heat oil in a large non-stick frying pan over a medium-high heat and cook sardines for 1-2 minutes each side. Remove to a side plate. Add onion to the same frying pan over a medium heat and cook for 5 minutes or until soft, stirring occasionally. Add tomatoes, paprika, parsley, garlic paste and extra water and cook, uncovered, for a further 5 minutes, stirring occasionally. Taste and adjust seasoning.

Return sardines to frying pan and spoon over the sauce. Serve with chopped parsley.

Tip: Sardines can often be purchased already cleaned and butterflied.

Patata y atún a la cazuela
Tuna & potato stew

Ingredients

400g fresh tuna steaks

400g all-purpose potatoes, peeled

60ml olive oil

1 medium brown onion, finely chopped

1 stick celery, finely chopped

2 garlic cloves, finely chopped

400g can chopped tomatoes

1 medium green pepper (capsicum)*, seeded and finely chopped

300ml fish stock

1 tablespoon chopped fresh oregano leaves

1 teaspoon freshly picked thyme leaves

½ cup chopped fresh flat-leaf (Italian) parsley

1 tablespoon baby capers*

1 hard-boiled egg, finely chopped

Flaked salt

Freshly cracked black pepper

Method

Cut tuna into 2cm cubes and set aside. Cut potatoes into pieces about the same size as tuna.

Heat oil in a large saucepan or frying pan over low-medium heat and cook onion, celery and garlic for 10 minutes, stirring occasionally. Add potatoes, tomatoes, pepper, fish stock, oregano and thyme and stir to combine. Cook for a further 20 minutes, partially covered, or until potatoes are cooked.

Add tuna, parsley and capers and cook for 3-4 minutes. Add the egg and gently stir to combine. Season to taste.

Tip: Swordfish or Spanish mackerel could be used instead of tuna.

* Refer to Glossary – Page 482

Merluza en salsa verde
Hake in green sauce

Ingredients

400g thick hake fillet, skinned (or blue
eye or monkfish)
2 medium zucchini (courgettes)*
20g butter
60ml olive oil
1 medium brown onion, thinly sliced
2 garlic cloves, finely chopped
125ml fish stock
1 teaspoon finely grated lemon rind
1 tablespoon lemon juice
½ teaspoon chilli paste*
Flaked salt
1 tablespoon olive oil, extra
2 teaspoons plain (all-purpose) flour
Boiled potatoes, to serve

Method

Pat fish dry with kitchen paper towel. Cut zucchini in half
lengthways, then thinly slice.

Heat butter and only 1 tablespoon of oil in a large frying pan over
medium-high heat and cook fish for 3-4 minutes each side or until
lightly browned and cooked through. Remove to a side plate and
keep warm.

Heat remaining oil in the same frying pan and cook onion and
garlic over medium heat for 8 minutes or until lightly golden, stirring
occasionally. Add zucchini and cook for a further 2 minutes or until
vegetables have softened, stirring occasionally. Add stock, lemon
rind and juice and chilli paste. Remove from heat and season to
taste with salt.

To make a paste to thicken the sauce, place the extra oil and
flour in a small bowl and mix well. Stir in 2 tablespoons of the pan
liquid to blend, then pour all the mixture back into the frying pan.
Return frying pan to the heat, then bring to the boil over medium
heat, stirring, until sauce thickens; simmer for 2 minutes stirring
occasionally. To serve, place sauce onto individual plates and top
with a piece of cooked fish. Or return fish to the frying pan and
spoon the sauce over. Serve with boiled potatoes.

* Refer to Glossary – Page 482

Mejillones a la Castellana
Castillian mussels

serves 4

Ingredients

2kg mussels*, cleaned and debearded
60ml olive oil
1 large brown onion, finely chopped
3 garlic cloves, finely chopped
2 teaspoons finely grated lemon rind
250ml dry white wine
Freshly cracked black pepper
¼ cup chopped fresh flat-leaf (Italian) parsley

Madrid is a landlocked city in the heart of the nation. Despite that, Los Madrileños, the people of Madrid, consume more seafood per head than any other European people. Great truckloads of mussels, freshly harvested from the protected inlets of Galicia, arrive early into the fish markets early each morning to keep up with the demand. This is a delicious way of preparing super fresh mussels with the richness of garlic, the tang of white wine and a fresh hit of green parsley.

Method

Rinse mussels and drain. Heat oil in a large frying pan over a low-medium heat and cook onion and garlic for 5 minutes or until soft and lightly golden, stirring occasionally.

Add mussels, lemon rind and wine. Cover with a lid and cook for 8-10 minutes or until the mussel shells open.

Season the mussels with pepper. Taste before adding any salt as the mussels have a delicious natural salty liquid when cooked.

Sprinkle with parsley and serve with crusty bread.

Note – Discard any mussels that don't open after cooking.

* Refer to Glossary – Page 482

Pulpo con tomate y alcachofas
Braised octopus with tomato & artichokes

serves 4

Ingredients

600g whole medium-large octopus, cleaned

60ml olive oil

1 large brown onion, finely chopped

2 cloves garlic, finely chopped

2 teaspoons smoked paprika*

400g can chopped tomatoes

125ml dry white wine

4 sprigs fresh thyme

4 whole cooked artichoke hearts*, cut into quarters

1 large zucchini (courgette)*, thickly sliced

¼ cup chopped fresh flat-leaf (Italian) parsley

Flaked salt

Freshly cracked black pepper

Cooked rice, to serve

Method

Cut octopus tentacles into pieces about 5cm long. Rinse under cold water and drain.

Heat oil in a large saucepan over medium heat and cook onion and garlic for 5 minutes or until soft, stirring occasionally. Add octopus, paprika, tomatoes, wine and thyme, then cover and bring to the boil. Reduce to a low-medium heat and simmer for 30 minutes. Uncover, stir and cook for a further 20-30 minutes or until octopus is tender (a skewer should insert easily into the thickest part of a tentacle) and the sauce has thickened slightly. Add artichokes and zucchini and cook for a further 5 minutes. Stir in the parsley and season to taste.

Serve with cooked rice.

Tip: Small baby octopus could also be and used and cooked whole in this recipe.

* Refer to Glossary – Page 482

Rodaballo relleno
Potato & mushroom stuffed turbot

serves 4

Ingredients

2 whole turbot (about 500g each),
cleaned and scaled

500g all-purpose potatoes, peeled and
cut into pieces

125ml milk

2 egg yolks

40g butter

2 tablespoons olive oil

1 medium brown onion, finely chopped

2 garlic cloves, finely chopped

200g button or Swiss brown mushrooms,
quartered and thinly sliced

2 tablespoons finely chopped fresh
flat-leaf (Italian) parsley

Flaked salt

Freshly cracked black pepper

1 tablespoon olive oil, extra

Lemon wedges, to serve

Method

Preheat oven to 200°C. Pat fish dry with kitchen paper towel.

Cut a pocket for the stuffing into the top of each turbot. To do this, cut into the flesh down to the bone that runs down the middle of the top-side of the fish. Then, using a small sharp knife, cut and lift the flesh on one side away from the bone; use small strokes of the knife and try not to cut through the flesh and skin. Repeat this process on the opposite side to create the pocket. Then place the fish on two oven trays lined with kitchen baking paper.

Bring a medium saucepan of salted water to the boil and cook potatoes until tender; drain. Add milk, egg yolks and only half the butter. Mash together.

Heat oil in a medium frying pan over a medium heat and cook onion and garlic for 8 minutes or until lightly golden, stirring occasionally. Stir in mushrooms and cook for a further 2 minutes or until soft. Add mashed potato and parsley to the pan and stir to combine. Season to taste. Allow to cool for 5 minutes.

Divide filling evenly between the fish by spooning it into the pocket. Dot fish with remaining butter and season with salt and pepper.

Bake in preheated oven for 20-25 minutes or until the flesh, is tender. Swap position of trays halfway during cooking. Serve drizzled with extra olive oil and lemon wedges.

Note – If turbot is unavailable, use whole flounder or sole as an alternative. The filling can also be used to stuff 4 individual fish (as in photo).

Gambas al ajillo
Garlic chilli shrimp

serves 4

Ingredients

2kg whole medium green shrimp*
(king prawns)

60ml olive oil

20g butter

2 garlic cloves, very thinly sliced

1 small fresh red chilli*, finely chopped
(see Tip)

¼ cup chopped fresh flat-leaf (Italian)
parsley

Pinch of sweet Spanish paprika*

Flaked salt

Crusty bread, to serve

Method

Peel and devein shrimp, leaving tails intact. Heat oil and butter in a heavy-based medium frying pan over a medium heat and cook garlic and chilli for 1-2 minutes or until lightly golden, stirring constantly.

Add shrimp and cook for about 6-8 minutes or until orange in colour. Toss occasionally during cooking.

Remove from heat, then add parsley and paprika and season to taste with salt.

Serve with crusty bread.

Tip: To reduce the 'heat' of the chilli, remove the seeds and discard; to make it hotter, use two chillies instead of one.

* Refer to Glossary – Page 482

Lenguado con setas y queso
Mushroom & cheese-topped sole

Ingredients

8 medium sole fillets

1 tablespoon olive oil

50g butter

2 eschalots*, finely chopped

200g button or Swiss brown mushrooms,
thinly sliced

150ml dry white wine

Flaked salt

Freshly cracked white pepper

50g manchego cheese*, finely grated

Method

Pat fish fillets dry with kitchen paper towel.

Heat oil and only half the butter in a large frying pan over a medium-high heat and cook the fillets for about 1 minute each side or until lightly brown on both sides. Remove from pan to a side plate and keep warm.

Heat remaining butter in the same frying pan over a medium heat and cook the eschalots for 5 minutes or until softened. Add mushrooms and cook, stirring, for a further 3-4 minutes or until the mushrooms are just tender. Add wine, bring to the boil and simmer, uncovered, until reduced by half. Season to taste.

To serve, place fillets onto a plate and top with sauce. Sprinkle with cheese.

Note – These fillets are from a flat fish and are rather thin compared with a round fish, such as monkfish, so 2 fillets per person is ideal. Flounder fillets are a good alternative.

* Refer to Glossary – Page 482

Fideuà
Seafood fideuà

serves 4

Ingredients

300g spagattini pasta*

600g medium whole green shrimp (king prawns)*

200g firm fish fillets (such as hake, monkfish, ling, Spanish mackerel), skin removed

2 tablespoons olive oil

½ leek, white part only, chopped

2 garlic cloves, finely chopped

2 ripe tomatoes, peeled and chopped

250ml hot fish or chicken stock

Pinch of saffron threads*

1 teaspoon mild Spanish paprika*

Flaked salt

Freshly cracked black pepper

300g mussels*, cleaned and debearded

2 tablespoons chopped fresh flat-leaf (Italian) parsley

2 teaspoons freshly picked thyme leaves

Lemon wedges, to serve

The Valencians love cooking in big pans. Their paellas, filled with all manner of seafood, are known all around the world. Less famous perhaps is the Valencian fideuá, like a paella but traditionally made with a macaroni-type pasta that's generally referred to as fideos. Here it is made with spagattini pasta.

Pasta is popular on the Spain's Mediterranean coast. Not the amazing range of 'different pasta for every sauce' like the Italians, but a handful including canelones and shell shapes called caracoles. Fideos are also used in escudella. The pasta cooks in the sauce soaking up the rich sofregit, the sofrito, of garlic, leeks and tomatoes and flavoursome stock. This is a great dish to make when entertaining friends – enjoy with a plenty of bread and a glass of chilled wine.

Method

Bring a large saucepan of salted water to the boil for the pasta. Break the pasta up into lengths, about 6cm long, and add to the boiling water; cook for 3 minutes. Drain and refresh under cold running water; set aside.

Leave 4 shrimp whole, then peel and devein the remaining shrimp. Cut fish into 2cm cubes. Heat oil in a large ovenproof frying pan or paella pan over a low-medium heat and cook the whole shrimp for 2 minutes each side; remove to a side plate. Add leek and garlic to frying pan and cook for 5 minutes or until soft, stirring occasionally. Add tomatoes, stock, saffron and paprika and stir to combine. Season to taste.

Add drained pasta, peeled prawns and fish to frying pan and toss to combine. Flatten the surface with the back of a wooden spoon, then push the mussels into the pasta. Bring to the boil and simmer, uncovered, for 10 minutes or until the mussels begin to open and the liquid reduces.

Lastly, place the frying pan under a hot grill for about 5 minutes or until the pasta is lightly golden. Sprinkle with parsley and thyme. Serve topped with reserved whole cooked shrimp and lemon wedges.

* Refer to Glossary – Page 482

Cangrejos a la Riojana
Crabs Riojan style

serves 4

Ingredients

6 whole green crabs (blue swimmer or small mud crabs)

2 tablespoons olive oil

1 large brown onion, finely chopped

2 garlic cloves, finely chopped

400g can chopped tomatoes

1 large green pepper (capsicum)*, finely chopped

1-2 small fresh red chillies*, seeded and finely chopped

1 teaspoon sugar

Flaked salt

3 spring onions*, finely sliced, to serve

Method

Clean crabs and cut in half (or quarters if they are large). Crack claws with the back of a heavy-bladed knife before cooking in the sauce, as it will make it easier to remove the flesh when hot with a claw pick.

Heat oil in a large deep frying pan over medium heat and cook onion and garlic for 8 minutes or until lightly golden, stirring occasionally.

Add tomatoes, pepper, chillies and sugar. Bring to the boil and, simmer, uncovered for a further 10 minutes. Season to taste with salt.

Add the crabs and spoon some of the sauce over them. Cover and cook for 10 minutes or until the shells turn orange in colour and flesh looks opaque and cooked.

Serve sprinkled with spring onions.

Tip: Provide a large bowl of warm water and lemon slices to rinse fingers while eating, plus some paper napkins. Paper bibs are also fun if they can be found.

* Refer to Glossary – Page 482

Coca de sardinas
Sardine & caramelised onion coca

serves 4

Coca is the bare canvas of Catalonian cooking. Here, we're painting it with a natural pairing of caramelised onions and fat sardines on top. Baked together, the onions sweeten, further moistening the coca dough, while the sardines cook to golden, crisp perfection.

Ingredients

1 quantity of coca dough (see recipe, page 346)

8 whole fresh sardines, cleaned and butterflied*

2 tablespoons olive oil

2 small red onions, thinly sliced

1 tablespoon balsamic vinegar

Pinch of sugar

2 tablespoons chopped pitted black olives

2 tablespoons chopped anchovy fillets*

2 tablespoons finely chopped fresh flat-leaf (Italian) parsley

Extra virgin olive oil, to serve

Method

Wipe over sardines with damp kitchen paper towel. Set aside.

Heat oil in a medium frying pan over a medium heat and cook onions for 10 minutes or until lightly golden, stirring occasionally. Add vinegar and sugar and cook, stirring, for a further 5-10 minutes or until onions are caramelised. Remove from heat and set aside to cool slightly.

Place olives, anchovies and parsley into a small bowl and stir to combine. Spread some olive mix onto the flesh side of the sardines; set aside.

Preheat oven to 200°C fan forced (220°C – no fan) and position a shelf close to the bottom of the oven, which will assist in a crispy base. Lightly grease a large oven tray or pizza tray.

Place coca dough onto a lightly floured board and divide into 4 portions. Roll each portion out into a round or rectangular shape and place on prepared tray. Top each coca with some caramelised onion, then place two prepared sardines, flesh side down, onto each coca.

Drizzle with oil and bake in preheated oven for 15 minutes or until dough is golden brown and crisp. Serve immediately.

Note – The fan-forced (or fan-assisted) oven function is perfect for cooking coca (pizza) where possible – or cook in a pizza oven.

* Refer to Glossary – Page 482

Suquet
Fish stew

serves 4

Ingredients

500g whole medium green shrimp
(king prawns)*

4 whole small squid, cleaned and skinned

100g monkfish fillets, skinned

100g swordfish steak

60ml olive oil

1 large brown onion, finely chopped

2 garlic cloves, finely chopped

1 small red pepper (capsicum)*, seeded
and finely diced

1 small yellow pepper (capsicum)*, seeded
and finely diced

400g can chopped tomatoes

1 teaspoon sugar

250ml hot fish stock

1 medium zucchini (courgette)*, finely
chopped

3 langoustine (scampi)*, cut in half
lengthways

Flaked salt

Freshly cracked black pepper

Fresh flat-leaf (Italian) parsley, to serve

Crusty bread, to serve

Barceloneta is a small neighbourhood of fishermen, a short walk from Barcelona's old town. Here, along the palm-lined promenade, are a number of restaurants offering seafood. In any number you'll find sarsuela, an eclectic fish stew in which the ingredients change from chef to chef. Its younger brother is the suquet, a subtle dish where the fish is king.

The sarsuela, on the other hand, is a much richer affair with a hearty sauce to be soaked up with crusty bread. The name itself means 'operetta', a sort of a variety show of different fish species.

Method

Peel and devein shrimp; discard shells. Rinse squid under cold water and cut into thin rounds. Cut the fish into 2cm cubes. Set aside.

Heat only 1 tablespoon of oil in a large deep frying pan over medium heat and cook the shrimp for 2 minutes or until lightly golden, turning during cooking; remove to a side plate.

Heat remaining oil in the same frying pan and cook onion and garlic over a low-medium heat for 10 minutes or until golden, stirring occasionally. Add the peppers, tomatoes, sugar and stock, then bring to the boil and simmer, uncovered, for a further 10 minutes. Add zucchini and fish and gently stir to combine. Cook for a further 5 minutes over medium heat. Lastly add the shrimp, langoustine and squid; gently stir again to combine. Simmer, uncovered, for 5 minutes or until the seafood is cooked.

Season to taste and serve with parsley and crusty bread.

238
gourmetpilgrim Spain

* Refer to Glossary – Page 482

Rape asado con tomate y avellanas
Monkfish, tomato & hazelnut bake

Ingredients

600g monkfish fillets, skinned (or blue eye or swordfish)

2 tablespoons plain (all-purpose) flour

60ml olive oil

4 thick slices French stick bread

2 garlic cloves, thinly sliced

200g very ripe tomatoes, chopped

60ml fish stock

2 tablespoons fresh flat-leaf (Italian) parsley

125g hazelnuts, roasted*, skinned and roughly chopped

Flaked salt

Freshly cracked black pepper

Method

Preheat oven to 180°C.

Pat fish dry with kitchen paper towel. Cut fish into 2cm cubes. Coat lightly with flour, shaking off the excess. Heat only 2 tablespoons of oil in a large frying pan over medium heat and cook bread slices for 2 minutes each side or until lightly golden. Remove, cool slightly and cut into large cubes.

Heat remaining oil in the same frying pan and cook fish over a medium heat for 1-2 minutes each side or until lightly browned. Transfer fish to an ovenproof casserole dish.

Using the same frying pan, cook garlic for 2 minutes over a medium heat, stirring constantly to avoid over browning. Stir in tomatoes, stock, parsley and hazelnuts, then bring to the boil and simmer, uncovered, for 5 minutes or until slightly thickened. Season to taste.

Spoon sauce over the fish and top with crisp bread cubes, pushing them very slightly into the sauce.

Bake in preheated oven, uncovered, for 20 minutes.

* Refer to Glossary – Page 482

Atún a la brasa
Char-grilled tuna with balsamic onions

Ingredients

4 x 150g tuna steaks (about 1cm thick)
or swordfish

125ml olive oil

Freshly cracked black pepper

Balsamic onions:

2 medium brown onions, halved and
thinly sliced

3 garlic cloves, crushed

1 tablespoon balsamic vinegar

1 tablespoon chopped fresh flat-leaf
(Italian) parsley

½ teaspoon mild Spanish paprika*

Flaked salt

Baby spinach leaves, to serve

Method

Pat fish dry with kitchen paper towel. Lightly rub only 1 tablespoon of the olive oil over the four steaks and season with pepper. Cover and set aside.

To make the balsamic onions, heat the remaining oil in a heavy-based saucepan over a low-medium heat and cook onion and garlic for 10 minutes or until lightly golden, stirring occasionally. Add vinegar, parsley and paprika and cook, uncovered, for a further 25 minutes, stirring occasionally. Season with salt to taste.

Cook tuna on a preheated char-grill or barbecue for about 2 minutes each side. Ideally, the middle of the tuna steak should remain a beautiful pink colour.

Serve tuna with balsamic onions and spinach leaves.

Tip: Ideally remove thick pieces of fish, such as tuna and swordfish, from the refrigerator 10-15 minutes before cooking to take the chill off and allow them to cook more evenly. Keep covered while standing.

242
gourmetpilgrim Spain

* Refer to Glossary – Page 482

Arroz negro con sepia y langostinos
Black rice with squid, shrimp & chorizo

serves 4

Ingredients

500g whole small-medium squid

500g whole medium green shrimp (king prawns)*

1.5-2 litres fish stock

2 tablespoons olive oil

1 medium brown onion, finely chopped

2 garlic cloves, finely chopped

½ red pepper (capsicum)*, seeded and finely chopped

½ green pepper (capsicum)*, seeded and finely chopped

60g Spanish chorizo sausage*, finely diced

1 teaspoon sweet paprika*

1 teaspoon flaked salt

360g short grain 'paella' rice* (such as Calasparra)

2 tablespoons fresh flat-leaf (Italian) parsley, to serve

Lemon wedges, to serve

Rice in Spain is so much more than paella. Paella pans are large and not suitable for the family apartment kitchen. Spanish cooks are far more adept at making silky smooth rice dishes in perols or heavy metal pots. This is a classic rice dish using both the flesh and ink of squid and the sweet flesh of king prawns or large shrimps. The ink gives the dish a wonderfully exotic shimmering black finish.

Method

Clean and skin the squid, reserving the ink sacs (see Note). Wash the squid hoods well under cold water. Cut the hood in half lengthways, then into strips. Set aside. Peel and devein the shrimp, reserving the shells. Place shells and stock into a medium saucepan and cook until the shells turn orange; strain liquid into a jug and discard the shells.

Heat oil in a medium frying pan over a medium heat and cook onions and garlic for 5 minutes or until softened, stirring occasionally. Add peppers, chorizo, paprika and salt, stir well and cook for a further 4 minutes or until peppers have softened.

Squeeze the black ink from the 3-4 squid ink sacs and add it to the pepper-chorizo mixture. Add the rice, squid and shrimp and only 1.5 litres of the prepared stock, reserving the remaining 500ml to use, if required.

Flatten out the mixture with the back of a wooden spoon to ensure it is covered with stock. Bring to the boil, then reduce heat to medium-low and simmer, uncovered, for 20-30 minutes or until rice is cooked and the stock absorbed. If the rice has too much 'bite', add remaining stock a little at a time, as needed, around the outside edge of the pan where the rice tends to take longer o cook. Remove from heat and cover with foil and a tea towel for 5 minutes before serving. Serve with parsley and lemon wedges.

Note – Squid's ink can also be purchased in small sachets from fish merchants. If taking the ink from the fresh squid look for a small sac that is a little shiny and black inside; wear disposable gloves, too.

* Refer to Glossary – Page 482

Langostas con salsa de tomate
Lobster with tomato & olive salsa

serves 4

Ingredients

2 whole medium-large green lobsters
(see Note)

Salsa:

60ml olive oil

1 medium red onion, finely chopped

125ml dry white wine

200g very ripe cherry or Roma tomatoes,
finely chopped

2 tablespoons finely chopped green
pitted olives

2 teaspoons baby capers*, chopped

2 tablespoons finely chopped fresh
flat-leaf (Italian) parsley

1 tablespoon freshly picked lemon
thyme leaves

Flaked salt

Freshly cracked black pepper

Extra virgin olive oil, to serve

Method

Preheat oven to 180°C.

Cut lobsters in half lengthways, remove digestive tract and wipe inside the head area with damp kitchen paper towel. (Avoid washing the flesh with water, as this can wash away natural sea flavour.) Place lobster halves, cut side up, onto a baking tray or into a heatproof dish.

To make the salsa, heat only 1 tablespoon of oil in a medium frying pan over a medium heat and cook onion for 5 minutes or until soft, stirring occasionally. Add wine and simmer, uncovered, until most of the wine evaporates. Remove from heat and add remaining oil, tomatoes, olives, capers, parsley and thyme. Season to taste.

Evenly spoon the salsa over each lobster half. Bake in preheated oven, uncovered, for 20 minutes or until the flesh is cooked (check just behind the head area).

Drizzle lightly with extra oil and serve.

Note – If possible, purchase live lobsters and ask the fish merchant to humanely kill them for you.

* Refer to Glossary – Page 482

Ensalada de bacalao con naranjas
Salted cod & orange salad

serves 4

Ingredients

600g salted cod*

125ml extra virgin olive oil

1 small red onion, very thinly sliced

10 black olives, pitted and halved

1 garlic clove, finely chopped

5 sun-dried tomato halves, thinly sliced

½ cup chopped fresh flat-leaf (Italian) parsley

1 tablespoon lemon juice

1 teaspoon smoked paprika*

3 medium oranges, peeled and thinly sliced

1 orange, juiced, extra

1 small bunch endive*, leaves only

Method

First, soak the salted cod; begin preparation the day before (36 hours before if possible). Brush any excess salt off the cod, place cod into a large bowl and cover with cold water. Refrigerate for 12 hours. Drain water and repeat soaking step twice. After soaking is complete, drain water and pat cod dry with kitchen paper towel.

Place skin side up onto an oven tray lined with kitchen baking paper and drizzle with only half the olive oil.

Preheat grill to medium-high and cook cod for 10-15 minutes or until skin is crisp and flesh is cooked. Remove and allow to cool slightly before flaking into large pieces, discarding any bones and skin.

Place cod into a large bowl. Add onion, olives, garlic, tomato, parsley, lemon juice and paprika. Toss to combine.

Add the orange slices. Drizzle with remaining oil and the extra orange juice and toss again.

Serve on a large platter with endive or plate up individual servings.

* Refer to Glossary – Page 482

Escabeche de pescados
Pickled fish with olives & vegetables

serves 4-6

Ingredients

500g monkfish fillets, skinned and boned
(or swordfish or Spanish mackerel)

35g plain (all-purpose) flour

125ml oil for shallow frying

Marinade:

60ml white wine vinegar

1 small red onion, halved and thinly sliced

1 medium carrot, thinly sliced

80g Spanish black olives*, pitted and
sliced

2 teaspoons capers*

1 teaspoon whole green peppercorns*

1 teaspoon dried oregano leaves

1 lime, juiced

½ teaspoon sugar

Light and slightly sharp with the tang of green peppercorns and capers, escabeche de pescados is a delicious way of preparing fish, particularly when you have a glut but still want to serve it in a few days time. Escabeche de pescados is a traditional method of preserving game in vinegar in the days before refrigeration. Today's escabeche recipes are much lighter and quite suitable for fish.

Method

Pat fish dry with kitchen paper towel; if necessary, cut fillets into 4-6 portions. Coat fish lightly with flour, shaking off the excess.

Heat oil in a large frying pan over a medium-high heat. Add fish and cook for 3-4 minutes each side or until lightly golden and cooked through. Remove to a side plate.

To make marinade, place vinegar, onion, carrot, olives, capers, peppercorns, oregano, lime juice and sugar in a medium saucepan, then cover and cook over low-medium heat for about 10 minutes.

Place a few pieces of the cooked fish into a large glass or ceramic bowl (see Note), then pour over some of the marinade. Repeat with a second layer and remaining marinade.

Cover the dish well with plastic wrap and refrigerate overnight.

Serve cold with crusty bread.

Note – When marinading any foods with acid (such as lime or lemon juice, vinegar or wine), avoid using metal bowls as the acid can react with the metal.

* Refer to Glossary – Page 482

Cocido de la monja
The nun's casserole

Ingredients

200g dried chickpeas

400g thick white fish fillets, skinned
(monkfish, swordfish or Spanish mackerel)

2 tablespoons olive oil

1 large brown onion, finely chopped

1 stick celery, finely chopped

1 medium red pepper (capsicum)*, seeded
and chopped

400g can chopped tomatoes

500ml water

Flaked salt

Freshly cracked black pepper

1 egg, lightly beaten

2 garlic cloves, crushed

2 tablespoon chopped fresh flat-leaf
(Italian) parsley

70g fresh breadcrumbs*

2 tablespoons olive oil, extra

Fresh oregano leaves, to serve

Method

Place chickpeas and 2 litres of boiling water into a large saucepan
and stand for 1 hour. Place saucepan of undrained chickpeas
over a medium heat, then cover and bring to the boil. Reduce
to medium-low heat and simmer gently for 40 minutes or until
tender. Drain and reserve.

Pat fish dry with kitchen paper towel and cut into 2cm cubes.
Set aside.

Heat oil in a large saucepan over a medium heat and cook
onion and celery for 8 minutes or until soft, stirring occasionally.
Add pepper, tomatoes, water and chickpeas and bring to the
boil. Reduce to medium-low heat and simmer, uncovered, for
20 minutes. Season to taste.

Meanwhile, place egg, garlic and parsley in a medium bowl and
mix well. Add breadcrumbs and mix well with your hands until it
becomes a thick paste. Form mixture into small round balls and
lightly fry in extra oil until golden. Drain on kitchen paper towel
and keep warm.

Add fish to chickpea mixture and stir gently to combine. Simmer
gently over medium-low heat for 3-4 minutes or until fish is cooked.
Serve with bread balls and oregano.

* Refer to Glossary – Page 482

La Parilla (The barbecue grill)

From wood-fired ovens, where suckling pigs are roasted, to plates of meaty tidbits sent to the table over a still glowing bed of coals, the Spanish love cooking with fire!

One of the greatest traditions at the heart of Spanish cooking is *la parilla* – the barbecue grill. It could be an outdoor barbecue in the country, where someone has shot a rabbit and then cooks it over a bed of coals from wood that's been collected from the forest. Or it could be a restaurant in a country town in which a little bricked area of the kitchen burns a few logs, over which is cooked a few steaks or half a chicken.

As the meat cooks it slowly releases its juices over the coals and the heat instantly vapourises the juices, sending up clouds of aromatic steam that envelope the meat, adding to the flavour.

Charcoal or *carbón* is more the norm in Spain and many dishes *a la parilla* are cooked on wood charcoal. It's a constant heat from a bed of glowing coals over which small birds, fish and vegetables are grilled. A quail cooked in this manner is absolutely delectable, the skin outside forming a deep brown crust that encases the juicy, sweet meat inside. Meat cooked over the parilla, unlike roasted meat, doesn't have time to loose moisture and is very juicy.

In fact, cooking over coals is technically roasting. Roasting is using the radiant heat from the coals, as opposed to an oven where food is cooked by the high air temperature. The flavours do not compare, and the Spanish understand this and have never truly gone down the path of electric and gas ovens. Even Joan Roca, the three-Michelin-Star chef of *El Celler de Can Roca* in Girona, uses oak logs in his kitchen to cook some of his dishes.

Restaurante grill

One of Spain's best restaurants is *Asador Etxebarri* in the hills of the Basque Country. Here, the chef selects different types of woods for different types of meats. Nearby, down on the coast, the fishing villages are famous for their restaurants that serve fish grilled outside on charcoal grills.

Calamares (Squid)

Jóse Rojas cooks some of the best calamari in Spain. From his tiny 20-seater restaurant – *Montalbán* in Poble Sec, Barcelona – he buys in fresh seafood daily from the market. He cleans his squid, slices it into rings, dips it in flour then drops it into very hot oil. The flour has barely had time to change colour when he scoops out the calamari, drains it for a scant second and sends it to the table. It's perfect. Soft, delicate and delicious.

He knows the art of cooking squid and octopus. It's an all-or-nothing affair. You either commit to a long, slow cooking process to break down the protein or fast cook it just long enough to set it. Or you serve it raw with a little seasoning.

The flat grill is another favourite for squid. A few minutes on a super-hot steel plate, a sprinkle of salt and a squeeze of lemon and then to the table. Some places stuff the squid with a few vegetables or other stuffing before slicing and serving it – so delicious.

Squid's tough cousin the cuttlefish, or *sepia*, needs to be handled in the slow-cooked style to bring out its lovely rich flavour and aroma.

Octopus is widely consumed across the Iberian Peninsula in bars and cooked in homes along the coast. It may be given a quick sizzle over the coals of a beachside barbecue or allowed to stew in a pot with a rich sauce. In bars, it is served Galician-style – over potatoes with paprika. This requires the octopus legs to be dipped in and out of boiling water several times then allowed to simmer in the water.

As always, the quality of the final product depends on the freshness of the raw materials. Visiting your local fish shop and letting them know what you're cooking, even placing an order in advance, is sometimes the best way to go.

Flash-fried, slow-cooked or eaten raw, squid is a Spanish delicacy.

Azafrán (Saffron)

The delicate golden strands of the saffron crocus are often referred to as the world's most extravagant spice.

A single purple flower emerges from the bare earth. It's autumn and the morning sun is yet appear over the horizon as the women of La Mancha, south of Madrid, start to harvest saffron.

The small flowers are laid in a basket and taken to a table inside the house. There the women carefully remove the bright yellow stamens and pistils and dry them out. The room is filled with the aroma of honey and straw – the distinctive smell of saffron.

Saffron, or *azafrán,* was introduced to Spain by the Moors. Gram for gram, it's often as expensive as gold, and just a few scant threads of quality saffron can add a fragrant note to a dish, and a delicate yellow hue.

The saffron story

Saffron enhances the delicate flavour of seafood and is often found lacing the sauce of white fish or in the juice with freshly cooked mussels. When cooked in the *sofrito* of paella, it imparts its musky honey and grass aroma to the rice, adding to layered complexity of flavours in the dish. It's also added to the sugar syrup in which apricots are cooked and often used to flavour creamy custards.

Due to the labour-intensive production process, the saffron harvest has dwindled in Spain in recent years; down from 6000 hectares of land under production in the 1970s to less 100 hectares today, and much of the saffron now used in Spain is imported from Iran. But the saffron produced in Spain is still considered to be some of the best in the world.

And cooks should note, a small canister of saffron threads is a great culinary investment and far superior to the cheaper saffron powder or, worse still, the imitation saffron.

Above: Harvesting crocus for saffron at Consuegra, Castilla – La Mancha, the site of a fortress thought to have been established by the Emperor Trajan.

Galicia

Galicia is one of Spain's most surprising regions. Hugging the northwest corner of the country on the Atlantic Coast, it seems to have more in common with its maritime neighbours Portugal and the United Kingdom than it does with the Spain of flamenco and Gaudí. Galicia is Celtic at heart and is sometimes described as the Ireland of the south – but with far better food.

Galicia's capital, Santiago de Compostela, is an ancient pilgrimage site wreathed in legend and spirituality and set to a soundtrack of bagpipes (called *gaitas* here). The discovery of the grave of the apostle St James in the 9th century established it as one of Christendom's holiest pilgrimage sites. Even today, more than a millennium later, the ancient cathedral built to house the apostle's remains attracts hundreds of thousands of pilgrims each year.

Despite being at the cultural crossroads of Christian Europe for many centuries, Galicia has maintained a unique culture that defines it from the rest of the country and continent. The Galician language is similar to Portuguese and the two neighbour-states share a sense of melancholy, called *saudade*, which comes from feeling isolated from the rest of the world. That's hardly surprising, given this is the boundary of Europe known, in less enlightened times, as *Finisterre* – the 'end of the earth'. Back then the Atlantic was called *Mare Tenebrosum*, the 'Dark Sea', and the shipwreck-strewn coastline around Cape Finisterre was the Costa da Morte, 'Death Coast'.

Spoils from the sea

This is still a harsh land at times but modern-day Galicia is also a triumph of humanity's determination to civilise its environment, not least through its cuisine. Galicia's diet essentially consists of a never-ending seafood banquet with generous side serves of meats, vegetables and cheeses, washed down with excellent wines.

Eating here is not about Michelin restaurants, though the region has a smattering of those. It's about fish, its freshness and variety. Santiago de Compostela's *Abasto* market routinely offers a choice of some 80 species of fresh fish and 50 types of seafood and shellfish including the mussels known as St James scallops, whose shells are the symbol of the Santiago de Compostela pilgrimage. The city even has a crustacean named after it, the *santiaguiño*, or slipper lobster.

Above all, Galicia is a land of octopus-eaters but its people also enjoy sardines, cod, crabs, barnacles, crayfish, razor clams and scallops. Many covet the snake-like lamprey (eel), sautéed with garlic, olive oil and pimentón.

Santiago de Compostela

Known in the middle ages as 'the end of the earth', Galicia is a maritime region – not least in its cuisine.

This intensive seafood diet is credited with Galicians' admirably low levels of cholesterol and heart disease – not a bad reward for eating octopus.

When it comes to meat, local tastes run mainly to pork and veal, with a big appetite for roasted ham, veal brisket and *unllas* (pig's trotters – also known as *manos de princesas*, 'princess's hands'). Like much of northern Spain, Galicia has been strongly influenced by Latin American eating habits introduced by the legions of expats who fled the region in the early 20th century to seek their fortunes in former Spanish colonies. Argentine-style barbecues are all the rage, with or without *chimichurri* sauce. And Galicians also share a love of *empanadas* with Argentines, only here the pies are family-sized and filled with whatever is in season at the time – cockle or sardines, fillet steak or the ubiquitous young turnip leaves called *grelos*.

A pious dessert

The Galician sweet tooth can be traced to convent kitchens that weaned the population on treats such as *Tarta de Santiago*, a flourless almond cake emblazoned with an icing-sugar Cross of St James. Almonds are big in Galician sweets and feature in many regional specialties, such as almond pie from Allariz and A Guarda's marzipan roll. For breakfast, it is common for Galicians to take a coffee and a couple of *Maria* (Marie) biscuits. Invented by Peek Freans of London, *galletas Maria* were mass-produced in Spain after the Civil War and swiftly became the country's favourite biscuit, as they are in many parts of the world, even Australia.

Galicia is home to one of Spain's most distinctive Denominación de Origen (DO) including protected cheeses, the conical *tetilla*, and *O Cebreiro,* a DO Galician cow's-milk cheese which has the shape of a chef's hat or mushroom.

Rias Baixas is globally renowned for the production of beautifully aromatic *albariños* but the nucleus of Galicia's wine industry is Ourense province. It is home to no fewer than four DO wines, *Valdeorras, Monterrei, Ribeiro* and *Ribeira Sacra,* which was first planted by the Romans.

Galicia's most notorious brew is *queimada*, a hot concoction of lemon, sugar, *aguardiente* (the local fire water), sometimes fruits and always seven coffee beans to represent the seven ancient provinces of Galicia. *Queimada* is said to cure coughs and colds, and, ironically, to protect the drinker against evil spirits.

Above: Subsistence farming, Concello de Laxe district, Galicia.

Opposite: Mussel boats anchored off Isla de Arousa and the port of Vilagarcia, Atlantic seaport for Santiago e Compostela, Galicia.

Madrid

Since Felipe II established it as the seat of the Spanish Empire in 1561, the Castilian Plateau capital of Madrid has attracted the cream of the country to its doorstep. Located in the geographical centre of Spain, this vibrant, dynamic European city is a product of the diversity of its people and traditions.

The Royal Houses of the Habsburgs and the Bourbons enriched Madrid with such monumental architecture as the Plaza Mayor and Retiro Park under the former, and the Baroque-style Royal Palace and Prado Museum under the latter.

A volatile history has shaped the character of the capital and its inhabitants but modern Madrid is, more than anything, a product of the hedonistic *Movida* social revolution that erupted from the streets after dictator Francisco Franco's death in 1975.

Movida! – freedom in a city of villages

Following a lifetime of oppression the city went wild with its newfound freedom, and creativity bloomed from the *barrios*, or local neighborhoods. Its countercultural mantras 'Madrid never sleeps' and 'Tonight everybody on the street!' were a rallying cry in the 1980s; today they are simply a statement of fact about life in this remarkable world centre.

Madrid's great attraction lies in discovering its *barrios* that partition its three million people into a collection of villages. Each has its own personality, from the raffish charm and excellent *tapas* culture of La Latina to the edgy migrant enclave of Lavapiés.

That's not to say the city is without star attractions. Highlights include the Modernista boulevard of Gran Vía, the spectacular stone Royal Palace, the 2000-year-old Temple of Debod – a present from Egypt to Spain in 1968 – and the Prado Museum with its priceless royal collection of treasures, including unforgettable works by Velázquez, Goya and Murillo.

And there's the Plaza Mayor, historic site of bullfights and heretic burnings, but these days thronged with tourists and locals enjoying the civic space known as 'Spain's backyard'.

Madrid is a city that, above all, knows how to live. *Madrileños* are social creatures who like a drink after work with perhaps a bite to eat, then a late dinner, then at least one more drink to end the evening. It is nothing unusual to find the streets gridlocked with traffic at 3am on a Sunday morning as city-dwellers party their way through the weekend.

Below: 'Andalucian sun in a bottle' – the famous Tio Pepe sign has stood above Puerto del Sol since the 1930's. Puerto del Sol ('Gate of the Sun') – originally the eastern gate of the medieval Madrid city wall – is the symbolic centre of Spain and the point from which all road distances are measured.

What this 'young' capital lacks in age, it makes up for with enthusiasm – truly a place of the people.

Right: Bacalao (dried salted cod) merchant at Mercat San Miguel, Madrid.

Over left: Plaza Mayor – Madrid's Central plaza – the site of markets and bullfights since the Middle Ages, and of trial and execution of heretics in the years of the Spanish Inquisition.

Over right: Roast suckling pig at el Botin, Madrid.

Being relatively young, Madrid has had to cobble together its own identity by cherry-picking the proudest cultural traditions and produce from all its autonomous communities and installing them in the capital. Andalucian gypsy settlers brought flamenco to Madrid and now the nation's most accomplished dancers and musicians flock here to perform in its terrific flamenco *tablaos*. The capital's bullfighting season has become the country's most glamorous, with fans crowding Plaza Santa Ana to catch a glimpse of their matador heroes.

Likewise in gastronomy, Madrid has assembled a distinctive food culture over the past 450 years, aided by the influx of immigrants from all corners of the country. Some dishes have been associated with Madrid for so long they are now considered 'native' – like *callos*, a stew of chorizo, blood sausage, paprika and various other animal parts including the stomach lining (tripe) of a lamb or calf. Or *cocido madrileño*, a hotpot of chickpeas, vegetables and various meats, often served in three courses as soup, vegetable-and-chickpea stew, and then meat.

Produce from the surrounding countryside is inextricably linked to the capital. From the Royal Palace gardens at Aranjuez comes asparagus (known as *pericos*) and strawberries, there's sheep's cheese and olives from Campo Real and beef from the Sierra de Guadarrama.

A waterless port city

Madrid makes no secret of its appetite for the spoils of its provinces. Every morning a convoy of trucks, planes and trains delivers the choicest consumables from all over Spain to the capital. So much so that Madrid, as far from the coast as it is possible to be on the Iberian Peninsula, is often referred to as the country's principal 'port' – the quality of seafood found here is without parallel. The pride of Galicia's fishing fleet is on sale each day at the San Miguel Market, and a favourite snack of city-dwellers is *bocadillo de calamares*, a bread roll stuffed with fried calamari and garlic mayonnaise.

Seafood aside, *Madrileños* have a particular penchant for offal, as seen in their beloved *cocido madrileño*, tripe stew, and local delicacies like *orejas a la plancha*, grilled pig's ears with spicy tomato sauce. Stuffed bull's tail is relished here as much as it is in the south of Spain and *cochinillo asado*, the roasted suckling pig of Segovia, is another typical plate of Madrid's restaurants.

Other regional transplants to local menus include garlic soup *(sopa de ajo)*, potato tortillas and baked bream. Fried *churros* – 'straight' doughnuts dipped in hot chocolate – are a common breakfast or late-night snack, while religious festivals are marked by sweet treats, such as the filled marzipan *huesos de santo* (bones of the saint) eaten on All Saints Day.

The culinary revolution that started in the Basque Country and Catalonia with *Arzak* and *elBulli* has infected Madrid's taste buds too, making the capital an international dining destination to suit all appetites – from avant-garde to ancestral.

Cantabria

From mountain stews to feasts from the ocean, the Cantabrian way of life is harsh but the epicurean rewards are plenty.

In many ways Cantabria is difficult to distinguish from its northern neighbours Asturias and the Basque Country, because each shares a similar history and geography. This is particularly true of Cantabrian cuisine, which fishes from the same sea and cultivates the same soil.

But there are enough unique characteristics to this region, in both character and custom, to trace a distinct Cantabrian identity. For starters, it is home to the endangered Cantabrian brown bear, several protected nature reserves and Spain's most celebrated prehistoric find – the Late Paleolithic paintings of the Altamira Caves, rediscovered in 1879.

The land is split geographically between the 101-kilometre coastline and an interior of seemingly endless mountains, including the Picos de Europa range. This northern stretch of coast is known as Green Spain for its lush vegetation and pristine landscapes. The bulk of the region's industry and its capital, Santander, are huddled along this habitable shoreline.

More than half the region sits at least 700 metres above sea level and life can be harsh in the fortified medieval villages or *castros* of the mountains. Families make a living from farming and cattle, most notably the *pasiegos* who live in the isolated southeastern enclave of *Vega del Pas*. They have farmed this cold, damp countryside for five centuries, moving stock from valley to valley in search of feed, establishing a network of stone shelters in their wake.

Their other notable legacy is *sobao pasiego*, a type of sweet butter cake spiked with anise liqueur and lemon that has become synonymous with Cantabria. Another well-known local dessert is *quesada pasiega*, a cottage-cheesecake made from cow's milk.

Right: Fishmonger, Mercat Central, Santander, Cantabria.

Below: Village of Santillana del Mar, Cantabria, site of the Cave of Altamira where the first Iberian prehistoric cave paintings were discovered in 1879.

Hearty fare for mountain dwellers, and fishermen

As well as heavy sweets, the mountain people have contributed dense stews to the local cuisine, including *cocido lebaniego*, a jumble of chickpeas, cabbage, eggs, bread, noodles and meats. *Cocido montañés* follows a similar recipe but uses dried beans instead of chickpeas. The villages of Bejes and Tresviso in Liébana are known for producing *picón* cheese, a soft blue made from a blend of cow, goat and sheep milks. Under its Denomination of Origin regulations, *Picón Bejes-Tresviso* must be left to mature for at least two months in the limestone caves that punctuate Liébana's valleys.

Fish is the staple diet of Cantabria's coastal dwellers. The *tapas* menus of virtually every bar and restaurant here will feature *rabas*, floured and deep-fried squid tentacles. *Sorropotún* is a thick stew of tuna or *bonito del norte*, slow-cooked in a clay pot with potatoes, green and red peppers, onions, bay leaves and paprika. The dish was originally eaten by fishermen to revive them after a day on the ocean but is now one of the region's most celebrated dishes. Abundant rivers provide a constant supply of freshwater fish such as salmon, which is cooked in a mixture of fish stock and milk to create *arroz santanderino*, rice Santander-style.

Winter antidote

Cantabria makes sweet *tostadillo* wines but its most famous drink is *Orujo de Liébana*, a potent eau-de-vie distilled from grape skins and pips. It is a clear spirit and, at more than 50 per cent proof, a sensible antidote to chilly Atlantic winters.

gourmet
pilgrim

Carne

Meat

Pork, beef, lamb and game – the Spanish are dedicated meat-eaters, with a repertoire of recipes to match.

Carne (Meat)

The Spanish taste for meat is a product of religious conquest and trial-by-diet.

Jamon is not the only meat in Spain, but walk into any café or bar and the stockpile of cured pork loins suspended from the ceiling may suggest otherwise. *Jamón, Serrano, ibérico de bellota…* whatever name it is known by, the Spanish live for ham. From its ears to its trotters and everywhere in between, pork is the pin-up meat of Spain.

It was not always so. In the 700 years of Moorish rule, meat was not nearly so central to the Spanish diet and pork was forbidden by the dominant religion. Pork is the meat of Christians and its consumption did not become widespread until the Reconquest of Spain in the late 15th century, when it was promoted as an item of religious faith as well as a tasty meal.

A test of faith

In 1492 the Catholic King Ferdinand and his wife Isabella retook the Kingdom of Granada for Christian Spain, banished the thriving Jewish population and forced Muslims to convert or leave. To test the strength of religious conversions among former Muslims it became commonplace to add pork to dishes. If you were a closet Muslim faced with a meal where the meat was pork, the vegetables had pork through them and the dessert was made with pork lard, there was not much room to hide your true faith. The cuisine of Christian Spain soon sorted the believers from the infidels.

Today, few parts of the pig are safe from the Spanish appetite. The cured loins of jamon are the most venerated meat of the animal but virtually no inch of the pig goes to waste. The inferior cuts and organs are ground into smallgoods of such permutation and combination that sometimes it can seem as if every village has a signature sausage.

Catalonia alone has 17 official types, from the blood-and-bread *botifarra negra* to the air-dried *fuet* – a long, thin pork sausage whose name means 'whip' – and the spreadable, garlicky *sobrassada*. Then there is Spain's most famous sausage, the chorizo, made from minced pork loin seasoned liberally with garlic and *pimentón de la Vera*, the country's premium smoky paprika.

Left: The *cortadore* slices jamon at El Rinconcillo – the oldest tapas bar in Seville, Andalucia.

The not-so-humble stew

Ham and pork products aside, if there is one meat dish that is known and enjoyed throughout the nation it is the *cocido*. This simple one-pot stew is less a formalised recipe than a combination of whatever is to hand – some meat, vegetables and aromatics – yet almost every one of Spain's 17 autonomous communities has its trademark *cocido* method.

Asturia's *fabada* is one of the most famous – a meat-lover's stew of shoulder pork, ham bones, chorizo, *morcilla* (blood sausage), white fabes beans and saffron. Extremadura has *caldereta de cordero*, a lamb stew flavoured with garlic, paprika, peppercorns and bay leaves. Madrid's hearty chickpea stew *cocido madrileño* is a one-pot wonder of marrow bones, streaky bacon, morcilla and chorizo – sometimes old hens, if there are any to be had – and winter vegetables like potatoes, turnips and cabbage. (Any leftovers were traditionally rehashed the following day in a tomato-based sauce to make a dish called *ropa vieja*, 'old clothes'.)

The Spanish capital is also renowned for *callos a la madrileña*, a dense sauce of tomatoes, onions and herbs simmered with ox tripe and snout, and a mix of other flavoursome meats like chorizo, black pudding and jamon. In the Atlantic northwest, Galicia has its *caldo gallego*, a pot-luck *cocido* usually involving pork belly and bacon with pulses, cabbage and turnip leaves. *Caldo gallego* is also one of Cuba's national dishes, introduced there by Galician emigrants in the late 19th century. Endlessly versatile, the *cocido* has endured through times of prosperity and poverty and evolved into some very distinctive regional specialties.

A Spanish roast – young and tender

The sometimes harsh expanses of the Castilian Plateau in central Spain have been dubbed the land of the roast, after the valiant dish that sustains the plains dwellers through long, cold winters. They like their meat young, so suckling pig, lamb and goat are always on the menu.

Castilian lamb, *lechazo*, is commonly roasted in a clay pan with little more than lard and salted water for seasoning. Suckling pig or *cochinillo* is the best-known dish of Segovia. Restaurants there pride themselves on baking the thyme-infused meat so tenderly it can be cut with the edge of a plate, a feat made easier by the fact that the piglets are just 15-20 days old and have been fed only on milk. The Madrid restaurant *el Botín* has been roasting these two Castilian specialties in *Calle Cuchilleros*, just beside the Plaza Mayor, since 1725.

La Caza – 'The Hunt'

Game is another key component of the Castilian diet. In the former imperial capital of Toledo red-legged partridge is stewed with bay leaves and garlic to make a dish fit for regal appetites. High up in the Pyrenees, Navarrese tastes run to wild birds – especially quail, dove, pigeon and partridge. Fattened quails are roasted in fig leaves and partridge is prepared in a special sauce of bitter chocolate, a recipe that has become a special occasion dish across Spain. Catalans have their own special occasion bird – the turkey. At Christmas-time the birds are stuffed with a heady mix of sausages including *butifarra* and Moorish heirloom flavours like pinenuts and raisins.

Catalonia also indulges its carnivorous tendencies in the wildly popular *fideos a la cazuela*, pot noodles loaded with ham and bacon, *botifarra* and assorted sausages, pork spare ribs and a smattering of tomato, onion and garlic to taste. In Navarra, lamb chops are stewed in a piquant tomato and chilli sauce called *chilindrón*. The Aragonese have a fondness for *chilindrón* too, adding it to everything from chicken to pork. In the mountains of Aragon the cuisine becomes even more rustic and meat-centric. *Espárragos montañeses* are not mountain asparagus, as the translation suggests, but lamb's tails boiled in salted water, dredged in flour and then deep fried.

The mighty *toro* (bull)

To understand just how much Spain loves meat, you only need to consider some of the Spaniards' favourite foods. In Seville and other bullfighting strongholds, *rabo de toro* – a hearty braise of bull's tail – is a crowd-pleasing favourite. The original Valencian *paella* contained rabbit and snails, not seafood. And that vegetarian vanguard from Andalucia, the chilled tomato soup *gazpacho*, is something much meatier in the interior of the Iberian Peninsula. In Castilla-La Mancha, the *gazpacho manchego* is not a soup at all but a gamey stew thickened with torn pieces of flatbread. The stew, traditionally seasoned with garlic and thyme, can be made with whatever the hunter brings home – quail, pigeon, rabbit or hare. Traditionally a huge pot of *gazpacho* is place in the centre of the table and everyone tucks in.

Right: Cooking meat at the *Festa medieval da Arribada*, Baiona, Galicia – a celebration of the March 1493 arrival of the caravel Pinta from Columbus's first voyage of discovery, which made Baiona the first port in Europe to receive the news of the discovery of the New World.

Opposite: *Salschicha* – handmade sausages at a market stall in Seville, Andalucia.

Tocinillo asado
Spiced roast pork

Ingredients

2.5kg leg pork, rind on
12 garlic cloves, peeled
60g flaked salt
2 tablespoons dried fennel seeds
2 teaspoons dried oregano leaves
1 tablespoon sweet paprika*
1 teaspoon ground white pepper
1 lemon, juiced
250ml red wine

A great sheet of golden garlic and fennel-infused crackling covers the tender joint of pork underneath. The initial searing heat of the oven sets the skin blistering on its way, while the longer time cooking at the lower temperature allows the red wine to evaporate and permeate the flesh. This is just as good cold.

Method

Preheat oven to 220°C.

Score the pork rind with a sharp knife. Make small incisions in the pork meat through the rind and fill with only 8 of the garlic cloves. Rub the salt all over the rind, especially into the scored areas.

Place remaining garlic, fennel, oregano, paprika, pepper and lemon juice into a mortar and grind with the pestle to form a paste. Rub paste over pork rind and flesh.

Place pork in a baking dish and add wine around the pork. Bake in preheated oven for 20 minutes, then reduce temperature to 180°C and bake for a further 1½-2 hours.

Remove dish from oven and cover loosely with foil to keep pork warm and rest for 20-30 minutes before carving.

Serve with roast vegetables, which can be added to the baking dish during the last 1 hour of cooking.

Note – Many butchers will score the pork rind for you or sell it already prepared.

272
gourmetpilgrim Spain

* Refer to Glossary – Page 482

Judías blancas con chorizo picante y tomate
Spicy sausage with butterbeans & tomato

serves 4-6

Ingredients

1 tablespoon olive oil

300g spicy chipolata sausages*

300g Spanish chorizo sausage*, sliced

1 large brown onion, thinly sliced

2 garlic cloves, finely chopped

1 teaspoon sweet smoked paprika*

250ml dry white wine

2 fresh bay leaves

400g can chopped tomatoes

250ml chicken stock

12 whole green olives

400g can butter beans, rinsed and drained

Flaked salt

Freshly cracked black pepper

Chopped fresh flat-leaf (Italian) parsley, to serve

Mashed potato, to serve

Method

Preheat oven to 180°C.

Heat oil in a large flameproof casserole dish or ovenproof saucepan over a medium-high heat and cook chipolata sausages for 3-4 minutes or until golden and almost cooked through, turning occasionally. Remove and set aside. Add chorizo sausage to dish and cook for 3-4 minutes or until lightly browned. Remove and set aside.

Reduce heat to medium, add onion and garlic cook for 3 minutes. Add paprika and wine and simmer, uncovered, for 3 minutes. Add bay leaves, tomatoes and stock, then cover and bring to the boil.

Return sausages to the dish and spoon the sauce over them. Cover and bake in the preheated oven for 20 minutes (or on a very low heat on the stovetop).

Stir in olives and beans and bake for a further 5-10 minutes. Season to taste.

Serve garnished with parsley and some mashed potato.

* Refer to Glossary – Page 482

Albóndigas con salsa de tomate
Meatballs in spicy tomato sauce

serves 4

Ingredients

600g lean minced pork
300g lean minced veal
4 garlic cloves, crushed
250g fresh breadcrumbs*
1 teaspoon ground coriander
1 teaspoon ground cumin
1 teaspoon ground cinnamon
1 teaspoon sweet smoked paprika*
1 egg, lightly beaten
Flaked salt
Freshly cracked black pepper
2 tablespoons olive oil for pan frying

Spicy tomato sauce:

1 tablespoon olive oil
1 medium red onion, finely chopped
2 garlic cloves, crushed
1 small fresh red chilli*, finely chopped
125ml white wine
400g can chopped tomatoes
1 tablespoon tomato paste*
125ml salt-reduced chicken stock
½ teaspoon cayenne pepper
60g fresh or frozen peas
Crusty bread and/or rice, to serve

"There is no such thing as waste in a Spanish kitchen – just opportunity," the saying goes. Take the lesser-loved cuts of meat, perhaps those too tough for grilling but without enough bone, gristle or fat for flavour. You mince it. You then take the bread that's now several days old and getting a little too dry, even for toasting and smothering in tomato and olive oil. Soak it in a little milk or water and add it to the meat. Flavour it with some vegetables and herbs from the garden, roll it into little balls and then fry them off in a pan. Make a sauce and let the juices of the meat, spices and garlic infuse into the sauce. Serve the meatballs with a great loaf of fresh bread to mop up the sauces and a little salad. This is the culture of albóndigas of which there are hundreds of recipes across the nation. This is just one.

Method

Place pork, veal, garlic, breadcrumbs, cumin, cinnamon, paprika and egg in a large bowl. Season with salt and pepper and using a gloved hand, mix ingredients together until mixture is smooth and leaves the side of the bowl. Cover and refrigerate mixture, for 30 minutes.

Roll tablespoonful of the mixture into small meatballs and place onto a large tray or plate. Heat only half the oil in a large frying pan and cook half the meatballs over medium-high heat for 2-3 minutes, or until browned all over. Remove to a side plate. Add the remaining oil and cook the remaining meatballs.

To make the sauce, heat the oil in a large frying pan over a medium heat and cook the onion, garlic and chilli for 5 minutes, stirring occasionally. Increase heat to high, add the wine and boil for 1 minute. Add tomatoes, tomato paste and stock, then simmer uncovered for 10 minutes.

Stir in the cayenne, peas and meatballs and simmer, uncovered, for a further 5-8 minutes or until sauce has thickened slightly. Season further to taste, if required.

Serve hot with crusty bread and/or rice.

* Refer to Glossary – Page 482

Pasta Asturiana
Asturian pasta

Ingredients

75g plain (all-purpose) flour

Flaked salt

Freshly cracked black pepper

600g pork fillet, cut into 2cm cubes

1 tablespoon olive oil

2 Spanish chorizo sausages*, halved lengthways and sliced

2 medium brown onions, thinly sliced

350g button mushrooms, thinly sliced

3 garlic cloves, finely chopped

400g can chopped tomatoes

1 green pepper (capsicum)*, deseeded and thinly sliced

250ml white wine

500ml salt-reduced chicken stock

150g dried spiral-shaped pasta

400g can butter beans, drained and rinsed

2 slices Serrano jamon or prosciutto, grilled until crisp, to serve

1 tablespoon chopped fresh flat-leaf (Italian) parsley, to serve

It can get cold in Asturias, particularly in the mountains. Fabadas, a hearty stew with pork and beans is a winter-warming classic. This dish draws from that rich heritage and in a very Spanish manner uses pork three ways: the braised solomillo or loin; the flavoursome chorizo sausage and is topped off with crisp jamon.

Method

Place flour into a plastic bag and season with salt and pepper. Add pork and shake until meat is lightly coated. Heat oil in a large frying pan or flameproof casserole dish over high heat and cook chorizo sausage for 2-3 minutes each side or until golden brown. Remove from pan, add pork and cook for 3-5 minutes or until golden; set both aside.

Reduce heat to medium, add onions, mushrooms, garlic, tomatoes and pepper and cook for 5-8 minutes or until soft but not browned, stirring occasionally. Add wine, bring to the boil and simmer, uncovered, for 10-12 minutes. Add stock and continue to simmer, uncovered, for a further 10-12 minutes.

Add pasta and cook for 5-8 minutes. Add butter beans and cook for a further 3-5 minutes or until pasta is tender. Serve sprinkled with jamon and parsley.

* Refer to Glossary – Page 482

Arroz de carne
Spiced meat & rice casserole

serves 4

Ingredients

1 tablespoon olive oil

2 garlic cloves, peeled

1 tablespoon chopped fresh flat-leaf (Italian) parsley

½ teaspoon saffron threads*

2 Spanish chorizo sausages*, skin removed and chopped

100g Serrano jamon* or prosciutto, chopped

100g spicy salami, chopped

2 pork sausages, skin removed, meat crumbled

1 medium red pepper (capsicum)*, sliced

150g artichoke quarters*

400g short grain 'paella' rice* (such as Calasparra)

500ml salt-reduced chicken stock

250ml white wine

4 eggs

25g grated manchego cheese*

Method

Heat oil in a large deep frying pan over medium heat and cook whole garlic cloves for 3-5 minutes or until lightly golden, stirring occasionally. Transfer to a mortar and pestle with a slotted spoon, add the parsley and saffron and crush to form a paste. Set aside.

Heat the same frying pan over medium-high heat and cook chorizo, jamon, salami and pork meat for 5-8 minutes or until golden brown, stirring occasionally. Add pepper, artichokes and garlic paste to the pan. Add rice and stir to coat.

Preheat oven to 180°C.

Place stock into a medium saucepan, then cover and bring to a gentle boil. Reduce heat to low.

Transfer rice mixture to a large flameproof casserole dish, add the wine and bring to the boil on the stovetop. Reduce heat and simmer, uncovered, until the liquid evaporates. Begin to add the hot stock, ladle by ladle, until all the liquid has been absorbed and the rice is just tender.

Whisk eggs in a bowl, add cheese, mix well and pour over rice. Bake in preheated oven for 10-15 minutes or until egg topping is golden and set.

Tip: This dish could be cooked just in the large deep frying pan and not transferred to a flameproof casserole.

* Refer to Glossary – Page 482

Pollo crujiente con pimentos rojos
Crisp spiced chicken with red pepper jam

serves 4

Ingredients

Red pepper and onion jam:
2 tablespoons olive oil

2 large red onions, finely chopped

1 large red pepper (capsicum)* finely diced

2 garlic cloves, finely chopped

1 small fresh red chilli*, seeded and finely chopped

1 teaspoon smoked sweet paprika*

¼ teaspoon cayenne pepper

125ml tomato puree (passata)*

2 tablespoons sherry vinegar*

2 tablespoons soft brown sugar

125ml water

Flaked salt

Crisp spiced chicken:
2 teaspoons ground cumin

2 teaspoons ground coriander

1 teaspoon smoked sweet paprika*

1 garlic clove, crushed

2 tablespoons lemon juice

4 Chicken Supremes (see Note)

Flaked salt

Freshly cracked black pepper

1 tablespoon olive oil

Method

To make the red pepper and onion jam, heat oil in a large saucepan over a low-medium heat and cook onions for 15-20 minutes until lightly golden, stirring occasionally. Add the pepper, garlic, chilli, paprika and cayenne. Cook for a further 10 minutes, or until pepper has softened, stirring occasionally. Add tomato puree, vinegar, sugar and water and bring to the boil. Reduce heat to low and simmer, covered, for 2 hours, stirring occasionally, until the jam is thick and pulpy and has darkened slightly. Season to taste with salt.

Place cumin, coriander, paprika, garlic and lemon juice in a large glass or ceramic bowl. Add chicken and coat well in the mixture. Season with salt and pepper.

Heat oil in a large frying pan over a medium-high heat and cook chicken, skin side down, for 3-5 minutes or until skin is golden and crispy. Turn and cook for a further 5-8 minutes or until cooked through.

Serve chicken with the red pepper and onion jam and a green salad.

Note – Chicken Supremes are the breast section of chicken with the wing bone attached. Chicken thighs and legs could be substituted, either as Maryland or individual pieces.

* Refer to Glossary – Page 482

Pollo a la cazuela
Chicken casserole

Ingredients

50g plain (all-purpose) flour

2½ tablespoons sweet smoked paprika*

Flaked salt

Freshly cracked black pepper

4 Chicken Supremes, (see Note)

2 tablespoons olive oil

8 eschalots*, thinly sliced

1 carrot, finely chopped

1 stick celery, finely chopped

4 garlic cloves, finely chopped

200g button mushrooms, quartered

1 teaspoon ground thyme

3 fresh bay leaves

2 strips orange rind

125ml orange juice

125ml white wine or Manzanilla sherry*

125ml salt-reduced chicken stock

12 Spanish anchovy-stuffed green olives

2 tablespoons fresh flat-leaf (Italian) parsley, to serve

Crispy or mashed potatoes, to serve

Method

Place flour, paprika, salt and pepper into a large bowl. Coat the chicken pieces in the seasoned flour, shaking off the excess.

Heat oil in a large flameproof casserole dish over a high heat and cook chicken for 5 minutes on each side or until golden brown. Remove chicken from dish and set aside. Reduce heat to medium, add eschalots, carrot, celery and garlic and cook for 8 minutes, stirring occasionally. Add mushrooms, thyme, bay leaves, orange rind and juice, wine and stock. Return chicken pieces to dish and spoon the sauce over the chicken.

Bring to the boil, then reduce heat to low and simmer, covered, for 30-40 minutes or until chicken is tender. Add olives in the last 10 minutes of cooking.

Serve with parsley and mash or crispy potatoes.

Note – Chicken Supremes are the breast section of chicken with the wing bone attached.

* Refer to Glossary – Page 482

Broquetas de pollo con salsa de yogur
Chicken skewers with yoghurt mint sauce

serves 4

Ingredients

700g chicken thigh fillets, cut into
2cm cubes

1 tablespoon olive oil

3 garlic cloves, crushed

2 spring onions, finely chopped

1 teaspoon freshly picked thyme leaves

2 teaspoons finely grated lemon rind

1 teaspoon ground cumin

1 teaspoon ground coriander

1 teaspoon ground fennel

½ teaspoon ground chilli

10-12 bamboo skewers, soaked
(see Tip)

Yoghurt sauce:

140g thick plain yoghurt

2 garlic cloves, crushed

¼ cup chopped fresh mint leaves

1 tablespoon caster (superfine) sugar

¼ teaspoon ground chilli*

2 teaspoons lemon juice

Flaked salt

Freshly cracked black pepper

Method

Place chicken into a glass or ceramic bowl. Add oil, garlic, spring onions, thyme, rind, cumin, coriander, fennel and chilli. Mix well and rub the marinade into the chicken. Cover and refrigerate for 1 hour.

Meanwhile, to make the yoghurt sauce place yoghurt, garlic, mint, sugar, chilli and lemon juice into a bowl and mix well. Cover and refrigerate until ready to serve.

Thread 3-4 pieces of chicken onto each skewer. Preheat barbecue or char-grill to medium heat. Cook chicken skewers for 12-15 minutes, turning occasionally, until evenly brown on all sides. Season to taste.

Serve skewers with yoghurt sauce.

Tip: Soak bamboo skewers in water before using to prevent them from burning too quickly on the barbecue or char-grill.

* Refer to Glossary – Page 482

Pollo con pimentos rojos y jamón
Chicken with red peppers & jamon

serves 4

Ingredients

1 large chicken, jointed (see Note)

Flaked salt

Freshly cracked black pepper

60ml olive oil

1 large brown onion, finely chopped

4 garlic cloves, thinly sliced

200g Serrano jamon* or prosciutto, cut into thin strips

4 roasted* red peppers* (capsicum), peeled and cut into wide strips

400g can chopped tomatoes

250ml salt-reduced chicken stock

2 tablespoons chopped fresh chives

Method

Lightly season the chicken pieces with salt and pepper. Heat oil in a large flameproof casserole dish over a medium-high heat and cook chicken in 2 batches until lightly browned on all sides. Return all chicken pieces to the dish, add onion, garlic and jamon and cook for 5 minutes, stirring occasionally.

Add peppers, tomatoes and stock to the dish and bring to the boil over a medium-high heat. Reduce heat to low and simmer, partly covered, for 40-45 minutes or until meat is tender and sauce has reduced and thickened.

Season further to taste, if required, and serve with chopped chives.

Note – To joint a chicken, use kitchen scissors to cut through the length of the breast bone. Turn the chicken over and cut down either side of the backbone to completely remove it. Cut the breast in half, so one piece has the wing attached, and cut through the leg joint to separate the drumstick from the thigh.

* Refer to Glossary – Page 482

Pato con papas y setas
Duck with mushrooms & potatoes

serves 4

Ingredients

4 large all-purpose potatoes, peeled and cut into 3cm dice

2 teaspoons flaked salt

2 teaspoons freshly picked thyme leaves

4 single duck breast fillets, skin on

375ml red wine

30g butter

Flaked salt

Freshly cracked black pepper

1 tablespoon olive oil

30g butter, extra

3 garlic cloves, finely chopped

250g portobello or Swiss brown mushrooms, sliced

2 tablespoons chopped fresh flat-leaf (Italian) parsley

Method

Place potatoes in a large saucepan of boiling salted water and cook until just tender; drain and set aside.

Place salt and thyme into a large, dry frying pan and heat gently over medium heat for 5 minutes, shaking pan regularly, until fragrant. Transfer to a mortar and pestle and cool slightly, then grind to a fine powder.

Score duck skin 3-4 times with a sharp knife and rub the salt-thyme powder into the skin. Heat a large frying pan over medium-high heat and cook duck, skin side down, for 6 minutes. Turn and cook for a further 6-8 minutes or until cooked to your liking. Remove from pan and cover loosely with foil to keep warm and rest while preparing rest of dish.

Tip off and discard excess fat from pan, reserving about 2 tablespoons. Add wine and bring to the boil. Using a wooden spoon, scrape up the cooking juices from the pan. Reduce heat and simmer until sauce reduces by half and is thick and syrupy. Whisk in butter and season to taste. Remove from heat and cover to keep warm.

Heat oil and extra butter in another large frying pan over medium-high heat and cook potatoes, stirring frequently, for 10 minutes or until potatoes are golden. Add garlic and cook for a further 2 minutes. Add mushrooms and cook for a further 5 minutes or until mushrooms are tender. Season to taste and stir in parsley.

To serve, slice each duck breast into 4 thick slices and serve on individual plates with potato and mushroom. Drizzle with sauce.

Codornices con panceta y pimento
Quail with pancetta and peppers

serves 4-6

Ingredients

6 whole quail, cleaned

2 tablespoons olive oil

Flaked salt

Freshly cracked black pepper

100g pancetta*, chopped

2 oranges (skin on), thinly sliced

50g butter

1 medium brown onion, finely chopped

6 garlic cloves, finely chopped

1 medium red pepper (capsicum)*,
finely chopped

1 large ripe tomato, finely chopped

4 sprigs fresh rosemary

1 fresh bay leaf

250ml red wine

1 tablespoon red wine vinegar

2 tablespoons brown sugar

2 tablespoons fresh flat-leaf (Italian)
parsley, chopped (optional)

Las cordonices, or quail, are so popular in Spain. These little birds live in the stubble of wheat fields and grasslands and are hunted for their deep pink flesh and delicate gamy flavour. With their skin sealed to golden brown then steeped in red wine, they impart the aroma of orange and the richness of the pancetta as they roast. This aromatic liquid is reduced to make a flavoursome sauce.

Method

Preheat oven to 180°C.

Place the quail into a large bowl, drizzle with only half the oil and season with salt and pepper. Rub the oil and seasoning into the quail. Fill the cavity of each quail with pancetta and orange slices.

Heat remaining oil and only half the butter in an ovenproof frying pan or flameproof casserole dish and fry the quail, turning occasionally, for 4-5 minutes or until browned all over. Remove with a slotted spoon and set aside.

Heat the same frying pan over medium heat and cook onion, garlic, pepper and tomato for 5-8 minutes or until soft. Add rosemary, bay leaf, wine, vinegar and sugar; stir to combine. Return quail to pan and spoon sauce over. Bake in preheated oven for 20-25 minutes.

Remove quail from pan to a side plate and cover loosely with foil to keep warm. Place frying pan over a medium-low heat and simmer, uncovered, until liquid has reduced to a sauce consistency. Add remaining butter and stir until melted and combined. Season further to taste, if required.

Serve quail with sauce and parsley.

* Refer to Glossary – Page 482

Faisán con furtos rojos
Pheasant with red fruits & cava

serves 4

Ingredients

2 x 1kg whole pheasants

60ml olive oil

1 large brown onion, finely chopped

4 garlic cloves, finely chopped

1 medium carrot, finely chopped

1 stick celery, finely chopped

Flaked salt

Freshly cracked pepper

4 sprigs fresh thyme

2 fresh bay leaves

250ml cava* (or sparkling wine)

100g pitted bottled cherries

100g fresh or frozen red currants

80g red-currant jelly

Drive through the hills surrounding Salamanca in pheasant season and you'll see groups of hunters, shotguns cocked over their arms, traipsing through forest set aside for hunting. The Spanish are mad about game. They love the dense toothsome texture and hearty, earthy flavours of the flesh.

The match of fruits in this dish highlights the gamy flavours, while the acid cuts through the richness. Pheasant can be ordered through quality butchers. Quail are suitable, but you'll need to use four to one pheasant and reduce the cooking time by half.

Method

Preheat oven to 180°C.

Cut pheasants in half lengthways with kitchen scissors and wipe inside with damp kitchen paper towel.

Heat half the oil in a large frying pan over a medium-high heat and lightly brown the skin side of the pheasants. Transfer to a baking dish and bake uncovered in preheated oven for 30-35 minutes or until tender. Cover loosely with foil for 10 minutes to keep warm while preparing the rest of the dish.

Meanwhile, heat remaining oil in a medium frying pan over a medium-high heat and cook onion, garlic, carrot and celery for 8-10 minutes or until golden, stirring occasionally. Season to taste. Add thyme, bay leaves and cava and cook for 3-5 minutes or until the liquid is slightly reduced. Add cherries, currants and currant jelly and stir to combine.

Pour sauce over the pheasant and serve.

Tip: When in season, fresh pomegranate seeds can be used instead of red currants.*

* Refer to Glossary – Page 482

Conejo al jerez
Rabbit in sherry sauce

Rabbit, or conejo, features very frequently in Spanish cooking. For a nation of hungry and passionate hunters, rabbit is always a welcome addition to the paella pan or the stew pot. Wild rabbit can be tough, so this method of marinating and slow cooking creates a dish with succulent flesh and a rich, spiced sauce.

Ingredients

Marinade:

150ml dry sherry or red wine

2 tablespoons red wine vinegar

2 garlic cloves, sliced

3 fresh bay leaves

1 cinnamon stick

4 whole cloves

1 teaspoon dried oregano leaves

¼ teaspoon ground allspice

1 teaspoon ground chilli*

Tomato sauce:

1 rabbit, cut into 6 pieces

60ml olive oil

2 medium brown onions, chopped

2 garlic cloves, crushed

2 tablespoons tomato paste*

80g whole green olives

Fresh oregano leaves, to serve

Method

To make the marinade, place sherry, vinegar, garlic, bay leaves, cinnamon stick, cloves, oregano, allspice and chilli in a separate bowl and mix well.

Place rabbit pieces in a large glass or ceramic bowl. Add the marinade ingredients to the rabbit, then cover and refrigerate overnight. Turn rabbit a couple of times, if possible.

Heat only half the oil in a large saucepan over medium heat and cook onions for 5 minutes or until soft, stirring occasionally. Add garlic and cook a further 3 minutes. Transfer mixture to a bowl and set aside.

Remove rabbit from marinade, reserving marinade mixture. Heat remaining oil in the same saucepan over medium-high heat and cook the rabbit in 2-3 batches for 8 minutes or until browned all over. Return onions to pan and add the marinade mixture, tomato paste and enough cold water to just cover the rabbit. Cover and bring to the boil then reduce heat to low and simmer for 1½-2 hours or until rabbit is tender and sauce has thickened. Add olives in the last 10 minutes to heat through.

Serve sprinkled with fresh oregano leaves and crusty bread.

* Refer to Glossary – Page 482

Cocido estofado
Rabbit & potato stew

When you have a small amount of meat and want it to go further you make a sauce and add some bread or, in this case, potatoes. This is classic comida de pueblo or 'food of the people' cooking. During the cooking time the juices soak into the potatoes, which makes them even more nourishing and delicious.

Ingredients

2 Spanish chorizo sausages*, thickly sliced

75g plain (all-purpose) flour

Flaked salt

Freshly cracked pepper

1-2 rabbits, jointed (see Tip)

60ml olive oil

2 medium red onions, thickly sliced

2 garlic cloves, sliced

1 green pepper (capsicum)*, seeded and thickly sliced

1 red pepper (capsicum)*, seeded and thickly sliced

1 long fresh red chilli*, finely chopped

8 medium all-purpose potatoes, quartered

Pinch of saffron threads*

250ml red wine

2 cinnamon sticks

1 teaspoon sweet smoked paprika*

2 fresh bay leaves

2 x 400ml cans chopped tomatoes

250ml salt-reduced chicken stock

Fresh flat-leaf (Italian) parsley, to serve

Method

Cook chorizo sausage in a large frying pan over a medium-high heat for 3 minutes or until lightly browned; transfer to a bowl and set aside.

Place flour into a large bowl and season with salt and pepper. Coat rabbit pieces in flour, shaking off the excess. Heat oil in the same frying pan and cook the rabbit in 2-3 batches over a medium-high heat for 4 minutes each side or until golden brown. Transfer to a bowl and set aside.

Add onions, garlic, peppers and chilli to the frying pan and cook for 10 minutes or until tender; remove and set aside. Next add potatoes and cook for 12 minutes or until golden. Add saffron, red wine, cinnamon sticks, paprika, bay leaves, tomatoes and stock.

Return onion mixture and rabbit to frying pan (for alternative cooking method, see Note) and stir to combine.

Cover and bring to the boil over a medium-high heat, then reduce heat to low and simmer for 35-40 minutes or until rabbit is tender.

Remove rabbit pieces and keep warm. Simmer the sauce, uncovered, for about 20 minutes or until reduced and slightly thickened. Return rabbit pieces to the sauce to heat through and adjust seasoning to taste.

Serve with parsley.

Tip: Either purchase rabbit pieces or ask your butcher to joint a rabbit for you.

Note – The mixture can be transferred to a large ovenproof casserole dish or baking dish with a lid and baked at 180°C for 40 minutes or until tender.

* Refer to Glossary – Page 482

Cabrito estofado
Aromatic braised kid (or lamb)

serves 4

Ingredients

80ml olive oil

800g diced kid or lamb

2 medium brown onions, finely chopped

4 garlic cloves, finely chopped

1 medium green pepper (capsicum)*, seeded and chopped

400g can chopped tomatoes

125 red wine

125ml salt-reduced beef stock

2 fresh bay leaves

1 teaspoon ground chilli*

Flaked salt

Freshly cracked black pepper

2 tablespoons chopped fresh flat-leaf (Italian) parsley, to serve

Saffron rice, to serve (see Note)

Method

Heat only 1 tablespoon of oil in a large flameproof casserole dish or ovenproof frying pan over a medium-high heat. Cook meat in 2-3 batches until lightly brown on all sides, adding extra oil as required. Set aside.

Reduce heat to medium, add onion and garlic cook for 3-5 minutes or until soft but not coloured. Add pepper, tomatoes, wine, stock, bay leaves and ground chilli and stir to combine.

Return meat to dish and stir to combine. Cover and simmer over low heat for 1 hour or until meat is tender. (For alternative cooking method, see Tip). Season to taste and sprinkle with parsley. Serve with saffron rice and steamed greens.

Tip: This dish could also be baked in the oven at 160°C for about 1 hour or until meat is tender.

Note – To make saffron rice, simply steep a pinch of saffron threads in a tablespoon of hot water for 10–20 minutes and add to rice as it is being cooked.

* Refer to Glossary – Page 482

Pierna de cordero rellena
Stuffed leg of lamb

serves 4-6

Ingredients

Stuffing:

60g minced pork

1 egg

25g fresh breadcrumbs*

40g roasted* pine nuts

60ml brandy

¼ cup chopped fresh flat-leaf
(Italian) parsley

Flaked salt

Freshly cracked black pepper

Lamb:

1.5kg butterflied leg lamb

50g chicken liver pâté or foie gras

1 tablespoon olive oil

1 medium brown onion, finely chopped

3 garlic cloves, finely chopped

2 medium carrots, finely chopped

3 fresh bay leaves

4 sprigs fresh thyme

60ml red wine

500ml salt-reduced beef stock

35g plain (all-purpose) flour

Sugar snap peas, potatoes and carrots,
to serve

Spain used to be the wool basket of Europe until someone took their Merino sheep to Australia. The rest is history. The Spanish still have a love of lamb, particularly lamb roasted with lots of expensive ingredients. Some Galician farmers' wives will dress up a leg of lamb with half a bottle of Cognac. Here, we're stuffing a butterflied leg with pork and pine nuts, a little rich pâté, trussing it up and roasting it until golden brown.

Method

Preheat oven to 180°C.

To make the stuffing, place pork, egg, breadcrumbs, pine nuts, brandy and parsley into a medium bowl and mix well. Season with salt and pepper.

Lay lamb out onto a board and spread with pâté. Top with stuffing, then roll up lamb and tie with kitchen string.

Heat oil in a heavy-based flameproof baking dish over medium-high heat and cook onion, garlic and carrots for 5 minutes, stirring occasionally. Add rolled lamb, bay leaves, thyme, wine and only half the beef stock. Bake in preheated oven for 45-50 minutes or until tender, basting regularly.

Remove lamb from dish and cover loosely with foil to keep warm and rest while preparing the gravy.

Place the same baking dish over a low-medium heat on the stovetop, add the flour to the pan juices and cook, stirring continuously, until mixture becomes a light brown colour.

Gradually pour in remaining beef stock, stirring, until smooth. Bring to the boil, stirring, and simmer for 2-3 minutes. Season further to taste, if required.

Serve sliced lamb with the gravy, accompanied with sugar snap peas, potatoes and carrots.

* Refer to Glossary – Page 482

Broquetas de cordero a la plancha
Char-grilled lamb skewers

serves 4

Ingredients

700g lamb backstraps or eye of loin,
cut into 2cm cubes

3 garlic cloves, finely chopped

125ml sherry

60ml olive oil

2 tablespoons ground cumin

1 tablespoon sweet smoked paprika*

1 teaspoon ground nutmeg

1 teaspoon ground turmeric

½ teaspoon cayenne pepper

1 teaspoon flaked salt

¼ cup chopped fresh flat-leaf (Italian)
parsley

10-12 bamboo skewers, soaked
(see Tip)

Lemon wedges, to serve

Method

Place lamb into a large glass or ceramic bowl. Add garlic, sherry, oil, cumin, paprika, nutmeg, turmeric, cayenne pepper, salt and parsley. Mix well and rub the marinade into the lamb. Cover and refrigerate for several hours or overnight, stirring 2-3 times.

Thread 3-4 pieces of lamb onto each skewer. Preheat barbecue or char-grill to medium heat.

Cook lamb for 10-15 minutes, turning occasionally, until evenly brown on all sides. Transfer skewers to a baking tray or plate, cover loosely with foil and rest for 2-3 minutes before serving.

Serve with a spinach or mixed leaf salad and lemon wedges.

Tip: Soak bamboo skewers in water before using to prevent them from burning too quickly on the barbecue or char-grill.

304
gourmetpilgrim Spain

* Refer to Glossary – Page 482

Chuletas de cordero en salsa
Lamb cutlets in chorizo tomato sauce

serves 4

Ingredients

Spice mix:

3 teaspoons ground cumin

2 teaspoons ground cinnamon

½ teaspoon smoked hot paprika*

½ teaspoon ground fennel

1½ teaspoons flaked salt

Lamb:

16 French-trimmed* lamb cutlets

2 tablespoons olive oil

150g Spanish chorizo sausage*, sliced

2 slices Serrano jamon or prosciutto*, sliced

1 large brown onion, halved and thinly sliced

400g can chopped tomatoes

Pinch of saffron threads*

Flaked salt

Freshly cracked black pepper

Fresh oregano leaves, to serve

Vegetables or salad, to serve

You can taste the food legacy of the Moors in this one dish. The spice blend in which these juicy little cutlets are cooked are reminiscent of Spain's occupation by Muslims. Spices were their calling card; some, such as cinnamon, they traded all the way from the Far East, others, such as saffron, from Persia. The pork chorizo and jamon in this dish mark the end of the Muslim era and the return to Christianity.

Method

To make the spice mix, place cumin, cinnamon, paprika, fennel and salt into a small bowl, mix well and transfer to a plate. Press the cutlets into the spice mixture, turning to coat both sides.

Heat oil in a large frying pan over medium-high heat and cook the lamb cutlets in batches for 2 minutes each side (depending on thickness) or until cooked to your liking. Remove from pan and cover loosely with foil to keep warm.

Return frying pan to heat, add chorizo, jamon and onion and cook for 5 minutes or until onion is lightly golden, stirring occasionally. Add tomatoes and saffron and cook for a further 10 minutes, stirring constantly. Add oregano and season to taste.

Serve lamb cutlets with the sauce, accompanied with vegetables or a small garden salad.

Hígado en vinagreta
Liver in sherry-vinegar sauce

serves 4

Ingredients

3 garlic cloves, roughly chopped

1 small fresh red chilli*, seeded and chopped

60ml sherry vinegar*

60ml water

½ teaspoon flaked salt

1 teaspoon mild paprika*

½ teaspoon freshly cracked black pepper

1 teaspoon chopped fresh oregano leaves

60ml olive oil

1 medium brown onion, thinly sliced

2 fresh bay leaves

650g calf's liver, sliced and cut into strips

Boiled potatoes, to serve

Method

Place the garlic, chilli, sherry vinegar, water, salt, paprika, pepper and oregano into a mortar and use the pestle to grind to a paste.

Heat only half the oil in a heavy-based frying pan over a medium heat and cook onion for 3-5 minutes or until soft but not coloured, stirring occasionally. Add herb-chilli paste and bay leaves, then cook for 3-5 minutes or until the sauce has reduced slightly.

Heat remaining oil in a separate large frying pan over a medium-high heat and cook the liver for 3-5 minutes or until lightly browned. Add liver to sauce mixture and cook over low heat for a further 2 minutes or until just cooked and heated through.

Serve with boiled potatoes.

* Refer to Glossary – Page 482

Chuletas de ternera con ensalada de patatas
Veal cutlets with warm potato salad

serves 4

Ingredients

1 tablespoon chopped fresh flat-leaf
(Italian) parsley
Pinch of saffron threads*
1 teaspoon flaked salt
120ml white wine
4 veal cutlets (225g each)

Warm potato salad:
700g kipfler potatoes, washed
4 spring onions*, diagonally sliced
2 sticks celery, finely sliced
¼ cup roughly chopped fresh flat-leaf
(Italian) parsley, extra
4 slices of Serrano jamon* or prosciutto

Dressing:
225g egg mayonnaise*
2 garlic cloves, crushed
1 tablespoon sherry vinegar*
2 tablespoons lemon juice

To cook veal:
75g plain (all-purpose) flour
1 teaspoon mild paprika*
1 teaspoon flaked salt, extra
½ teaspoon freshly cracked black pepper
2 eggs, lightly beaten
75g dry breadcrumbs
Olive oil for pan frying

Method

Place parsley, saffron and salt in a mortar and pound with the pestle to form a paste. Transfer paste to a glass or ceramic bowl. Add wine and mix well. Add cutlets to bowl and rub marinade into the flesh. Cover and refrigerate for 1 hour.

Meanwhile, to make the warm potato salad, place potatoes into a large saucepan and cover with cold water. Bring to the boil and cook for 20 minutes or until tender. Drain and cool slightly, then peel potatoes and diagonally cut into 2cm-thick slices. Place slices in a large bowl, add spring onions, celery and parsley and gently stir to combine.

Dry fry* jamon in a medium frying pan over a medium-high heat for 2 minutes each side or until crisp. Remove and cool.

To make the dressing, place the egg mayonnaise, garlic, vinegar and lemon juice in a small bowl and mix well. Add the dressing to the potatoes and toss until well coated. Break the jamon into pieces and sprinkle on top of the salad close to serving.

Place flour, paprika, salt and pepper onto a plate. Place beaten eggs into a shallow bowl. Place breadcrumbs into a second shallow bowl. Coat veal in seasoned flour, shaking off excess, then dip into egg and, lastly, breadcrumbs.

Heat oil in a large frying pan over a medium-high heat and cook cutlets for 6-8 minutes on each side or until well browned and tender. Serve with potato salad.

* Refer to Glossary – Page 482

Rabo de buey estofado
Braised oxtail

Ingredients

75g plain (all-purpose) flour

2 teaspoons dried oregano leaves

1 teaspoon mild paprika*

½ teaspoon cayenne pepper

½ teaspoon flaked salt

½ teaspoon freshly cracked black pepper

1.5kg oxtail, cut into sections
(see Tip)

20g butter

1 tablespoon olive oil

2 medium brown onions, finely chopped

3 garlic cloves, finely chopped

1 small fresh red chilli*, finely chopped

2 medium carrots, finely chopped

1 stick celery, finely chopped

250ml white wine

250ml red wine

60ml brandy

2 fresh bay leaves

250ml tomato puree (passata)*

Pinch of saffron threads*

250ml salt-reduced beef stock

10 small chat potatoes, halved

Flaked salt, extra

Freshly cracked pepper, extra

Green beans, to serve

The name refers to the tail of a bull. It's cheap meat, mostly bone and sinew. But in this recipe it undergoes a dramatic transformation to make a sweet and succulent meal. The slow cooking breaks down the flesh to create a super-sticky, lip-smackingly beautiful dish. It's rich with vegetables, cooked-down tomatoes and nice slug of brandy, red and white wine and a hint of saffron.

Method

Place flour, oregano, paprika, cayenne, salt and pepper into a large bowl and mix well. Coat oxtail in the flour mixture, shaking off the excess. Heat butter and oil in a deep heavy-based saucepan or flameproof casserole dish over medium-high heat and cook oxtail in 2-3 batches for 8 minutes or until browned all over. Remove and set aside.

Reduce heat to medium and cook onions for 5 minutes or until soft. Add garlic, chilli and carrots and cook for a further 5 minutes, then add celery and cook for 2 minutes or until vegetables begin to soften.

Pour in wines and brandy, then bring to the boil and simmer, uncovered, until mixture has reduced by a third. Return oxtail to the saucepan with bay leaves, tomato puree, saffron and stock and bring to the boil. Reduce heat to low, then cover and gently simmer for 2½ hours, stirring occasionally (for alternative cooking method, see Note).

Add potatoes and simmer, covered, for a further 30 minutes or until potato is tender and oxtail is falling off the bone. Season to taste.

Serve with steamed green beans.

Tip: Ask your butcher to cut the oxtail into pieces.

Note – This dish could also be cooked in a casserole dish in a slow oven (about 120°C) for about 3-4 hours or until oxtail is tender. Add potatoes, cover and return to the oven for a further 45 minutes.

* Refer to Glossary – Page 482

Carrilleras de ternera
Slow cooked beef cheeks

Ingredients

500ml red wine

500ml Manzanilla* sherry

1 large carrot, finely chopped

1 leek, white part only, finely chopped

1 medium brown onion, finely chopped

1 stick celery, finely chopped

5 sprigs fresh thyme

1 fresh bay leaf

4 garlic cloves, unpeeled and lightly crushed

1 teaspoon sweet smoked paprika*

6 (about 1.5kg) beef cheeks

Flaked salt

Freshly cracked black pepper

2 tablespoons olive oil

500ml veal jus*

800ml salt-reduced chicken stock

2 tablespoons tomato paste*

12 slices jamon* or prosciutto, baked until crispy (optional)

This is perhaps the most delicious part of the animal. Full flavoured and slow cooked in red wine and sherry, it's one of the most deliciously silky dishes in the world. Not every butcher carries beef cheeks so you'll need to place an order well in advance. Don't be frightened about the long cooking time; cheeks need a lot of low, slow heat to achieve the delicate texture.

Method

Place wine, sherry, carrot, leek, onion, celery, thyme, bay leaf, garlic and paprika into a large glass or ceramic bowl and stir well. Add beef cheeks and stir to coat in the marinade. Cover and refrigerate for 6-8 hours.

Remove the cheeks from the marinade and drain, reserving the liquid. Strain the liquid, keeping aside both the liquid and vegetables separately. Lightly season the beef cheeks with salt and pepper.

Preheat oven to 160°C.

Heat oil in a large flameproof casserole dish or cast-iron pot over medium-high heat. Add the beef cheeks and cook in 2 batches until well browned on both sides. Remove beef from the dish and set aside.

Return dish to heat, add the vegetables from the marinade and cook over medium heat for 5 minutes or until slightly caramelised. Add the beef cheeks and pour over the reserved marinade. Bring to the boil, reduce heat and simmer, uncovered, for 5 minutes, skimming any fat from the surface.

Add veal jus, stock and tomato paste and bring to the boil. Remove from heat, cover the dish and bake in preheated oven for 3½ hours or until meat is tender.

If the sauce is a little thin, return the dish to the stovetop. Remove meat from dish and cover loosely with foil to keep warm, then simmer the sauce, uncovered, until it thickens and reduces slightly.

Serve with baked jamon.

* Refer to Glossary – Page 482

Solomillo de ternera al queso azul
Fillet of beef with blue cheese

serves 4

Ingredients

½ cup finely chopped fresh flat-leaf (Italian) parsley

2 tablespoons finely chopped fresh oregano leaves

2 tablespoons finely chopped fresh rosemary leaves

4 x 200g beef eye-fillet steaks (see Tip)

1 tablespoon olive oil

1 large brown onion, halved and thinly sliced

2 garlic cloves, finely chopped

125ml white wine

185ml pure (single) cream

150g Spanish blue cheese* (such as Cabrales), crumbled

Asparagus, to serve

Method

Preheat oven to 100°C.

Place parsley, oregano and rosemary on a plate and gently mix. Press beef steaks into herb mixture.

Heat oil in a large frying pan over a medium-high heat and cook beef for 4-5 minutes on each side (for medium-rare) or until cooked to your liking. Remove from pan and cover loosely with foil and place into the oven to keep warm. Wipe out pan with kitchen paper towel.

Return frying pan to medium heat and cook onion and garlic, stirring occasionally, for 3-5 minutes or until soft but not coloured. Add wine to deglaze the pan and simmer, uncovered, for 2 minutes or until reduced by half. Add cream and blue cheese and simmer, uncovered, for a further 2-3 minutes or until combined.

Serve steak with blue cheese sauce accompanied with asparagus.

Tip: Remove beef from the refrigerator 20-30 minutes before cooking to take the chill off and allow for more even cooking.

Jamón (Jamon)

Just like a fine wine, producing the highest quality jamon and then aging it to perfection requires a lot of skill – with mouth-watering results.

Right: The art of the *cortadore* – slicing jamon along the grain to reveal the full cross-section of flavours in the muscle.

Over left: How to savour fine jamon – *lonchas* – ultra thin, mouth size slices.

Over right: A *cortadore* assesses his produce in the *secadero* (drying rooms), Valle de los Pedroches, Andalucia.

To the Spaniards, ham is much more than cured pork. It is a cultural tradition dating back to the Middle Ages and a source of national pride. Spain consumes more ham per capita than any other nation, which is entirely understandable to anyone who has tasted the pleasure of freshly sliced *jamón*.

The majority of hams consumed, around 90 per cent, are *jamón Serrano* (mountain hams) made from white pigs, the legs salted and then hung from the rafters to cure according to age-old village tradition. The remaining 10 per cent are Iberico hams from the endemic Iberian boar, a black beast with slender legs and *pata negra*, black hooves, by which you can usually identify these lovely joints. The most treasured and expensive iberico ham is *ibérico de bellota*, the acorn-fed, aromatic and intensely flavoured flesh bred from a unique alliance between man, animal and nature.

Iberico production is confined to the south-west of Spain where the *dehesa* pasturelands abound with oak trees that provide wood for fuel, cork for wine and, most crucially, fodder for pigs. According to the strict Denomination of Origin (DO) rules governing the production of *ibérico de bellota*, each pure-bred pig must have one hectare of dehesa to feed in during the autumn *montanera*, or fattening period, when acorns fall and greedy animals double their weight. Each pig can bolt down 10 kilograms of acorns a day, gaining an extra kilogram in weight every 24 hours.

Free range finesse – and time

Pigs fed exclusively on free-range acorns and grasses produce the finest quality *ibérico de bellota* hams. Lesser hams such as *recebo* and *cebo* have more grain and compound feed in their diets so lack the heady aroma and nutty, oleic acid flavours of their exclusively acorn-fed superiors. *Bellota* hams are also hung for longer in the *secaderos* or factory drying rooms to mature, like fine wines. The entire process, from birth to table, of producing *jamón ibérico de bellota* takes more than four years, hence the price for a single seven kilogram ham is several hundred euros.

Despite its sometimes extravagant cost, *jamón* is a fundamental staple of the Spanish diet. Around a third of homes and every café and bar worth its salt proudly displays a *jamonero*, the vice-like device used to hold the ham steady during carving. Jamon is always eaten at room temperature, kept moist and fresh by covering the cut with a layer of sliced fat or a tea-towel.

The best-known and most sought after *jamón* brands are *Joselito*, *Julián Martín* and *Cinco Jotas*. Officially protected DO *jamón* include *Guijuelo*, *Los Pedroches*, *Huelva* and *Dehesa de Extremadura*. Extremadura has the broadest prairielands in the country, spanning more than one million hectares – the ideal environment for fattening *pata negra*.

JULIÁN MARTÍN – *Jamón in the family*

First there was wine tourism, now there is *jamonturismo* – guided tours of the factories that produce Spain's national pride.

In the industrial city of Guijuelo just south of Salamanca, Julián Martín is the pioneer of this new form of tourism, inviting ham fanciers inside its aromatic warehouses to discover the extensive process by which *jamón* is created.

Visits begin in the salting pits where *iberico* hams are rested for at least a week to drain and season. Any excess salt is rinsed off before hams are hung in temperature-controlled rooms to gather mould, which forces any residual salt inside the leg and enhances flavours. They are then cleaned and hung, for at least two years, in the upper-floor *secaderos* where they dry naturally in the plains breezes. Julián Martín slaughters 100,000 pigs each year, which means that at any one time there will be roughly 200,000 hams hanging in its store-rooms, presenting a deliciously Gothic still-life for visitors.

The company's master-carver or *cortador*, Juan Vicente Delgado, is the man charged with quality-testing each ham during the maturation process. Using a small plastic prong called a *cala*, he samples each ham in two or three places along the femur vein to ensure the blood has drained properly. Like a master vigneron, Delgado can tell how well a ham is maturing simply by smelling the *cala*. The company's biggest clients, including leading Spanish department store El Corte Inglés, visit the factory a year before hams are fully matured to choose the ones they want. Some bring their own cala to perform their own tests, but most trust Señor Delgado to choose the best for them.

Tours also explore the *obradores* where pork sausages such as chorizo, *salchichón* and *lomo ibérico* are prepared, and the drying rooms where they hang for about four months with the provenance and manufacturing date of each sausage carefully tagged.

By far the highlight of the tour is the end, when guests stop merely looking at produce and finally get to taste it. Served simply with bread and ample bottles of Manzanilla wine, visitors gorge on chorizo, *lomo*, sausage and superb *jamón ibérico* against a backdrop of hundreds of thousands of hams hanging in the *bodega*.

www.julianmartin.es

La caza (The hunt)

In Spain, hunting game is a national obsession – followed closely a taste for game meats.

Across the Spanish countryside there are small black-and-white signs nailed to trees by the roadside reading *coto privado de caza*, or private reserve for hunting.

Game is a national obsession. Spanish love their wild animals almost as much as they love eating them. Perhaps it's part of Spanish machismo, perhaps it's their passion for strong flavours. Perhaps, for wealthy city dwellers, it is part of their ongoing longing to be connected to their magnificent countryside. Whatever the case, game is on the menu in Spain.

Wild Slow Food

Because these animals lead a life in the wild, walking long distances to find food and often running away from predators, they have developed strong muscles and can be tough. Traditional Spanish game recipes call for long periods of marinating in wine and, sometimes, strong liquor. This is followed by long, low and slow cooking times to break down the strong flesh, resulting in rich dishes with a lot of sauce.

Wild game is expensive and illegal in some areas. Farmed venison, rabbit, quail, pheasant and partridge are available almost year round, are consistent in quality, and have been humanely dispatched. Farmed game isn't as costly as wild caught game, doesn't have the same strong flavour and requires less cooking time.

The curious cook who searches out these animals and cooks them in the Spanish style will follow in the footsteps of generations of great cooks and won't be disappointed.

> **To market, to market**
>
> A good starting point to witness the Spanish love of game is at the markets. Rabbit and hare hang in fur, rigid and not refrigerated, slowly gaining deeper, richer flavours. Pheasant, quail and partridge, still in feather, wait for a buyer; and venison and wild boar are also popular. They are all on show in the markets in every town and big city.

Chorizo (Chorizo)

This flavoursome sausage is so omnipresent it's practically an emblem of Spanish cuisine.

Deep red sausages hang from hooks in the ceiling. There are hundreds of them, slowly drying in the chill air. These are chorizo, a sausage that's used extensively in Spanish cooking.

The chorizo is made from chopped pork that's mixed with herbs, garlic, salt and smoky Spanish paprika. As they dry, naturally occurring bacteria transform lactose in the flesh into lactic acid. This not only gives the cured chorizo a lively and fresh acidic finish but also makes the sausage too acidic for bad bacteria to flourish.

More than 50,000 tonnes of chorizo are produced in Spain each year. In the north of the country, the chorizo are given a light smoking to help preserve them in the more humid environment.

A sausage that sizzles

Cured chorizo look and feel like small salami and are generally used as a snack, as well as in cooking. When chorizo are fried, the red, flavoursome fat rendered from the sausage is reserved and used in other dishes – perhaps in which to fry some *migas* (breadcumbs) or spread on a toasted roll as a breakfast snack.

Another fattier variety of chorizo is sold fresh and used in stews such as the *cocido*, a stew of many meats and vegetables. As the *cocido* cooks, the chorizo releases the flavour of the garlic and paprika.

A butcher who makes chorizo in his *chacinería* will probably also make a cured pork loin called *lomo curado*. This involves taking a whole pork loin and smearing it in a paste of garlic, herbs and Spanish paprika and allowing it to slowly cure.

Finding the real deal

Sourcing good chorizo outside Spain can be a vexed issue. The name chorizo has been often misappropriated by butchers and, as a result, there are some very lame sausages sold as 'chorizo'. Cooks who really want to cook traditional-tasting Spanish food should buy their chorizo from Spanish butchers, Spanish grocery stores or good quality delicatessens.

Castilla-León

The largest of Spain's 17 autonomous regions shares borders with nine regions and one country, Portugal, and sprawls across one-fifth of the country's total landmass. This is frontier land where holy wars were fought for centuries between Christians and Muslims for control of the Iberian Peninsula. Today it abounds with palaces and castles and, at Segovia, one of the world's most perfectly preserved Roman aqueducts, which is as inspiring now as when it was constructed in 1AD.

The kingdoms of León and Castilla united in the 13th century to repel Muslim imperialists in the south but the region of Castilla-León is only a few decades old. Castilla was cleaved into north and south after General Franco's death, when the modern, democratic Spain took shape, and Castilla-León is the northern half, encompassing such eminent cities as Salamanca, the ancient seat of learning whose university dates from 1218, and Segovia with its *alcázar*, a Disney-perfect palace that was a favourite sanctuary of Spanish kings.

The remnants of the region's starring role in the reconquest of Christian Spain from the Moors are on display everywhere – in Ávila's daunting defensive walls that date from the 11th and 12th centuries, and León with its centuries-old Gothic cathedral, a seminal landmark on the Christian pilgrimage route of St James.

The granary of Spain

Long before it became a religious battleground the Romans introduced cereals to this region and Castilla-León is today often referred to as the granary of Spain, for its abundance of wheat, barley, rye and oats. In common with the rest of the central steppes, it also has a big appetite for chickpeas, lentils and dried beans of all descriptions. The vegetable harvest is substantial and includes beetroot and potatoes, but plains dwellers are primarily eaters of tender young meat.

The Castilian plateau is the land of roasted meats and the people of Castilla-León like theirs tender – in texture and in age. Milk-fed lamb or *lechazo* is simply cooked, just roasted with a little water and salt and served with a salad of lettuce and tomato. Segovia is renowned for its *cochinillo*, roasted suckling pig no more than 20 days old with flesh so supple it can be sliced by the edge of a plate. *Cabrito* or baby goat is also common.

In Salamanca, local tastes run to beef, especially the *calderillo bejarano* stew of beef shank or rib cooked with vegetables, paprika, bay leaves and sometimes chilli. Salamanca also invented the *hornazo*, a pie loaded with chorizo, pork loin, jamon Serrano and boiled eggs.

The world's finest ham hails from here, but there is so much more to this fertile region.

Below: The old town of Miranda de Ebro and medieval church of Santa Maria, Castilla y Leon.

A region of meat specialties – and the world's finest ham

Just south of Salamanca lies the city of Guijuelo, home to arguably Spain's finest hams and sausages, including the sublime, acorn-fed, *jamón ibérico de bellota*.

The region is one of Spain's least populous, its broad plains sparsely punctuated with clusters of farmhouses and, more rarely these days, a *palomar* or dove cote. These adobe pigeon houses provided fertiliser for crops and food for tables, inspiring such enduring recipes as Valladolid's *pichones estofados*, pigeon stewed with diced vegetables, garlic and bay leaves. Rabbit is another favourite cheap eat, usually stewed but also roasted, fried and barbecued.

León introduced *botillo* to the Castilian diet, a sausage (*embutido*) made from pigs' tails, ribs and sundry other offcuts, smoked and seasoned with paprika, oregano and garlic. It is traditionally fried until it bursts, then served with potatoes. Many cities have a signature *embutido*, such as Burgos's black pudding and the bread and pork-fat *farinato* from Ciudad Rodrigo.

Mule drivers from León are credited with having introduced salt cod to the central plains and Castilla-Léon shares the local fondness for *bacalao al ajoarriero*, salt cod braised with garlic and piquillo peppers. Freshwater trout from León and Zamora is grilled simply with oil and lemon.

There are said to be more than 1500 types of fungi growing in the region, which has given rise to recipes such as pigeon stuffed with *boletus* and *setas* sautéed with ham, as well as a peculiar form of tourism called *micoturismo*, where visitors explore mushroom-picking routes and feast on fungi at local restaurants.

Pork tends to get star billing in these parts but Castilla-León is also Spain's largest beef producer and woolgrower. Its substantial stocks of sheep, cows and goats provide the raw material for cheeses, ranging from the creamy, spiced goat's milk *Queso del Tiétar* from Ávila to the manchego-like *Zamorano* DO, a hard, drum-shaped cheese made with ewe's milk.

The mighty Duero River irrigates the valleys of the Ribera del Duero, one of Spain's most distinguished winemaking regions and revered for its tempranillos. Castilla-León's 12 Denomination of Origin (DO) wine regions include Rueda – known for its juicy *verdejos* and, more recently, for sauvignon blancs – Toro's full-bodied reds and floral rosés from Cigales.

For centuries Castilians and Leonese have been weaned on sweet pastries baked by nuns in the region's myriad convents, so it's no surprise regional desserts tend towards the ecclesiastical. Perhaps most typical are the *yemas de Santa Teresa*, bite-sized cakes of sugar and egg yolks invented by the barefoot Carmelites to use up yolks leftover from local vineyards, where eggwhites are used to clarify wines.

Aragón

It may be the nation's biggest producer of the prized truffle, but this region is loved for its rustic, earthy cuisine.

The medieval Crown of Aragon was a great European power in the 14th and 15th centuries, with its territories extending from Catalonia to Greece, via Sardinia, Corsica, Malta and the Italian peninsula. Aragon was also, memorably, the motherland of Catherine, the unfortunate first wife of England's King Henry VIII. But modern-day Aragon is perhaps best described as the great outdoors of Spain.

This northeastern border region is home to the stunning Ordesa National Park – with picturesque gorges and a geography that ranges from the highest peak in the Pyrenees to the longest river in Spain, the Ebro.

Mountain pastures and forests in the north give way to valleys and fertile fields before the region rises again to meet the soaring Sistema Iberico. Most of Aragon is a giant basin flanked by mountains, which makes it the ideal adventurer's playground for canyoning, hiking, horse riding, rock-climbing and skiing.

Culturally, Aragon is a land of Roman and Romanesque remains, of Christian and Moorish castles and grand cathedrals that were the spiritual fortress of the fledgling Spanish empire against Islam. The capital, Zaragoza, was originally called Cesaraugusta under the Romans, then Sarakusta under the Moors, before assuming the mantle of capital of the Crown of Aragon.

A region of herders

The climate is harsh and the Aragonese are notoriously hardy folk with a simple but superbly nourishing cuisine. The River Ebro breathes life into the valley, watering crops of wheat and barley, grapevines and orchards of peaches, cherries and apples.

Rural Aragonese have always been herders and that tradition persists today – cattle, sheep, pigs and goats form the four pillars of the local diet. The region's farmers have had centuries to tinker with raw produce and their efforts have resulted in the hams of Teruel that are dried in the arid sierra to produce memorable jamon Serrano, the first agricultural product to win Spanish Denomination of Origin (DO) protection.

Below: Sheepfold, Teruel, Aragon.

Opposite top: Strings of garlic hang at the market in the Plaza Mayor, Leon, Castilla y Leon.

Opposite bottom: Vineyards of the Ribera del Duero and the medieval castle of Penafiel, Castilla y Leon. The mountain below the castle is riddled with caves traditionally used to ferment wine. Chimneys built to ventilate the caves dot the landscape surrounding the castle.

Above: Jaca Citadel, Jaca, Aragon. Constructed in the 15th and 16th centuries to defend against the threat from the Huguenot armies of neighbouring France, the citadel is one of only two complete pentagonal military fortifications in Europe.

Right: Hay fields and the Pyrenees Mountains, Huesca, Aragon.

Their lamb, too, is legendary. Aragonese lamb or *ternasco* is milk-fed for at least 50 days then dispatched between 70 and 90 days, to be roasted and served with potatoes and *alioli* sauce. DO protection also extends to peaches from Calanda, olive oil from Bajo Aragón, as well as a quintet of wine regions.

The sparseness of Aragonese cuisine can be seen in dishes such as *chireta*, inside-out sheep intestines stuffed with offal (lungs, tripe, heart) and rice, then flavoured with bacon, ham, garlic, parsley and cinnamon. It's known as the 'haggis of Aragon'.

There's a similar austerity in the appetite for snails, the easy meat casseroles of lamb, pork or chicken commonly in a *chilindrón* sauce of red peppers, tomatoes and onion, and in that staple of rural Spain, *sopa de ajo*, a garlic and bread soup enhanced with whatever is to hand – peppers, paprika, maybe some ham or chorizo.

Calves or sheep's tails are known euphemistically as *espárragos montañeses*, 'mountain asparagus', and breadcrumb fry-ups (*migas*, often flavoured with chorizo-like longaniza sausage and onion) are as popular here as in other provincial areas.

The Aragonese are hunters and in times of plenty their tables welcome wild boar simmered in sherry and a regal soup of pigeon and truffles.

Rabbit, chicken and partridge can be prepared *escabeche*-style, a basic pickling process of cooking the meat in vinegar and oil with garlic and other aromatics (bay, thyme, cumin), then leaving it to marinate for anywhere from a day to a week. Trout makes a fine *escabeche* too, and there are ample stocks of the freshwater delicacy in the rivers of Aragon. Salt-cod is prepared the basic *ajoarriero* way with garlic and peppers, as well as a *la baturra*, with potatoes and eggs.

Alcohol also dominates in a dessert dish from the Tena Valley called *las sopetas*, or 'drunk peaches'. The fruit is soaked in red wine and served as a drink.

Crespillos, borage leaves battered and fried and served with honey or sugar, are typical of Aragonese ingenuity in the kitchen.

gourmet
pilgrim

El pan
Bread

As the old Spanish
saying goes, 'A meal
without bread is no
meal at all.'

El pan (Bread)

Whatever the variety, a quality loaf is an essential addition to every Spanish meal.

Bread, or *pan*, is served with every meal in one way or another. It's used to fill up a growing family at breakfast, lunch and dinner, and it's the basis of many pintxos and montaditos.

Different town, different bread

Any town or village of a decent size should have at least one panadero, or baker.

In the south, the local bread will be large, round loaves with a light tan crust and super white, slightly dry crumb. In the north, the bread changes dramatically with a lot more variation. In Catalonia, there's the thick-crusted *pa de pagès,* or country bread, which is particularly suitable for making *pa amb tomàquet.*

Old women at the market at Santiago de Compostela in Galicia sell giant loaves of cornbread by weight, slicing off brick-sized pieces and weighing the bread before simply wrapping it in paper.

Some of the more rustic breads don't rise to lofty heights and remain squat and dense – perfect to carry in a satchel with a piece of cheese when working in the fields or the olive groves. The Basques are particularly good bakers and, as well as the French-inspired baguettes, some bake a dark-crusted, spongy loaf called *sopako.*

Even stale bread rises again

Days after a loaf has been at its freshest, it gains a second life when it becomes an ingredient in another dish. It may be grated and mixed with fish to make *albóndigas de atún* in Andalusia – a remnant of the influence of the Jewish community on the cuisine of Spain prior to the years of the Inquisition.

Bread past its prime may be roughly turned into migas, which are then salted, fried and served with onions and oranges, perhaps with jamon or chorizo, or even with eggs. Slices of stale bread might be soaked in sweetened flavoured milk then fried to make torrijas. Or they could be used to make a cold *gazpacho* soup, or to thicken a sauce.

Serve a loaf of your own freshly baked bread on a breadboard alongside the dishes you make from this book for the final touch of authenticity to your meal. A good loaf of pasta dura bread, bought from the local market or Italian baker, will do if you're in hurry, or a quality loaf of sourdough works as well. It just needs a firm crust that you can hold on to while you're sopping up the juices from your plate.

Spanish folk wisdom:

'If there's not enough to go around, then make a sauce.' A sauce with fish or a cut of meat extends the dish to at least another one or two extra people, as the sauce will be mopped up with bread.

Migas con chorizo
Fried breadcrumbs with chorizo

Ingredients

1 loaf white, stale (2-3 days old) bread,
cubed (see Note)

150ml water

½ teaspoon flaked salt

60ml olive oil

1 chorizo sausage*, thinly sliced

150g manchego cheese*

Migas are breadcrumbs – fried breadcrumbs. They're also a delicious and salty little treat. Unlike commercial breadcrumbs, migas are a variety of sizes; from the size of the tip of one's thumb to quite small particles.

They're salted, sometimes by being splashed with salty water, left for a while and then fried, sometimes deep-fried, in the fat in which a spicy chorizo was fried. A fried egg could be laid over the top, perhaps some fried onions and there, in minutes, is a very cheap but extremely filling meal. One thing can't be left unsaid, and that is that the Spanish are very particular about their migas, passionate to the point of obsession. But when you eat a good plate of them you'll understand why.

Method

Place bread cubes into a large bowl. Place water and salt in a small jug and mix well, then evenly pour over bread, a little at a time. Toss the bread, ensuring that it is not too wet. Stand uncovered for 2 hours, tossing occasionally.

Heat oil in a large frying pan over medium heat and cook chorizo for 3-4 minutes or until crisp. Remove to a side plate, leaving the pan juices behind. Add bread cubes to the pan and cook over medium-high heat until golden.

Return chorizo to the frying pan to heat through. Serve with chunks of manchego cheese or another favourite cheese.

Note – The staler the bread (and drier the crust) the more traditional the dish. Use a good bread knife to slice it up, or once sliced just tear the bread into smaller pieces.

* Refer to Glossary – Page 482

Bocadillo
Bocadillo

Ingredients

2 fresh baguettes
Manchego cheese*
Membrillo (quince paste)*
Sliced jamon* or prosciutto
Red onion, thinly sliced

You could describe it as a bread roll but it's so much more. It's a small bite, a snack, a tasty respite. Bocadillos are a Spanish obsession. You could be in a café in Córdoba or a train station in Toledo and there would be a plate of bocadillos on offer.

A crusty baguette sliced lengthways and stuffed with a few fine slices of jamon or some wedges of warm potato tortilla. They're never buttered nor over stuffed. The fillings tend not to be moist – perhaps some aged manchego cheese and a fine slice of membrillo or quince paste. There's a satisfying crunch as one's teeth bite through the rustic crust and then the salty sweet hit of the filling.

Method

Cut baguette in half lengthways and fill with your choice of fillings. Here, one baguette is filled with jamon and thinly sliced red onion and the other with manchego cheese and membrillo.

The choice of delicious fillings is endless: consider tuna, potato omelette, chicken, tomato, cooked egg, roasted red pepper (capsicum) and rucola.

* Refer to Glossary – Page 482

Montaditos
Montaditos

Ingredients

Fresh baguette
Smoked salmon
Red onion, thinly sliced
Canned sardines
Manchego cheese*
Membrillo (quince paste)*

While the bocadillo is a fun, rough-and-ready snack, the montadito is a slightly more refined affair. Basically, it's a slice of large baguette onto which tasty toppings, such as smoked salmon, fried fish, cheese, jamon or even caviar, are placed. They're not dissimilar to pintxos one would find in a bar in the Basque Country, except there they prefer to layer their snacks with seafood smothered in mayonnaise.

Method

Cut baguette into slices, cutting at a slight angle to make larger slices on which to lay your choice of toppings.

Here, our montaditos are topped with smoked salmon and red onion, canned (drained) sardines, manchego and membrillo.

As with bocadillo, the choice of delicious toppings is endless.

* Refer to Glossary – Page 482

Ensaimada
Sweet Mallorcan bread scroll

serves 3

Ingredients

14g active dry yeast
125ml warm water
85g caster (superfine) sugar
500g plain (all-purpose) flour
Pinch of salt
50g pork lard, melted and cooled until warm
50g butter, melted and cooled until warm
1 egg, at room temperature, lightly beaten
2 tablespoons olive oil
Icing sugar, to serve

It's breakfast time on the Mediterranean island of Majorca. The guesthouse has an old-fashioned cook who hand makes her ensaïmadas. It's made with sourdough and rendered lard or, in her language, saïm. It's the pastry of Majorca, perhaps of Jewish or Arabic origin.

The olive oil has been replaced with pig fat in recent centuries, giving a definite sweetness and Christian overtone. Here, they sometimes fill the ensaïmada with angel hair, a type of candied melon or even sobrasada, which is a paste of fatty pig meat spiced with lots of Spanish paprika.

It takes a little time to get the rhythm of the rolling and folding of the method but the result is truly worth the effort. It's worth remembering to have some fruit, coffee and even some conserves ready for when they come out of the oven. Then, let them rest a day or two and toast them in the oven to bring them back to life.

Method

Place yeast and water into a bowl. Sprinkle with only 1 tablespoon of sugar, mix and leave in a warm place until it begins to foam slightly.

Sieve flour into a separate large bowl and add the salt, yeast mixture, lard, butter, egg, oil and remaining sugar. Mix well until a soft dough forms.

Once the dough comes away from the sides of the bowl turn it out onto a lightly floured work surface. Knead lightly.

Place the dough into a clean, lightly oiled bowl and cover with a slightly damp clean tea towel. Put bowl and dough into a warm place to leave to rise for about 1½-2 hours.

Line a large baking tray with kitchen baking paper.

Return dough to the lightly floured work surface and divide into three portions. Roll each portion into a long snake (cylinder shape). Coil and loosely roll up. Place onto prepared tray, cover again with a tea towel and allow to double in size.

Meanwhile, preheat oven to 180°C. Bake ensaimadas for 15-20 minutes or until they are lightly browned and sound hollow when tapped. Serve dusted with icing sugar.

Tip: Cover ensaimadas loosely with foil if they appear to be browning too quickly yet still require longer cooking.

Torrijas
Fried bread

Ingredients

1 large French bread stick or brioche loaf
160ml milk
6 free-range eggs*
1 lemon, rind only, finely grated
1 orange, rind only, finely grated
50g butter
2 tablespoons caster (superfine) sugar
1 teaspoon ground cinnamon
Ice cream, to serve

Nothing is wasted in a Spanish kitchen. Here bread or, even better, brioche is given a second lease of life by being drenched in egg and milk that's infused with citrus flavours, then fried in butter and dusted with cinnamon sugar. The exterior is golden brown and the interior soft, just like rich custard.

Method

Cut French stick or brioche into 10 slices, cutting at a slight angle to make larger slices. Place slices flat into a large baking dish.

Place milk, eggs and rind into a large bowl and mix well. Pour mixture over the bread. Stand for 15 minutes, turning over after 7 minutes (do this gently to avoid breaking the bread).

Heat only half the butter in a large non-stick frying pan over medium heat and cook half the bread for 2-3 minutes each side or until lightly golden. Repeat with the remaining butter and bread.

Combine sugar and cinnamon and sprinkle over the warm cooked bread.

Serve hot with ice cream.

* Refer to Glossary – Page 482

Cocas saladas
Savoury Catalan flatbread

serves 3-4

Ingredients

1 quantity of coca dough (see recipe next page)

2 tablespoons olive oil

1 teaspoon dried oregano leaves

250g cherry tomatoes, halved

70g raisins

40g baby spinach leaves

40g pine nuts

Flaked salt

Freshly cracked black pepper

A coca is a blank canvas of thin dough onto which Catalans paint the food of their town or village, depending on the season or the festival. Think pizza but without herbs or cheese and add a whole lot of Catalan passion. The plural is coques and comes from the Latin 'coquere' – to cook.

A coca amb recapte is a flat bread onto which whatever the specialty of the area gets cooked; it could be anchovies or botifarra, a peppery sausage. One version, coca amb pinyons, has it cooked with pine nuts, sugar and a touch of anise. Some are cooked with pine nuts, spinach and raisins, other with sardines, parsley and garlic, some with sugar and fruit.

What a coca is not is an overladen affair. It will have a generous amount of just a few ingredients to bring a beautiful flavour to the baked dough without overwhelming it. For the flavouring is not the point – it is a dish that comes from a time when food wasn't plentiful, so the ingredients on top were used sparingly to add excitement to an otherwise plain piece of baked bread. That said, a few slices of this, some salad and a glass of red wine makes a wonderful casual meal.

Method

Preheat oven to 200°C fan-forced (or 220°C – no fan) and position a shelf close to the bottom of the oven, which will assist in a crispy base. Lightly grease a 24cm x 31cm baking tray.

Roll out the dough on a lightly floured work surface to fit the baking tray. Brush the dough with only half the oil and prick the base randomly with a fork.

Sprinkle dough with oregano, then top with tomatoes, raisins, spinach and pine nuts. Drizzle with remaining oil and season with salt and pepper.

Bake in preheated oven for 20-25 minutes or until base is crisp and golden. Serve.

Note – The fan-forced (or fan-assisted) oven function is perfect for cooking coca where possible – or cook in a pizza oven.

* Refer to Glossary – Page 482

Cocas dulces
Sweet Catalan flatbread

serves 3-4

Ingredients

1 quantity of coca dough (see recipe, below)

2 teaspoons olive oil

2 tablespoons caster (superfine) sugar

1 large apple, quartered, cored and thinly sliced

40g glace fruit, thinly sliced

Method

Preheat oven to 200°C fan-forced (or 220°C – no fan) and position a shelf close to the bottom of the oven, which will assist in a crispy base. Lightly grease a 24cm x 31cm baking tray.

Roll out the dough on a lightly floured work surface to fit the baking tray. Brush the dough with oil and prick the base randomly with a fork.

Sprinkle dough with only half the sugar, then top with slices of apple and glace fruit. Sprinkle with remaining sugar. Bake in preheated oven for 15 minutes or until base is crisp and golden. Serve.

Note – The fan-forced (or fan-assisted) oven function is perfect for cooking coca where possible – or cook in a pizza oven.

Masa de coca
Coca dough

Ingredients

4g active dry yeast

180ml lukewarm water

250g strong (baker's) flour

2 tablespoons olive oil

10g butter, at room temperature

1 teaspoon salt

Pinch of sugar

Method

To make dough, combine the yeast and water in a bowl and allow to sit in a warm place until it begins to foam slightly. Place the flour into a separate bowl and make a well in the middle. Add the yeast mixture, oil, butter, salt and sugar and mix well. Using your hand, bring the dough together and add a little extra flour if the dough is a little sticky.

Turn out the dough onto a lightly floured work surface and knead for about 5 minutes or until smooth.

Place into a clean, lightly oiled bowl and sit in a warm place again for 1 hour or until the dough doubles in size.

Pan campestre
Campestre bread

Ingredients

500g strong (baker's) flour
120g brown rice flour
120g rye flour
120g barley flour
140g wheat flour
2 teaspoons salt
40g fresh yeast
700ml warm water

Made with half baker's flour and half wholemeal flours, such as brown rice, rye and barley, this is a good heavy, moist loaf with plenty of flavour and lasting power. Pack it into a picnic basket with a bread knife and some cheese and it would be easy to think you were a campesino, person of the land, taking a day off.

Method

Sift the flours into a large bowl and stir in the salt.

In a small bowl, dissolve the yeast with only 125ml warm water, using a fork to break up any lumps. Add a tablespoon of flour mixture and whisk with a fork. Set aside in a warm place for 10 minutes or until it has risen slightly and looks slightly foamy.

Make a well in the centre of the flours, then pour in the yeast mixture and half the remaining water. Work the mixture, gradually drawing the flour into the water until a soft dough forms, adding more water if required.

Turn onto a lightly floured surface and knead well for 10 minutes or until smooth and elastic. Divide the dough into 6 portions and roll each into a ball. Place each ball into a clean, lightly oiled bowl or onto a large oiled tray, then cover with a damp clean tea towel. Leave in a warm place for 1-1½ hours or until double in size.

Lightly grease 2 large baking trays.

To make each loaf, take one ball of dough and knock back*. Then roll out on the floured work surface to form a rectangle. Fold the dough from one end into the middle then the other end into the middle, which will result in covering the first folded end. Turn the dough so the open seam ends are facing you and roll again into a rectangle and repeat the folding process.

Next, roll out the dough again into a rectangle about 1cm thick. This time, starting from the longest edge, roll up the dough (as if rolling a Swiss or jelly roll) until it meets the other long edge into a long tapered log about 35cm long. Use a razor blade to make diagonal slashes along the length of the log.

Place onto prepared tray, then cover and leave in a warm place for about 1 hour or until almost double in size. (You can fit one or two logs on each tray at a time.) Meanwhile, preheat oven to 250°C.

Bake bread for 10-15 minutes or until golden. When you tap the base, it should sound hollow when cooked. If there are two trays going into the oven at the same time, rotate the trays between shelves once during cooking. Cool on wire racks.

Tip: When kneading, be firm with the dough to assist in developing the gluten, so the bread will rise to its fullest.

348
gourmetpilgrim Spain

* Refer to Glossary – Page 482

Pan de grano con chilis
Chilli cornbread

Ingredients

220g plain (all-purpose) flour
3 teaspoons baking powder
200g maize flour (fine polenta)
60g granulated sugar
1½ teaspoons salt
2 eggs, at room temperature
350ml buttermilk
185ml sunflower oil
1 tablespoon red chilli* paste
100g manchego* cheese, finely grated

Method

Lightly grease and line the base and sides of a shallow 20cm round cake pan.

Preheat oven to 200°C.

Combine the flour and baking powder and sift into a medium bowl. Add the maize, sugar and salt, and stir to combine.

Place the eggs, buttermilk, oil and chilli into a large bowl and whisk to combine. Pour liquid into the dry ingredients. Mix well.

Spoon half the cornbread mixture into the prepared pan, spreading it out with a spatula to the edges and smoothing the surface.

Sprinkle evenly with the cheese, not going right to the edge. Spoon in the remaining cornbread mixture and smooth out to the edges.

Bake the bread in the preheated oven for 30 minutes or until lightly golden. To test if the cornbread is cooked, insert a skewer into the middle of the bread and it should come out clean, with no wet dough sticking to the skewer.

Serve warm or cold.

Note – Jalapeno peppers could be used instead of the chilli paste. Add to your taste preference.

Tip: Ideally, don't put the cornbread into a deep cake pan as the top will not crack as well and it may not become as golden.

* Refer to Glossary – Page 482

Pan rústico
Rustic bread

Ingredients

275g strong (baker's) flour
275g rye flour
2 teaspoons salt
2 x 7g sachets active dry yeast
375ml lukewarm water
extra flour, for dusting

Method

Combine the flours and sift into a large bowl. Add salt.

In a small bowl, dissolve the yeast with only 60ml water. Set aside in a warm place for 10 minutes or until slightly frothy.

Make a well in the centre of the flours and pour in the yeast mixture and the remaining water. Work mixture with a clean hand, gradually drawing the flour into the water until a soft dough forms. Add more water as required to moisten all the flour and to form the soft dough.

Turn onto a lightly floured work surface and knead well for 10 minutes or until smooth and elastic. Place into a lightly oiled bowl or onto a large, oiled tray. Cover with a damp clean tea towel and leave in a warm place for 1-1½ hours or until doubled in size.

Punch down* then form into a round loaf shape. Place onto prepared tray and leave covered in a warm place to prove again for about 1 hour or until almost doubled in size.

Meanwhile, preheat oven to 180°C.

Lightly dust loaf with extra flour and cut three slashes into the top of the loaf with a sharp knife. Bake the bread in the preheated oven for 25-30 minutes or until well coloured, or golden. Tap the base and a hollow sound should be heard when it is cooked.

Cool on a wire rack.

* Refer to Glossary – Page 482

Comida para llevar
(Street food)

The Spanish, generally speaking, are far too civilised to eat on the street. Where's the pleasure in eating on the street? And where's the wine? Much better to find a table somewhere and settle in, or to bar-hop between bites.

Occasionally, however, Spaniards let their guard down and eat on the go, or at least on the footpath. For a quick bite there's nothing quite like a *bocadillo*, a 'little mouthful' of bread roll usually filled with jamon or chorizo and cheese. In many cities, Madrid especially, *bocadillos* are stuffed with fried calamari, peppers and mayo. It's a delicious, decadent little snack.

Business-like Catalans in Barcelona often don't have time for a leisurely lunch so instead they queue en masse for a freshly toasted *entrepá*, grilled baguette sandwiches are filled with some sort of sausage, often the spreadable *sobrasada*, and onion. Barcelonians are also fond of *bikinis* – toasted ham and cheese sandwiches.

You'll see the Spanish clutching bags of *pipas* or sunflower seeds on the go, and ice creams are popular too, especially among Andalucians sweltering through typically scorching summers. Another excellent antidote to searing heat is Valencia's *horchata*, a nutty, sweet, milk drink made from the tubers of the tigernut, served chilled in tiled emporiums called *horchaterías*, or from mobile kiosks offering icy-cold refreshment on the run.

The tapas culture

Tapas isn't strictly streetfood but in some quarters – such as Santiago de Compostela or Valencia's old city – thirsty, hungry crowds can spill out of bars and onto cobbled lanes for al fresco drinking and dining. Several bars in Santiago's Rua do Franco, known as the street of 100 taverns, offer free tapas with drinks and do a roaring trade in plates of '*crocodile*' – very thin pork steaks, dripping in oil, that are a favourite of tipsy students.

Piping hot and sugary *churros*, doughnuts, are best enjoyed outdoors with a pot of melted chocolate, just as they have been for centuries. Chocolate has been a pet delicacy of the elite since the conquistadors first returned from the New World with xocolatl in the 15th century. Drinking it warm for breakfast is quite normal in Spain; add *churros* if you're particularly peckish.

Festivals of food

The country's packed roster of regional festivals routinely involve locals gathering in the streets to feast on the local specialty, whether it be truffles in Teruel or bull's tail in Pamplona. In Galicia, the public passion is for octopus. Octopus sellers or *pulpeiras* hawk plates of grilled pulpo from street kiosks, while Lugo and O Carballiño both host festivals in honour of the eight-limbed creatures. During Lugo's weeklong Fiesta de San Froilán, townsfolk consume around 90,000 kilograms of octopus, stewed in copper cauldrons and served at street banquets.

Galician pies or *empanadas* make excellent picnic fare. They are filled with whatever takes the fancy – from cockles and mussels to mushrooms, rabbit and apples – and baked in a wheat or cornflour pastry. Not quite street food, perhaps, but the perfect meal for the great outdoors.

Los años del hambre
(The hunger years)

Modern Spain may be a gastronomic paradise, but the years of poverty and deprivation are a not-so-distant memory.

In times of conflict food can be both power and comfort. During the Civil War of 1936-1939, Spaniards had little of either. Accounts from that grim era recall how Madrileños survived on meager rations of bread and rice, putrid oil and whatever they could scrounge on the streets or the black market. "Aching hunger, rather than lack of munitions, has become Leftist Spain's gravest problem," Time magazine observed in 1938.

Unfortunately for Spaniards, the end of the war proved the start of more than a decade of intense deprivation known as *Los Años de Hambre*, 'the Hunger Years'. The bitter spoils of General Francisco Franco's victory were a country divided, destroyed and, in some cases, starving to death. It is said that even the dogs and cats disappeared from the streets during this time.

An isolated country

Franco's obstinacy in refusing offers of outside help to rebuild Spain were compounded by a United Nations embargo that further isolated and devastated the nation. Ration cards introduced as an emergency measure in 1940 remained a fact of life until 1952. By 1945 the standard of living was a third what it had been a decade earlier, agricultural output was halved and Spain's economy trailed its former colonies in Latin America. Argentina, once the slave of Spain, came to its rescue with wheat shipments; in one of its well-publicised charity dashes, First Lady Eva Perón defied the UN embargo in 1947 to deliver food supplies to a desperate mother country.

Those destitute years did not necessarily alter the methods of Spanish cooking – soups and stews are well-suited to poverty – but the quality and quantity of food suffered noticeably. Porridges and *migas* (fry-ups of breadcrumbs and other leftovers and scraps) were prevalent. The Iberian appetite for offal served Spaniards well, when they could get their hands on it.

While many rural dwellers flocked to the cities in the hope of survival, others retreated back to the land in the hope of growing enough food to eat. Therefore, as other western societies became increasingly urbanised, Spain turned to its peasant roots. By the end of the 1950s, more than 60 per cent of Spaniards were still classed as poor, eking an existence from agriculture. Spain did not recover sufficiently to join the industrialised world until the 1960s.

Previous page: Port of Ciutadella de Menorca, Balearic Islands.

Right: A field kitchen and Government troops in the main street of Buitrago, north of Madrid, during the Spanish Civil War.

The legacy of *la cocina de los campesinos* (peasant cooking)

This extended period of austerity perhaps explains the enduring popularity of hard-scrabble dishes, like *sopa de ajo* (garlic soup) and *migas* (fried breadcrumbs) in a country that is now at the vanguard of innovative global cuisine. It also explains the how the *María* (Marie) biscuit became a favourite breakfast treat for millions of Spaniards.

Invented by the English Peek Freans bakery in 1874, this sweet biscuit was sold in Spain but it did not become the country's favourite *galleta* until the 1940s, when the nation's bakeries began making them en masse to use up the (short-lived) wheat surplus immediately after the end of the Civil War.

El queso
Cheese

Spanish cheese
tells a tasty story
of the diverse
landscapes
of the Iberian
peninsula.

El queso (Cheese)

The diverse Iberian landscape produces an equally diverse abundance of dairy produce

Spain is a land of extremes. While the rain clouds gather on the damp green coast of Galicia, the sun bakes the desert-like lands of Almeria in the south.

Most of the nation is not covered in lush pastures – the Castilians describe the central plateaus as *'nueve meses de invierno y tres meses de infierno'* – nine months of winter and three months of hell.

Despite the extremes – perhaps even because of them – Spain produces some wonderful cheeses. Cow's milk cheeses are produced in the lush north-west coast, while sheep and goat's milk cheeses dominate elsewhere.

The cheeses of Spain reflect the land on which the animals that produce the milk were grazed. Spanish cheeses popular outside of Spain include:

Manchego – the cheese from La Mancha

La Mancha is a hot, dry region. The sheep specific to this place are the hardy *manchega* breed, who make short work of grain stubble, native shrubs and anything else that comes under their noses.

The cheese made from their milk is easily identified by the basket-like impression made by the mould. This harks back to the days when cheese was made in moulds made from woven reeds. After rennet is added, the milk is warmed and the curds are cut into very fine pieces. They're poured into the moulds and pressed several times to remove the liquid whey. The cheeses are then immersed in a brine that helps to form the skin and are then aged for anything from 60 days to several years, depending on the size of the individual cheese.

Manchego is creamy yellow in colour, with cracks forming along the curds and often small crystals that form during the aging process. It's a sweet cheese; sharp and tangy with a hint of earth and even flavours of the 'dairy' in which it was made or 'cave' in which it was aged. In Spain, it's often used in cooking, or served as a *tapa* or in a *bocadillo* with quince paste.

Mahón

Made on the island of Menorca from cow's milk, the young cheeses are rubbed with *pimentón* to give a dark stain to the rind.

Its irregular shape comes from being made in cloth and being pressed into shape on a table. The cheese is then soaked in brine and matured.

Cheese etiquette

The Spanish don't share the French culture of the cheeseboard as an interlude in a meal. Instead, they love their cheese in *bocadillos*, as a *tapa* and in cooking. In restaurants, where there is more of a French dining influence, you may find cheeses offered at the end of meal as a final course.

Valdeón

The Picos de Europa are a magnificent range of limestone mountains dotted with tiny villages and, being a National Park, is home to more wildlife than humans. Up in these hills are a series of limestone caves that are essential in the maturing of one of Spain's best cheeses, *Valdeón*.

Made with a blend of cow, sheep and goat milk, it's a creamy blue cheese that's inoculated with *penicillium roqueforti*, the same mould that gives Roquefort cheese its blue mould.

Once wrapped in sycamore leaves, the 2.5 kilogram rounds of cheese are taken up to the moist caves to mature for several months where the veins of blue colonise the cheese. Salty and tangy, it's a beautiful cheese that goes well with dried fruit and powerfully tannic red wines or even sweet fortified wines.

Above: Making cheese on the farm, Cuitadella de Menorca, Balearic Islands.

Right: Artisan goat & sheep milk cheese's, for sale at roadside, Morella, Valencia.

Murcia al Vino

This fine goat's cheese from the Murcia, has the blush of red wine on the rind and a creamy pale interior.

The Murcian goats produce large volumes of milk that are made into this semi-hard cheese with a rind hardened by brine, wine and marc, which is the grape pressings that are left after wine making.

Perhaps because of the use of wine in its production, it's a full flavoured, slightly fruity cheese that lends itself to being enjoyed with medium-bodied red wines.

Torta del Casar

Out west of Spain, where the low undulating croplands give way to rocky ground, is a little town called Casar de Cáceres. One of Spain's most idiosyncratic cheeses is made here – Torta del Casar.

It's made from raw sheep's milk that's heated to just above blood temperature, then a tea is added to it, which is made from the flowers of the local thistle or *cardo*. Enzymes in the flowers break down the milk just as rennet does. The curds are hooped and pressed and the cheese is placed in a brine bath. Soon afterwards, it's dressed in a thick band of lace, which holds the flaccid cheese in shape while letting it breathe. It's then matured, being turned twice a day for several months. The result is a small, creamy cheese with a yellow rind.

It's decapitated when served and the creamy interior is stirred to make a stringy pâté.

With a rich, creamy texture, it has the delicate aroma of sheep's milk and an intriguing flavour that is at once sweet and bitter.

Tetilla

Like almost all Galician cheeses, the *tetilla* is made from the milk of Galicia's *rubia* breed of cattle.

The curds are formed in a conical mould then immersed in brine. Matured for just a few weeks, it's soft, tart and stringy. It's often served with quince paste as either a *tapa* or dessert.

San Simón

Another Galician cheese made in a similar manner to the *tetilla* but smoked over birchwood. Excellent with Oloroso sherry.

Availability

Due to import restrictions, some Spanish cheeses may not be available in some countries.

Castilla-La Mancha

The vast and sparse tablelands of Castilla-La Mancha have produced two unforgettable icons of Spain – *Don Quixote de la Mancha* and *manchego* cheese. This region, geographically the heart of the nation, has played a seminal role in Spanish history. Castilla means castle and the name references the treasury of fortresses and *alcázares*, held alternately by Christians and Moors through the ages, which still decorates the central plains of the Iberian Peninsula.

Castilla-La Mancha is home to the former Spanish capital of Toledo, a city ruled by Romans, Visigoths, Moors and Christians and the anchor of Catholic Spain since the 6th century. This fortified settlement beside the River Tagus became "The Imperial Toledo" in the 12th century under the Emperor of all the Spains, Alfonso VII.

Today, this monumental city and the relatively new region of Castilla-La Mancha play a less pivotal role in Spanish history. But tradition lives on in this region of giant windmills immortalised in Miguel de Cervantes classic book and of honest, authentic cuisine that has sustained the hardy plains dwellers for centuries.

Cream of the crop

Eclipsed these days by the more glamorous regions of Madrid, Catalonia and Basque Country, Castilla-La Mancha is Spain's quiet achiever when it comes to agriculture and livestock, the industries that drive the local economy. Sheep have been raised on this arid but fertile plateau for 4000 years; olives, wheat and wine since Roman times. It is also home to Spain's biggest onion crop, some of the country's largest cheese factories (to meet the insatiable demand for *manchego*) and more land under vine than anywhere in Europe. Meanwhile, the small village of Princesa de Minaya in La Mancha is said to produce the finest saffron in the world.

Among its grocery list of Denomination of Origin-protected (DO) products, the region can lay claim to wines, cheese, watermelon, lamb and saffron from La Mancha, honey from La Alcarria and purple garlic from Cuenca province.

Gastronomy in Castilla-La Mancha traces its roots to simple shepherds' meals eaten on the meseta. Dining habits have not changed much since Don Quixote was around – bread, meat, cheese, vegetables and wine still sustain the plains people.

Highlights of the local cuisine include *pisto manchego*, a ratatouille-like dish based around tomatoes, zucchinis (courgettes), onions and green peppers and usually served with boiled eggs or fried potatoes. *El salpicón* is a one-pot wonder of minced veal with onion, tomato, garlic, parsley and pepper.

Below: 'Imperial Toledo' – inhabited since the Bronze age, an important centre of the Roman and Moorish empires, and a former capital of the Spanish empire

Right: The ancient windmills of Alcazar de San Juan, La Mancha, at sunset. Introduced to the Iberian peninsula by the Moors sometime around the 12th century, the windmills of the La Mancha region were made famous in the medieval novel *Don Quixote de la Mancha*.

The home of famous manchego cheese is a high-achieving gastronomic all-rounder, also boasting quality wine, lamb, saffron and honey.

Below: Harvest of the saffron crocus, Consuegra, Castilla-La Mancha.

Right: Plaza Mayor and the gothic Basilica de Nuestra Senora de Gracia, completed in 1257, Cuenca, Castilla-La Mancha.

The soup kitchen

Gazpachos de pastor is not a cold soup but a bubbling pot of mixed meats – maybe game, rabbit, lamb – stewed with aromatic vegetables like onion, tomato and garlic, thickened with chunks of stale bread and seasoned with sweet paprika, rosemary and thyme. Another bread-based dish is *migas de pastor*, breadcrumbs fried in animal fat with bacon and garlic. There's also a sweet version of breadcrumbs soaked in milk and melted chocolate.

Garlic soup, *sopa de ajo*, served with bread, and maybe some cumin or paprika, helps fortify Castilians for the bitterly cold winters of the steppes. Lamb and goat are eaten young and roasted over wood fires.

The beautiful city of Cuenca, whose medieval houses seem to teeter on a cliff edge, is known for a dish called *morteruelo* – a pâté made from pork livers, partridge, hen, hare, ham and spice. Cuencans also enjoy *zarajos*, lamb's intestines wound around two sticks and then fried or oven-baked. Another staple of inland Spain, salted cod, is prepared in various ways including *atascaburras* ('donkey-clogger'), a basic mountain dish of potatoes, cod and garlic.

Manchego cheese – a national icon

Under Spain's Denomination of Origin laws, *manchego* cheese is made only from the milk of Manchego ewes. It can be eaten young (*tierno*) when it is soft and creamy, partially cured after three months, or fully mature after six months when the texture has firmed and the cheese has developed its characteristic tang.

Castilla-La Mancha's extensive vineyards have a reputation for producing cheap bulk wine but in recent years the region has distinguished itself with increasingly elegant reds and more rounded whites. DO La Mancha is regarded as the world's largest single wine region, with production sprawled across four provinces. The most respected regional wines come from La Mancha and Valdepeñas, known for its red-white blend *clarete*, but Almansa, Méntrida and Mondéjar also produce DO quality drops.

Castilians are typically Spanish in their fondness for sweets. The Moors introduced marzipan but these days it is the nuns, especially in Toledo, who ply a brisk trade in almond confectionary sold from the doors of convents. The sisters wisely steer clear of *bizcochos borrachos* or 'drunken biscuits', a dessert of sponge cake spiked with brandy, cinnamon and lemon.

Asturias

The Principality of Asturias is wedged in northwest Spain between the dramatic coastline of the Cantabrian Sea and the natural barricade of the Asturian Ranges and the Picos de Europa massif in the south. Its villages and cities house a treasury of pre-Romanesque architecture, ancient hilltop forts and Paleolithic rock art.

Its people have always had a reputation for being fiercely independent – as the Romans and Moors both discovered when they tried to conquer this stubborn, rugged land.

El país de los quesos – the land of cheeses.

The mountain pastures of the south sustain sheep, cattle and goats from which farmers obtain meat and such a bounty of dairy products that the region is renowned as *el país de los quesos*, the land of cheeses.

Of the 20 handmade Asturian cheeses only four have protected, Denomination of Origin (DO) status. *Gamonedo* is a semi-smoked, hard cheese made from milk strained through a traditional sieve of firmly braided horse and cow hair, and then salted and air-dried in high mountain huts. *Cabrales*, named after the town in southeast Asturias where it is made, is a blue-vein cheese made from cow, goat or sheep's milk and left to mature in mountain caves that have been owned by the same families for generations. Just 37 dairies produce the greenish-blue *Cabrales*, which is the region's most famous cheese.

Elaborate cheese-making rituals aside, Asturian cuisine is unsophisticated but rooted in the freshest produce from earth and sea. Its most typical dish is *fabada*, a stew of soft white *fabes* or beans cooked with ham fat, black pudding and other pork products. Another common bean stew is *fabes con almejas*, made with fresh clams and best served with crusty bread.

Below: *el escanciado* – the traditional method of pouring *sidra* in a *sidreria* (ciderhouse), seen here in a ciderhouse in Oveido, capital of Asturias.

Right: Villar de Vildas, Somiedo, Asturias. The Asturians are of Celtic origin, and have many traits in common with other Celtic peoples, not least the traditional highland folk music of the Asturian *gaita* or bagpipes.

Seafood, stews & *sidra*

Seafood from the Bay of Biscay is essential to the diet. Two favourite local ingredients come together in *merluza a la sidra*, hake with cider sauce. *Caldereta* is a pot-luck casserole of the day's fresh-caught seafood (shrimps, crayfish and giant scorpion fish are standard) while *oricios*, sea urchins, are a coveted delicacy. Wild salmon and trout throng mountain rivers, like the Sella, and are usually prepared with a *cava*-based sauce.

The common base for non-seafood stews is *compango*, a hearty mix of chorizo, Asturian *morcilla* or black pudding, pork shoulder and bacon that is designed to insulate against the cold, wet winters. *Bollo preñao* (literally, pregnant bread roll) is the fast food of choice – a golden cornbread roll stuffed and baked with spicy, cider-cured chorizo, and available at any bakery.

Cider or *sidra* is the preferred tipple in Asturias, where the apple juice is traditionally fermented in chestnut barrels and then drunk liberally at fiestas and in *sideria* or cider houses. Pouring it is an art form; the bottle is hoisted high above the barman's head with the right hand while the left hand holds the glass at waist level and tilted slightly. The cider should flow slowly and ceremoniously into the glass, barely touching its edge and, naturally, not a drop should be spilled.

From sea to mountain – nature sets the menu in rugged Asturias, including a remarkable lode of dairy produce.

gourmet
pilgrim

Postres
Dessert

Dessert in Spain
is a simple affair
which celebrates the
rich history of the
national cuisine.

Postres (Dessert)

Simple and sweet is the theme of the Spanish dessert

Desserts are not complicated affairs by any stretch of the imagination – often a simple plate of fresh and delicious fruit will be offered at the end of the meal. A few slices of melon, some ripe figs, some bananas from the Canary Islands, perhaps some tiny strawberries – so fragile that they never left their hometown of Aranjuez until a rail line was constructed to Madrid.

Many homes will have a collection of preserved *melocotón*, peaches, or *albaricoques*, apricots, bottled by the matriarch in early summer or purchased from a market.

A tangy taste

But if dessert is served, one of the most distinctive flavours is the combination of cinnamon and citrus peel that's infused into milk or cream. Whole sticks of cinnamon and wide strips of lemon, and perhaps orange, are gently warmed to extract the essential oils from the rind.

The finer the peeled rind, the greater the chance the oils have to escape from it. These infused creams or milks are sweetened and form the basis of custards and flans.

The Spanish love their *cremas*, or baked custards, and *leche frita*, or fried milk custards – the ultimate in sweet comfort foods.

Spanish cooks and chefs take pride in preparing these dishes with perfect smoothness and silkiness, taking great care when cooking eggs to increase the heat gradually to avoid splitting and lumpiness. They also take great care in choosing their eggs. One classic dessert *tocino de cielo*, or 'bacon from heaven', is perhaps the world's sweetest custard, but relies on excellent quality of eggs to achieve the rich yellow colour.

As sweet as honey

Honey is the other key ingredient in Spanish desserts. Bees are kept in the orchards and gardens of Spain to pollinate the flowers. As a result, there's a diverse range of honeys produced across the nation, with flavours ranging from thick and floral to fine and subtle. They're used extensively in desserts, from flavouring a pastry or glazing a sweet crust, to pouring on fresh *cuajada* junket.

While the Spanish may not consume desserts in volume, they make up for it in the intensity of sweetness. The sweet-toothed legacy of the Moors' is celebrated on a daily basis in Spanish desserts.

Something a little richer

Dried fruit and nuts are also an acceptable dessert. Perhaps some sweet, fortified wine may be poured over the fruit and nuts to enrich the dish a little.

Ground almonds add body and richness to the fillings of tarts and puddings, such as the delicious *Tarta de Santiago*.

Pine nuts are popular on the Mediterranean coasts and in the south where the pine trees grow in the hills behind the coast. They're planted as wind breaks, and for the sweet little seeds that are harvested from the pine cones. Pine nuts are generally toasted to intensify their flavour and give the creamy pale exterior a golden hue.

Peras al vino
Pears cooked in red wine

Ingredients

4 medium pears (firm but ripe)
60ml lemon juice
250ml dry red wine
2 cinnamon sticks
220g white (granulated) sugar
8 lemon slices
250ml water

Out the back of almost every Spanish country home is a small orchard. Gnarled olive trees grow on the top of the slope where the soil is poor while the cherries grow at the bottom where the soil is rich and the wind less harsh. The apple and pear trees are in between, some are ancient with their limbs covered in lichen. Cooked in lightly spiced wine syrup, these pears are a perfect dish for a cool autumn night.

Method

Peel pears and rub with lemon juice.

Place the wine, cinnamon sticks, sugar, lemon slices and water into a medium saucepan that will be just large enough to fit the pears. Cook mixture over low-medium heat, stirring, until sugar dissolves. Bring to the boil, then reduce the heat and simmer, uncovered, for 15 minutes.

Add pears and simmer, partially covered, for 20-30 minutes or until tender, carefully turning occasionally to ensure even colouring. Remove from heat and cool pears in syrup. (Leave to soak in the syrup overnight, if possible.)

Remove pears from the liquid and set aside. Simmer the syrup over high heat, uncovered, for about 15 minutes or until it thickens slightly.

Serve the pears whole, drizzled with the syrup.

Flan de naranja
Orange custard flan

serves 4

Ingredients

Spray oil, to grease

60ml water

275g caster (superfine) sugar

1 strip orange rind

200ml orange juice, strained

1 cinnamon stick

7 free-range* egg yolks, at room temperature

1 free-range* egg, at room temperature

This is a variation of the classic Spanish flan with the sauce enriched with orange juice and a little orange peel. Citrus peel is used extensively in Spanish cooking, where thinly peeled wide strips are taken from the fruit. This not only increases the ability to extract the essential oils but also makes it easier to remove the peel when finished.

Method

Preheat oven to 170°C.

Lightly grease 4 x 125ml ramekins or moulds with oil spray (use fingers to rub and spread the oil around) and place them in a baking dish.

Place water and only 75g of the sugar into a small saucepan and cook gently, stirring, over a low heat without boiling until the sugar dissolves. Increase the heat to a gentle boil and cook, uncovered, for about 20-30 minutes or until the mixture is golden and smells like caramel. Quickly pour and divide the toffee between the ramekins and tilt to cover the bases. Set aside.

Place orange rind and juice, cinnamon stick and remaining sugar into a medium saucepan and cook, stirring, over a low heat without boiling until the sugar dissolves. Increase the heat, bring to the boil and cook for 2 minutes or until the mixture is slightly syrupy. Leave to cool for 10 minutes.

Place egg yolks and whole egg into a medium bowl and beat with a wooden spoon. Pour the partly cooled orange syrup onto the eggs, stirring constantly until well combined. Pass the mixture through a sieve into a large jug, then pour into the moulds and place them into a small baking dish.

Pour enough boiling water into the baking dish until it comes halfway up the side of the ramekins. Bake in preheated oven for 20-25 minutes, then carefully remove the ramekins from the water and cool to room temperature. Chill completely in the refrigerator (about 3 hours).

To serve, dip moulds in hot water for 10 seconds, then invert on to serving plates.

* Refer to Glossary – Page 482

Leche frita
Fried milk

Ingredients

500ml milk

1 cinnamon stick

1 strip lemon rind, about 6 cm long

1 vanilla bean*, split lengthways

140g unsalted butter

300g plain (all-purpose) flour

150g caster (superfine) sugar

4 free-range* eggs, at room temperature, separated

85g fresh breadcrumbs*

Vegetable oil for shallow frying

1 teaspoon ground cinnamon, to serve

55g caster (superfine) sugar, extra, to serve

This is the comfort food of millions of Spaniards. It's so simple yet so delicious. Milk is infused with lemon, cinnamon and vanilla. It is sweetened and then thickened into custard. Once set it's cut into bite-sized pieces and rolled in breadcrumbs, fried and dusted with cinnamon sugar. Good on its own or even better with a scoop of cinnamon ice cream.

Method

Lightly grease a 27cm x 17cm rectangular cake pan and line base and long sides with kitchen baking paper.

Place milk, cinnamon stick, rind and vanilla bean into a medium saucepan and bring to a gentle boil. Remove from heat. Strain into a medium heatproof jug, discarding cinnamon stick, rind and bean.

Melt butter in a large heavy-based saucepan over medium heat and stir in only 225g of flour. The mixture will form a loose clump around your spoon. Reduce heat to low and stir for 30 seconds, then stir in sugar and gradually pour the warm milk into the saucepan, stirring constantly. Continue to stir for about 10 minutes or until a smooth mass forms and leaves the side of the pan.

Remove from heat and stir in egg yolks one at a time, beating well after each addition. Spread the custard mixture in the prepared cake pan, smoothing the surface. Refrigerate for 1 hour or until firm and set.

Place egg whites into a small bowl and lightly whisk until frothy. Lift the set custard from the pan, place onto work surface and carefully cut into pieces (such as triangles). Dip pieces into the remaining flour to lightly coat all sides, shaking to remove excess flour. Dip into eggwhites, then the breadcrumbs. Press the crumbs onto the set custard. Set aside.

Heat oil in a large heavy-based frying pan. Cook custard pieces in batches for about 1 minute each side or until lightly golden. Drain on crumpled kitchen paper towel. Combine cinnamon and sugar and sprinkle over pieces. Serve immediately.

Tip: Perfect served with stewed fruit, such as rhubarb.

Tarta de Santiago
St James tart

Ingredients

Dough:

100g unsalted butter, at room temperature

70g caster (superfine) sugar

1 free-range* egg, at room temperature, lightly beaten

200g plain (all-purpose) flour, sifted

Filling:

4 free-range* eggs, at room temperature

200g caster (superfine) sugar

1 tablespoon finely grated lemon rind

1 tablespoon finely grated orange rind

40ml orange juice

1 tablespoon lemon juice

300g almond meal

½ teaspoon ground cinnamon

Icing (confectioner's) sugar, to decorate

Pilgrims have been making their way to Santiago de Compostela since the Middle Ages. From around Europe they walked, making their way through France and eventually finding the green wet shores of Galicia. The way was marked with scallop shells and the pilgrims carried a scallop shell on themselves. There in Santiago they found the supposed resting place of St James the Disciple, his bones re-interred after being 'discovered' during the crusades.

The cathedral built above the crypt is a magnificent edifice and is still the destination of thousands of pilgrims every year. They make their way by foot and, now, mountain bike. Pilgrims often take back home a delicious tart with an almond filling dusted with the cross of the Order of Santiago as a souvenir.

Method

Preheat oven to 200°C. Lightly grease, flour and line a 26cm round springform cake pan with kitchen baking paper.

To make the dough, place butter and sugar into a large bowl and beat with electric beaters for 5 minutes or until pale yellow in colour. Add egg and beat for a further 30 seconds. Fold in flour and shape mixture into a dough.

Transfer the dough to a lightly floured work surface and roll out to a circle larger than the cake pan (about 30-32cm). Use a rolling pin to lift and transfer the dough to the pan. Position the dough to cover the base and part way (about 3cm) up the sides of the pan. Trim the dough once inside the pan to even up the top edge.

Line the pan with crumpled kitchen baking paper weighted down with baking beads and bake blind* in preheated oven for 10 minutes. Remove the paper and beads and bake for a further 5-10 minutes or until lightly golden. Place cake pan onto a wire rack and allow to cool in the pan.

Reduce oven temperature to 180°C.

To make the filling, place eggs and sugar into a large bowl and beat with electric beaters until combined and pale yellow in colour. Fold in the lemon and orange rind, juices, almond meal and cinnamon. Stir well to combine.

Spoon filling into the prepared crust and return to the oven. Bake in preheated oven for 30 -35 minutes or until golden and cooked through. Allow to cool completely in the cake pan. Release the pan's springform and transfer the cake to a serving plate.

To decorate this cake in the traditional way, place a stencil of the Cross of the Order of Santiago on top of the cake, sprinkle icing sugar over it and remove stencil. Serve.

Note – A stencil for the Cross of the Order of Santiago can be found on page 490.

* Refer to Glossary – Page 482

Flan de almendra
Almond pudding with honey

serves 4

Ingredients

600ml milk
120g almond meal
140g caster (superfine) sugar
1 teaspoon vanilla extract*
4 free-range* eggs, at room temperature
2 free-range* egg yolks, at room temperature
Spray oil to grease
120g honey, warmed, to serve
2 oranges, cut into segments, to serve

Method

Preheat oven to 160°C.

Place milk, almond meal, sugar and vanilla into a medium saucepan. Bring to just below the boil over medium heat, stirring occasionally. Remove from heat and set aside.

Place eggs and yolks into a medium bowl and mix until just combined (do not over beat or aerate as this will cause unattractive bubbles in the finished custard).

Slowly whisk the hot milk mixture into the egg mixture, whisking constantly. Lightly grease a 1 litre heatproof mould (or six x 160ml individual moulds). Pour the mixture into the mould then place the mould into a large baking dish. Carefully transfer it to the oven. Pour enough boiling water into the baking dish until it comes halfway up the sides of the mould.

Bake in preheated oven for 20-25 minutes or until the pudding is set in the centre.

Allow to cool for 15-20 minutes before turning out onto a serving plate.

Serve drizzled with warm honey and topped with orange segments.

Tip: Puddings can also be cooled completely and then turned out. It may be necessary to just slightly loosen the edges before up-turning the mould.

* Refer to Glossary – Page 482

Tarta de manzana
Apple tart

In the middle of autumn in the south of Spain, when the apples are ripe but still have a little sharpness, they are peeled and sliced, then laid out on sheets of puff pastry. They're then baked with nuts and sweetened with sugar or honey – simple yet beautifully honest.

Ingredients

1 sheet puff pastry*
40g butter, melted
35g crushed hazelnuts
2 medium apples, peeled, cored and sliced
2 tablespoons raw sugar
1 teaspoon ground cinnamon

Method

Preheat oven to 220°C. Line a baking tray with kitchen baking paper.

Cut the pastry into quarters to make 4 squares. Place onto the prepared tray. Using a sharp knife, score a thin border about 5mm in from the edge of the pastry (not cutting all the way through). This will assist the edge of the pastry to puff up a little during the cooking.

Lightly brush pastry with butter and sprinkle the middle of the square with crushed hazelnuts. Layer apple onto the pastry and sprinkle with sugar and cinnamon.

Bake in preheated oven for 15 minutes or until golden.

Serve immediately with ice cream or cream.

* Refer to Glossary – Page 482

Tarta de higos
Fig cake

serves 8-10

Figs are perhaps one of the most painted fruits found in the Baroque still-lifes in Madrid's Prado Museum. Fat, ripe and fertile, their sweet flesh bursts open revealing those delicious little seeds. All that beauty and flavour is captured in this upside-down cake.

Ingredients

5 fresh figs (not too soft)
90g golden syrup
200g butter, at room temperature
200g caster (superfine) sugar
1 teaspoon vanilla extract*
3 eggs, at room temperature
200g self-raising flour, sifted
125ml milk

Method

Preheat oven to 180°C. Lightly grease and line the base and side of a round, 20cm-deep cake pan with kitchen baking paper.

Wipe figs with damp kitchen paper towel and cut in half. Lay halves cut side down around the outer edge of the cake pan and place 2 halves (depending on size) in the middle. Warm golden syrup slightly in a microwave, then drizzle evenly over the figs. Set aside.

Place butter, sugar and vanilla into a large bowl and beat with electric beaters for at least 10 minutes, occasionally scraping down the sides, or until light and creamy. Add the eggs one at a time, beating well after each addition.

Add flour and milk alternately to the butter mixture, in two batches, folding in with a large metal spoon and beginning and ending with flour.

Spoon mixture into the prepared cake pan. Bake in preheated oven for about 60 minutes or until a skewer comes out clean when inserted into the centre. If the cake begins to brown too much, shield it with some foil until the cake is cooked.

Allow the cake to stand in the pan for 5 minutes before turning out onto a serving plate. Serve the cake fig side up.

* Refer to Glossary – Page 482

Brazo de gitano
'Gypsy's Arm' rolled sponge cake

serves 6-8

Ingredients

35g plain (all-purpose) flour

25g cocoa powder

40g icing (confectioner's) sugar

5 eggs, at room temperature, separated

55g caster (superfine) sugar

1 teaspoon vanilla extract*

250ml thickened cream*

1¼ teaspoons rum extract

1 tablespoon caster (superfine) sugar, extra

1 tablespoon icing (confectioner's) sugar, extra

Gypsies live across Spain and feature heavily in Spanish arts and culture. While the traditional name of 'Gypsy's arm' may not be politically correct, it doesn't belie the fact that this is a very delicious thin chocolate sponge rolled around a filling of sweet rum-flavoured whipped cream.

Method

Preheat oven to 180°C.

Lightly grease a 32cm x 25cm Swiss roll baking pan. Line the base and sides with kitchen baking paper.

Sift flour and cocoa, set aside. Sift icing sugar into a separate bowl. Place egg whites into a large bowl and beat with electric beaters until soft peaks form. Beat in the sifted icing sugar in two batches. Set aside.

In another larger bowl, beat egg yolks with electric beaters, then add caster sugar and vanilla and beat until thick and pale yellow in colour. Fold the flour mixture into the egg yolks in two batches, folding and turning with a large metal spoon. Next, fold in about a third of the beaten egg whites and fold with the spoon to gently loosen the mixture. Lastly, fold in the remaining egg white in two batches.

Pour batter into the prepared pan and spread evenly. Bake in preheated oven for 15 minutes. Turn sponge out onto a clean tea towel, peel away the baking paper then carefully roll up the hot sponge along the long edge into a tight roll. Allow to sit in the tea towel until completely cold.

Place the cream into a medium bowl and beat with electric beaters until thick, then add rum extract and caster sugar to taste.

Unroll the cake and evenly spread with the cream before rolling up the cake again like a jellyroll.

Dust with extra icing sugar and slice to serve.

Tip: Real rum can be used instead of the rum extract.

* Refer to Glossary – Page 482

Arroz con leche
Rice pudding

Ingredients

1 litre milk

150g short grain 'paella' rice* (such as
Arborio or Calasparra)

200g caster (superfine) sugar

1 cinnamon stick

1 lemon, rind only, finely grated

Pinch of salt

20g butter

Ground cinnamon, to serve

Arroz con leche or rice cooked in milk is one of the great foundation dishes of every Spanish home cook. Rice is cooked in sweetened milk that's infused with spice and citrus to make a dessert to warm the flesh and the soul. For a touch of decadence, let a few pieces of dark chocolate melt into it while it's still hot.

Method

Place milk, rice, sugar, cinnamon, rind and salt into a medium heavy-based saucepan and mix well.

Slowly bring mixture to the boil over low heat, stirring occasionally with a wooden spoon. As the pudding thickens, stir more frequently to avoid the rice sticking to the bottom of the pan. Cook for 25-35 minutes or until thick and the rice is tender. Add butter and stir through. Remove cinnamon stick and discard.

Serve pudding warm or cold in individual cups or dishes sprinkled lightly with ground cinnamon.

* Refer to Glossary – Page 482

Helado de canela
Cinnamon ice cream

serves 4-6

Ingredients

1 litre milk

1 cinnamon stick

2 strips lemon rind, about 6cm long

6 free-range* egg yolks, at room temperature

350g white (granulated) sugar

1 teaspoon vanilla extract*

Fresh mint leaves, to serve

Helado is Spanish for ice cream. Come summer, the Spanish go ice cream mad, a short sweet respite from the hot sun. Good restaurants will have an ice cream churn and the progressive ones love to experiment with novel flavours. Cinnamon is a classic flavour and cinnamon ice cream goes well with every sweet dish.

Method

Place only half the milk, cinnamon stick and rind into a medium saucepan. Heat milk over low-medium heat until it comes to a very gentle simmer. Remove from heat and set aside.

Place egg yolks into a medium bowl and lightly beat. Add sugar and remaining milk and mix well. Add the egg mixture to the saucepan.

Return saucepan to low-medium heat and allow the mixture to come to a gentle simmer, stirring continuously. Don't let the mixture boil.

Use a slotted spoon to remove and discard the cinnamon stick and rind. Stir in the vanilla.

Transfer mixture to a metal loaf pan or square cake pan and freeze until set.

Serve in individual dessert glasses decorated with mint.

Note – Ideally don't store the ice cream for more than a couple of days as ice crystals may form.

* Refer to Glossary – Page 482

Tocino de cielo
'Heaven's bacon' (toffee custard)

serves 10-12

Despite the name, there's no pork product in this super-sweet egg custard, but it's still extremely rich. Small slivers served with fresh fruit make a refreshing desert, while a piece with cake and coffee is a decadent way of enjoying the afternoon.

Ingredients

2 tablespoons water

320g caster (superfine) sugar

250ml water, extra

1 teaspoon vanilla extract*

7 free-range* egg yolks, at room temperature

3 free-range* eggs, at room temperature

Method

Preheat oven to 180°C.

Place first measure of water and only 120g of sugar into a small heavy-based saucepan over a low-medium heat. Stir with a metal spoon, without boiling, until sugar dissolves. Allow mixture to come to the boil and cook for about 10 minutes or until golden in colour.

Remove from heat and pour straightaway into an ungreased 20cm square cake pan, tilting the pan to cover the base with toffee.

Place the extra water, remaining sugar and vanilla into a large saucepan and cook, stirring, over a medium heat, without boiling, until sugar dissolves. Bring to the boil, reduce heat and simmer, uncovered, for a further 10-15 minutes or until mixture forms a syrup consistency. Remove from heat and allow to cool for about 15 minutes.

Place egg yolks and eggs into a medium bowl and beat with electric beaters until smooth. Slowly add the syrup in a stream, beating continuously. When all the syrup has been added, strain the mixture through a fine sieve over the toffee in the pan.

Bake the Heaven's bacon in a water bath* in preheated oven for 20-25 minutes or until just set when the tip of a knife comes out clean when inserted in the centre of the custard.

To serve, fill a baking dish with boiling water, then dip the cake pan in the hot water and hold for 30 seconds to loosen the caramel. Use a small knife to run around the edges of the pan. Turn out the Heaven's bacon onto a serving plate, so the caramel toffee is on the top.

* Refer to Glossary – Page 482

Natillas
Natillas custard

This is a simple Spanish egg custard made with cornflour, giving it a super-smooth, silky texture. It can be served by itself or with fruit, hot or cold. Dusted with cinnamon and redolent with citrus, it's a delicate and delicious Spanish classic.

Ingredients

750ml milk

125g caster (superfine) sugar

1 teaspoon finely grated lemon rind

2½ tablespoons cornflour

5 free-range* egg yolks, at room temperature, lightly beaten

Ground cinnamon, to serve (optional)

Fresh fruit, to serve (optional)

Method

Place milk, sugar and rind into a medium saucepan and heat gently over a low-medium heat until it comes to a gentle simmer. Remove from heat.

Place cornflour into a bowl and whisk in half the hot milk mixture. Stir in the egg yolks then return this mixture to the saucepan with the remaining milk.

Stir custard continuously over a low heat until the mixture just comes to a gentle boil and coats the back of a wooden spoon. Remove from heat.

Pour into individual glasses or dishes. Serve warm or cold, sprinkled with cinnamon or with some fresh seasonal fruit.

* Refer to Glossary – Page 482

Filloas Gallegas
Galician pancakes

serves 4

Ingredients

Filling:

200g soft cream cheese or mascarpone*

55g caster (superfine) sugar

1 teaspoon finely grated lemon rind

1 tablespoon lemon juice

Batter:

150g plain (all-purpose) flour

440ml milk

2 eggs, at room temperature

10g butter, melted

Spray oil to grease

55g raw sugar, to serve

200g strawberries, hulled and sliced, to serve

With its ample rainfall and green grass, Galicia is one is one of the few places in Spain with a culture of dairy foods. Galicians use creamy fillings inside their filloas, which are light, thin and lacy pancakes often served on festival days. Sometimes they flavour the cream with a little lemon rind or orujo, a grappa-like spirit.

Method

To make the filling, place cream cheese, sugar, lemon rind and juice into a medium bowl. Mix well to combine and set aside.

To make the batter, sift flour into a medium bowl and make a well in the centre. Place milk and eggs into a measuring jug and mix with a fork until just combined. Pour about 125ml of the milk mixture into the flour, then use a wooden spoon to gradually incorporate some of the flour. Continue to gradually add more of the milk mixture until all the flour and milk is incorporated and a thin batter forms. Lastly, add the melted butter and lightly whisk until smooth. Cover batter with plastic wrap and set aside at room temperature for 30 minutes. If mixture is a little too thick after standing, add a little extra milk.

Preheat oven to 150°C. Line a baking tray with kitchen baking paper.

Pour batter into a jug. Heat a 20cm non-stick frying pan over medium-low heat for 1 minute. Spray the pan away from the heat to lightly grease. Holding the pan in one hand, pour approximately 2 tablespoons of the batter into the centre of pan while quickly tilting pan in a circular motion to swirl batter and evenly cover the base. Cook for 1 minute or until the edges of the pancake curl slightly.

Using a metal spatula, gently lift the edge of the pancake to ensure it is light golden and lacy underneath. Use the spatula to loosen the crepe from the pan and turn it over. Cook for a further 1 minute or until light golden underneath. Slide onto prepared baking tray and cover loosely with foil. Place in preheated oven to keep warm. Repeat with remaining mix.

To serve, spread cream filling over the pancakes, roll up, then sprinkle with sugar and serve with strawberries.

Dulce de membrillo
Quince paste

Ingredients

1kg fresh quinces
1 lemon
125ml water
700g white (granulated) sugar

When one makes a batch of quince paste it comes as no surprise to find that quince is a member of the rose family. The delicate aroma of sweet roses fills the kitchen as the flesh of the quince slowly cooks down. The sweetness of thin slices of quince paste on a cheese platter matches the saltiness of cheese, such as manchego or the classic blue Valdeón, whilst enhancing the aroma.

Method

Peel and deseed the quinces, then chop. Using a small sharp knife or potato peeler, remove rind from the lemon in long pieces, avoiding the white pith. Juice the lemon.

Place quinces, lemon rind and juice and water into a large saucepan and bring to the boil. Cook, slightly covered, over medium heat for about 30 minutes or until the quinces are soft. Remove rind and discard. Use a stick blender to process the quinces in the saucepan until almost smooth.

Add sugar and stir well to combine. Cover and cook over a very low heat for 3-3½ hours, stirring occasionally, until quinces become a smooth ruby-coloured paste.

Transfer warm mixture to a flat slab pan or dish. Cover and chill.

Serve as part of a cheese platter or with toasted bread.

Tip: Membrillo can be stored, covered, in the refrigerator for up to 3 months.

Plátano fritos
Banana fritters

Ingredients

1 egg, at room temperature, lightly beaten
125ml milk
2 tablespoons caster (superfine) sugar
20g butter, at room temperature
1 tablespoon runny honey
1 teaspoon finely grated orange rind
1 egg white, extra
Pinch of salt
100g plain (all-purpose) flour
Sunflower oil for deep frying
4 large bananas, ripe but firm
40g icing (confectioner's) sugar
2 teaspoons ground cinnamon

Method

Place egg, milk, sugar, butter, honey and orange rind into a large bowl and mix well.

In a separate bowl, whisk egg white and salt until soft peaks form. Add egg white to the milk mixture then sift in the flour in three batches, folding it in to form a smooth thin batter.

Preheat oven to 150°C. Heat oil in a deep fryer or heavy-based saucepan.

Peel bananas and slice diagonally into large pieces. Dip banana into the batter, allowing the excess to drain. Cook in batches in the hot oil until lightly golden.

Drain cooked banana fritters on a wire rack, which is sitting on an oven tray. Keep fritters warm in the preheated oven while you cook the remaining banana.

Sprinkle lightly with icing sugar and cinnamon and serve with a good scoop of ice cream.

Sabayón de cava
Egg custard with cava

serves 4

Ingredients

8 free-range* egg yolks, at room temperature

150g caster (superfine) sugar

250ml cava* (or sparkling wine)

125ml thickened cream*

Fresh berries or fruit, to serve

Cava is Spain's answer to champagne. It's the sparkling wine to start a meal and is the breakfast of champions. With its slightly sweet bready aroma it makes a perfect custard that when blended with whipped cream makes a sabayon that matches perfectly with berries or perhaps a fruit tart.

Method

Heat a saucepan of water that is large enough for a medium heatproof glass bowl to sit over the top.

Place egg yolks and sugar into a medium heatproof glass bowl and use a whisk to beat them for about 3 minutes until pale yellow in colour. Add the cava, then place the bowl over the simmering water – ensure the water does not come into contact with the base of the bowl (as this will overcook the egg yolks).

Whisk the sabayon continuously until it thickens and is the consistency of custard. This takes about 15-20 minutes.

Remove the glass bowl to a larger bowl filled with some ice and a little water. Place the hot bowl directly onto the ice to cool it down, stirring occasionally.

Whip the cream until soft peaks form; when the sabayon is cold, stir in the cream.

Serve chilled with fresh berries or seasonal fruit.

Tip: This sabayon can be made a few hours in advance and stored, covered, in the refrigerator – ideally the day you intend to serve it.

* Refer to Glossary – Page 482

Crema Catalana
Caramelised Catalan custard

serves 4

Ingredients

1 lemon

1 litre milk

1 cinnamon stick

8 free-range* egg yolks, at room temperature

300g caster (superfine) sugar

80g cornflour

100g caster (superfine) sugar, extra

There's a hiss of heat and a small white puff of smoke as the chef finishes off another Crema Catalana. He puts the branding iron back into the coals ready to caramelise the sugar on the next.

Crema Catalana is the very similar to France's crème brûlée or England's Trinity Cream. It's dear to Catalans who serve it on 19 March, which is St Joseph's Day, when it's called Crema de Sant Josep. Whoever discovered this delicate custard that's made with rich egg yolks, a little cinnamon and a hint of lemon, sprinkled with sugar and then scorched with a branding iron or flame, could be canonised themselves, as it's a true masterpiece.

As branding irons are hard to come by these days, so many use a propane gas canister fitted with a little flame torch. Caramelising the sugar under a grill turned up high works nearly as well but be careful not to overcook the custard.

Method

Using a small sharp knife or potato peeler, remove rind from the lemon in long pieces, avoiding the white pith.

Place rind, milk and cinnamon into a medium saucepan and bring to a gentle simmer over medium heat. Remove from heat and cool slightly. Strain into a heatproof jug.

Place egg yolks, sugar and cornflour into a large bowl, then add milk mixture, a little at a time, and whisk to loosen the mixture. Add remaining milk and mix well.

Return the mixture to the saucepan and whisk over low heat until the mixture forms a thick custard.

Pour into 4 x 1-cup serving dishes or ramekins. Chill until custard is firm and set.

Before serving, generously sprinkle the top of each custard with the extra sugar. Burn with a hot flame gun or place under a preheated grill until a toffee forms. Serve immediately.

* Refer to Glossary – Page 482

Flaó
Cheese mint tart and aniseed

serves 6-8

Ingredients

Dough:

60ml olive oil

60g pork lard, at room temperature

60ml water

2 tablespoons aniseed liqueur (such as Pernod)

2 teaspoons whole aniseeds or fennel seeds

320g plain (all-purpose) flour, plus extra for dusting

1 tablespoon caster (superfine) sugar

Pinch of salt

Filling:

380g quark* or mascarpone*

2 free-range* eggs, at room temperature

75g caster (superfine) sugar

2 teaspoons finely grated lemon rind

1 tablespoon lemon juice

4 fresh mint leaves, finely chopped

2 tablespoons icing (confectioner's) sugar, to serve

This tart is from the island of Ibiza. The base is flavoured with a little kick of aniseed, thanks to a good dash of liqueur and some actual aniseeds. The rich, sweet filling is laced with flecks of fresh mint, giving a delicate foil to the creamy sweet cheese. Enjoy with coffee or a small glass of anise liqueur.

Method

To make the dough, place oil, lard, water, liqueur, seeds, flour, sugar and salt into a large bowl. Stir with a wooden spoon until the ingredients form a soft dough. Turn the dough out onto a lightly floured work surface and knead for about 10 minutes or until soft and no longer sticky. (Use a little extra flour if necessary – just sprinkle it on the work surface and knead it into the dough.) Wrap dough in plastic wrap and refrigerate for 1½ hours.

Preheat oven to 200°C. Lightly grease a 26cm round, 4cm deep springform pan.

Clean the work surface, dust again with flour and roll out the dough into a thin round at least 40cm in diameter. Carefully transfer the dough round to the prepared pan, pressing dough into the bottom and sides of the pan, allowing the excess to hang over the top edge. Refrigerate again for 20 minutes, then trim the excess dough and randomly prick the base with a fork.

Line the pan with crumpled kitchen baking paper weighted down with baking beads and bake blind* in preheated oven for 10 minutes. Remove the paper and beads and bake for a further 10 minutes or until lightly golden. Allow to cool.

Reduce oven temperature to 180°C.

To make the filling, place quark, eggs, sugar, lemon rind and juice and mint into a food processor and process until just smooth. Pour the mixture into the prepared crust and return to the oven. Bake for 25-30 minutes or until just set when tested with a knife in the centre.

Place cake pan onto a wire rack and allow to cool in pan.

Release the pan's springform and slide the tart onto a flat serving plate. Dust with icing sugar and serve at room temperature.

Tip: If the top is browning too much during the final stages of baking, shield the tart with a piece of foil to prevent further browning.

* Refer to Glossary – Page 482

Macedonia al cava
Fresh fruit salad with cava syrup

serves 4-6

Ingredients

1½ kg mixed fresh fruit in season
(we used apple, strawberries, peach,
nectarine, grapes, pomegranate and figs)

1 lemon, juiced

Cava syrup:

125g granulated sugar

250ml water

60ml cava*

Method

Make the fruit salad with your choice of fruit – try to have a variety of colours and textures. Drizzle the lemon juice on cut fruit, such as apples and pears, to prevent browning.

To make the syrup, place the sugar and water into a small, heavy-based saucepan over low-medium heat. Bring to a gentle boil without stirring. You can gently shake the saucepan but avoid stirring as sugar crystals may form.

Simmer over low heat, uncovered, for 10 minutes.

Remove from heat and gradually add the cava. Stir to combine.

Transfer the syrup to a heatproof jug and set aside to cool to room temperature (avoid stirring).

Pour the cooled syrup over the fruit just prior to serving and very gently combine.

Serve with fresh cream or ice cream and, of course, chilled cava.

* Refer to Glossary – Page 482

Cataluña
(Catalonia)

Barcelona

Since Romans settled Barcelona around the start of the Christian era it has always been an outward-looking city, open to ideas from the rest of the world. In the Middle Ages, when it was aligned with the Crown of Aragon, Catalonia took a more active interest in the outside world by colonising the Mediterranean as far as Naples and Athens. Even today the so-called *paisos Catalans*, the lands where Catalan culture predominates, extend from Valencia via French Roussillon to Alghero in Sardinia.

Catalonia's broadmindedness is coupled with an intense pride among Catalans in their culture, language and achievements, all of which have flourished again since Spain's disparate regions emerged from dictatorship in 1975.

The 1992 Barcelona Olympic Games were the culmination of a period of self-determination after which Catalonia put on its best face to the world – and liked what it saw reflected back. Ever since it has been one of the most popular destinations in Europe, attracting around 20 million visitors each year. But at its heart, Catalonia remains an uncomplicated place where traditional lifestyle and cuisine reign.

Layers of history – a cosmopolitan cuisine

Like the people of Galicia and the Basque Country, Catalans exist within Spain as a historic nationality – a people apart from the rest of the Iberian lands. While cosmopolitan Barcelona may seem like the quintessential 21st century city, venture outside the capital and there are hundreds of villages by the sea or isolated in the mountains where life has not changed a great deal since the start of the 20th century.

But Catalonia is not backward. As the world renowned restaurant *elBulli* has shown, Catalans can take the best ideas on the globe and incorporate them into something wonderful and new. Catalan cuisine has base notes of Roman (this land has always been the coastal route to the Iberian Peninsula), an aromatic overlay of the Moors, liberal helpings of the New World, and side dishes of anything the locals encountered and enjoyed on their travels around the world.

To understand their passion for imported ideas and products look no further than the tomato. This humble fruit discovered in the Americas is now one of the most recognisable symbols of Catalan culture and honoured every day in the national breakfast dish *pa amb tomàquet*, toasted bread smeared with tomato, good olive oil and a crush of sea salt. Maybe topped with an anchovy.

Cuisine Catalan-style: simple yet sophisticated with the perfect marriage of produce from land and sea.

Left: A bounty of *botifarra* displayed at a sausage specialty shop in Camprodon, Catalonia.

Above: Vineyards of the Penedes wine region – the home of Cava – during the grape harvest. The dramatic mountains of Montserrat dominate the skyline of the entire region surrounding Barcelona.

A bounty of *botifarra*

If there is one food that defines Catalonia, perhaps it is *botifarra*, an umbrella term that covers a multitude of sausages or *embotits*. *Botifarra* comes in all makes and colours, from the standard black banger of pork and blood to *botifarra de huevo*, a white sausage made with egg that is eaten during Lent, *dolça amb poma i nous*, a sweet *embotit* with apple and nuts, and, most infamously, the chocolate *botifarra*.

Catalans tend to believe they live in god's own country, surrounded by an abundance of superior produce. They have everything on their doorstep: the Ebro delta in the south supports rice plantations and salt pans; the Mediterranean provides endless seafood; the vineyards of *Penedès* ply them with excellent wine and the villages of the interior supply the region with rustic delights. Roasted meats, such as pork and veal, are popular and often matched with fruits rather than vegetables – duck with pears is common. The mountains also provide mushrooms, rabbit, snails and calçots, a kind of spring onion flame-grilled and dipped in spicy, nutty romesco sauce.

Picadas or sauces are generally made from ground aromatics like garlic, herbs, olive oil and dried bread. Aside from *romesco*, Catalonia is renowned for its *allioli, samfaina* – fried aubergine, tomatoes and peppers – and *sofregit* or *sofrito*, very slowly cooked onions and tomato in olive oil.

413

gourmetpilgrim Spain

The best of both worlds

As in Australia, the Catalans have an appetite for 'surf and turf', or *mar i muntanya* as they like to call it. The unorthodox combination of mountain and sea leads to preparations like chicken with lobster, or the Catalan salad common along the coast of lettuce and tomato with a mixed marriage of sliced *botifarra* sausage and plump Catalonian anchovies. Catalans also like to marry sweet and savoury in the one plate, as with a sauté of anchovies and apples or *elBullí*'s gelato of anchovy and watermelon.

In the north of Catalonia on the Costa Brava, the residents may be more casual in the way they dress but they will always serve the best food they can afford. Maybe this helps explain *elBulli* phenomenon.

Lest anyone get the idea that Catalan cuisine is overly sophisticated, bear in mind a staple of the local diet is lard. It is often paired with olive oil to lend an extra depth to the flavour to dishes. And much of the region's agricultural output is still farmed by cooperatives of small landholders, like those who produce Catalonia's *Denominación de Origen* olive oil and the 'brotherhoods' of fishermen who trawl the Mediterranean coastline. These fishermen are responsible for *suquet*, a traditional bouillabaisse-like stew of whatever is freshly caught – monkfish, mussels, shrimp and calamari.

Like all Spaniards, Catalans too, have a hopeless sweet tooth, perhaps most famously expressed in the *crema catalana*, a sugary custard with burnt caramel top. Crème brûlée, Catalan style.

Below: Rice fields of the Ebro delta, Tarragona region, Catalonia.

Right: City of architecture – view of the uber-modern Agbar Tower and the Sagrada Familia Basilica, Barcelona. Designed by famed Catalan architect Antoni Gaudi, the masterplan for the eclectic church includes a total of 18 spires and 3 distinct facades. The basilica has been under construction since 1882, and is expected to be completed in 2025.

Dulces
y galletas

Sweets & biscuits

The Spanish have
a renowned sweet
tooth and a store of
recipes to satisfy it.

Dulces y galletas
(Sweets & biscuits)

The Moors left the deepest impression on the sweet Spanish palate and their legacy is most obvious today in the last stronghold of Moorish rule, Andalucia. Desserts and sweets there commonly feature honey, almonds, cinnamon, cloves and fruits – all innovations of the Arabs.

They also introduced olive oil to the Spanish *pastelería*, an ingredient still commonly used today in simple oil cakes (*tortas de aceite*) and biscuits like *pelusas*, melting moments flavoured with lemon and anise. Oil is an essential ingredient, too, in the ubiquitous *churros* – the elongated doughnuts that pass for breakfast on the Iberian Peninsula. These are usually dipped into a pot of dense chocolate, an innovation souvenired from the Aztecs by 16th century conquistadors.

The Arabs are also ascribed with having popularised sugar, that most essential ingredient of any sweet treat. Moorish texts dating back to the 11th century dictate the optimum conditions for Spanish sugar cane cultivation – plant the crops in March, on a plain sheltered from the east wind and near to water.

Moreish staples

Marzipan is synonymous today with the city of Toledo, whose convents and bakeries feed the habits of the sugar-and-almond addicted. It comes in myriad shapes and sizes from the heart-shaped *corazones* filled with sweet egg-yolk paste to the *anguilas* or eels, lavishly decorated with edible silver *dragée* balls, that are an essential addition to the Christmas table.

Turrón is another indispensable Christmas treat throughout Spain. Tempting towers of this more-ish nougat fill shop windows every December. The most famous versions are made in the Valencian region at Jijona and Alicante. Both are made from the classic mix of almonds, egg yolks, honey and sugar but Jijona *turrón* is soft and chewy while Alicante's is firm and crunchy.

Alfajores, derived from the Arabic words for filling and nectar, are sugar-dusted fingers of dried fruits, such as figs and sultanas, with honey, almonds and hazelnuts. They are spiced with cinnamon, cloves and lemon and often laced with a slosh of sticky Pedro Ximénez black sherry for good measure.

Sweet treats are an Iberian article of faith – closely linked to the religious calendar.

Sweets of the sacristy

Despite overwhelmingly Arabic origins, most Spanish confectionery owes its continued existence to the religious festivals of the Christian calendar.

Many distinctive sweets are inextricably linked to *Nochebuena*, Christmas Eve, when family feasts invariably culminate in decadent displays of sweets. *Mantecados*, rich and crumbly shortbread-like biscuits made with lard instead of butter are a typical Yuletide treat, often wrapped, like chocolates, in different coloured papers to identify the tastes – anise, lemon, almond. *Pestiños* are honey-flavoured fritters flavoured with sherry, cinnamon, cloves and anise.

But the star of the Christmas-time confections is the *Roscón de Reyes*, a sweet, ring-shaped bread studded with dried fruit and nuts and filled with custard, marzipan or candied fruits. Traditionally eaten at Epiphany on January 6, the cake takes centre-stage in celebrations as guests search their slice for either a figurine of a king or a dried bean. Whoever finds the figurine is said to have a year of good luck ahead; whoever finds the bean must pay for the cake.

Other sacred sweets include the *buñuelos de cuaresma*, a cream-filled fried doughnut eaten on Holy Wednesday in Catalonia; Cadiz's Holy Week *gañote*, a fried dough twist with lemon, sesame and cinnamon; marzipan rolls filled with sweetened egg yolk known as *huesos de santo* ('saint's bones') and eaten all over the country on All Saints' Day, and the *Mona de Pasqua* or Easter Cake, presented by godparents to their godchildren on Palm Sunday. Usually adorned with almonds, the cake has succumbed to modern tastes and is now more likely to be fashioned into elaborate chocolate forms or luridly coloured, edible sculptures.

For those rare occasions when there are no religious events to be celebrated, Spaniards have a plentiful supply of heathen sweets such as Majorca's famous *ensaimadas*, sugar-dusted pastry coils, and the breakfast cupcakes called *magdalenas*.

And then there is always the flan. Almost every region has its own version of this custard pie with caramel sauce, much like France's *crème caramel*. *Leche frita*, literally fried milk, is a variation on the custard theme, as is the cold vanilla and cinnamon custard *natillas*.

Above: Nuns bake biscuits in the kitchen of El Convento de Santa Clara, Burgos, Castilla y Leon.
Opposite: A busy indoor Churreria in Madrid.

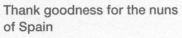

Thank goodness for the nuns of Spain

The convent bakeries of the Catholic Church are the repository of a sweet culinary history that has evolved from centuries of cross-pollinated ideas and techniques bequeathed by Moors, Aztecs, Jews and Christians. It is the nuns, and the country's packed calendar of religious festivals and holy days, that ensure the enduring popularity of these age-old confections.

Churros and the churrería

Outside the Jerez de la Frontera market is one of the happiest men in the world. Domingo is the local *churrero*, or *churro* maker.

He has a great metal pot filled with a paste made from flour, salt, water, butter & eggs that he swings in a circular motion over a pot of hot oil, the exuding paste forming a great coil of frying dough. From the bubbling oil he lifts the now golden *churros* onto a tray. He cuts them into portions with a pair of scissors, dusts them in sugar and wraps them in paper. His customers wander to the outdoor café next door and order a *café con leche*, and a mug of thick sweet hot chocolate for dipping the *Churros*.

Churros are a great little deep-fried treat to be consumed at any time of the day. They're basically little sticks of fried dough – the classic, super-sweet breakfast of *Madrileños*, but just as perfect for afternoon tea or a late-night snack when you've finished with *tapas*.

There are *churrerías* – simple *churro* shops – in the base of many apartment blocks in the cities of Spain.

Most city dwelling Spaniards live in small apartments so tend to congregate in the public areas in and around their apartment blocks. In the evening and at night this will be the *tapas* bars and restaurants, during the morning, however, will be a time when people, feeling like a sweet deep-fried treat, will gather in the *churrería* waiting for their *churros* to fry while they catch up on gossip and other important family business.

Churros
Churros

Ingredients

300ml water
Pinch of salt
50g butter, cubed
200g plain (all-purpose) flour
2 eggs, at room temperature
Vegetable oil for deep-frying
60g caster (superfine) sugar

Method

Place water, salt and butter into a large saucepan and bring to the boil over medium-high heat.

Reduce heat to medium, add flour all at once and stir vigorously over heat until the dough comes away from the sides of the saucepan. Remove from heat and set aside for a few minutes to cool slightly.

Lightly whisk the eggs in a small jug or bowl. Pour about half the eggs into the dough and beat well to combine, then add remaining egg, beating until eggs are well combined and dough is shiny and smooth. Heat oil in a deep fryer or heavy-based saucepan. Spoon the dough into a large piping bag fitted with a large star-shaped nozzle.

Carefully pipe three 10cm snail shapes into the hot oil, using a knife to cut the ends. Deep-fry until lightly golden all over.

Remove with a slotted spoon and drain on kitchen paper towel. Sprinkle with sugar while hot. Repeat with remaining dough.

Serve with 'Hot chocolate – Spanish style' for dipping (see recipe, page 470).

Carquinyolis
Almond bars

Ingredients

125g raw (skin-on) almonds

200g plain (all-purpose) flour

2 teaspoons baking powder

125g caster (superfine) sugar

1 teaspoon finely grated lemon rind

1 teaspoon ground cinnamon

1 egg, at room temperature, lightly beaten

1 egg, at room temperature, separated, extra

When you have the best almonds in the world, like the Catalans do with their flat sweet marcona almonds, you use them in all manner of dishes, such as this baked sweet treat. Carquinyolis are sometimes broken into breadcrumbs for a picada but are just as good with a hot cup of tea or coffee.

Method

Place almonds into a colander and wash with cold water. Allow to drain well.

Preheat oven to 200°C. Line two large baking trays with kitchen baking paper.

Sift flour and baking powder into a medium bowl. Stir in sugar, rind and cinnamon. Make a well in the centre of the flour mixture and add the whole egg and egg white.

Mix well to form a dough, then knead in the almonds. If the dough is a little sticky, use slightly damp hands to roll level tablespoons of the mixture into small log shapes. Place about 2cm apart onto prepared oven trays. Lightly brush logs with lightly beaten egg yolk.

Bake in preheated oven for 10-15 minutes or until golden. Leave to cool on the trays.

Turrón de Jijona
Soft almond & rosemary nougat

Ingredients

225g honey

125g caster (superfine) sugar

3 small sprigs fresh rosemary

1 egg white, at room temperature

200g blanched almonds, roasted* and chopped

175g ground almond meal

1 lemon, rind only, finely grated

In the hills near Alicante is a small town with a museum dedicated to turrón or nougat. Jijona is typical of such towns in Spain where a handful of families still make food products that combine traditional skill with modern technology. Turrón is a blend of egg whites folded though hot honey or sugar syrup and dotted with roasted almonds. Sometimes turrón is wrapped in rice paper and sold in a disc or in boxes.

Traditionally a Christmastime treat, it has now found a greater year-round audience. It's not difficult to make at home and just requires a little patience. The quality of the ingredients will determine the end result; good-quality honey, fresh eggs and almonds will give you turrón so delicious you may want to wrap it in decorative paper and give it away as a gift. Or keep it for yourself as a treat.

Method

Line the base and sides of an 18cm square cake pan with kitchen baking paper.

Place honey, sugar and rosemary in a medium heavy-based saucepan and cook, uncovered, over low-medium heat for about 15 minutes, stirring often with a wooden spoon until sugar dissolves and mixture thickens. Remove from heat.

Beat egg white with a whisk until foamy. Add this to hot honey mixture and stir well. Return saucepan to medium heat and stir continuously for 10 minutes. Reduce heat to low and continue to cook the mixture until it becomes a light caramel colour. Stir often, especially around the inside base of the saucepan as this is where the mixture may catch and possibly burn. Remove the rosemary with tongs and discard.

Remove saucepan from heat and add the almonds, almond meal and rind. Stir well with a spoon, then working fast because the turrón sets quickly, pour the mixture into the prepared pan as quickly as possible. Use the back of a metal spoon dipped in water to flatten the mixture in the pan.

Set for 5-6 hours, then remove from the pan and cut into pieces.

Note – This soft-style turrón cuts well. Keep pieces in an air-tight container in a cool, dry place for up to 1 month.

* Refer to Glossary – Page 482

Magdalenas
Magdalenas

Ingredients

2 eggs, at room temperature
180g honey, soft and runny
80g butter, melted
1 tablespoon orange blossom water*
1 teaspoon finely grated orange rind
200g self-raising flour, sifted
Icing (confectioner's) sugar to serve

It's part of life in the big cities to get a copy of the daily paper, perhaps El Mundo or El País, order a café con leche (milk coffee) with a magdalena and take a break. While you're reading the football scores or about the latest strike you can quietly dunk this sweet little cake into your coffee, knowing that everyone around is doing the same.

Method

Preheat oven to 180°C. Lightly grease a 6-hole Texas (180ml) muffin pan.

Separate the eggs and place the yolks into a small bowl and the whites into a separate clean medium bowl. To the yolks, add the honey, butter, orange blossom water and rind and mix well. Whisk the egg whites until stiff peaks form.

Fold the flour into the egg-yolk mixture in three batches, then fold through the egg whites.

Spoon mixture evenly into the prepared muffin pan and bake in preheated oven for 15 minutes or until lightly golden.

Allow to stand in the muffin pan for 5 minutes. Remove to a cooling rack and dust lightly with icing sugar while still warm.

* Refer to Glossary – Page 482

Chuchos
Chocolate filled doughnut logs

A kind of pet sounding word, Chucho is sometimes used as a nickname in Spain. Chuchos, however, are little log-like doughnuts, sometimes filled with custard, other times, as here, with chocolate. A little plate of serious fun, and a perfect snack.

Ingredients

14g active dry yeast

75ml milk, warmed

300g plain (all-purpose) flour

50g caster (superfine) sugar

Pinch of salt

½ lemon, rind only, finely grated

80g unsalted butter, cubed, at room temperature

2 eggs, at room temperature, lightly beaten

100g dark chocolate (60-70 per cent cocoa content), cut into 20 pieces

Vegetable oil for deep-frying

2 tablespoons caster (superfine) sugar, extra

Method

Place yeast and warm milk in a small bowl, mix and leave in a warm place until the mixture begins to foam slightly.

Place flour, sugar, salt and rind into a large bowl and make a well in the centre. Add yeast mixture, butter and eggs. Mix well and knead in the bowl to form a soft dough. Transfer dough to a large clean, lightly oiled bowl. Cover with a clean, damp tea towel and leave for about 1 hour or until double in size.

Preheat oven to 150°C. Line a baking tray with kitchen baking paper.

Divide the dough into 20 equal portions and roll out each piece into a circle (about 8cm in diameter) on a lightly floured work surface. Place a piece of chocolate at one end. Fold over the dough to enclose chocolate and roll to form a cylinder, pressing ends firmly to seal. Place about 5cm apart onto the prepared tray while you make the remaining chuchos.

Heat oil in a deep fryer or heavy-based saucepan and cook chuchos 3-4 at a time until lightly golden.

Drain cooked chuchos on a wire rack, sitting on an oven tray. Sprinkle with extra caster sugar. Keep warm in preheated oven while you cook the remaining chuchos.

Panellets
Almond & pine nut balls

Come All Saints Day in Catalonia and panellets are a popular treat. A ball of sweet potato and almond that's rolled in pine nuts then roasted until golden. They are served with sweet Vi ranci, the local sweet wine, or moscatell.

Ingredients

400g peeled sweet potato
100ml water
350g caster (superfine) sugar
400g ground almond meal
1 egg, at room temperature, separated
1 tablespoon finely grated lemon rind
200g pine nuts

Method

Preheat oven to 180°C. Line two baking trays with kitchen baking paper.

Cut sweet potato into large pieces and steam until tender. Remove to a bowl and mash until almost smooth. Cool.

Place the water, sugar, almond meal, egg yolk, rind and sweet potato into a large bowl and mix well.

In a separate clean bowl, lightly beat the egg white until frothy.

Using your hands, roll tablespoons of mixture into balls. Lightly brush each ball with egg white, then gently press some pine nuts into each.

Place half the balls about 2cm apart onto prepared baking trays. Bake in preheated oven for 12-15 minutes or until lightly golden.

Cool for 10 minutes on trays before transferring to a wire rack to cool completely. Repeat with remaining balls of dough. Serve.

Polvorones
Shortbread cookies

The name polvorón is a giveaway to the light, powdery texture of this shortbread; it sounds like pulverise. Quite often they are made exclusively with pork lard and eaten at Christmastime. They're surprisingly sweet and delicate.

Ingredients

300g plain (all-purpose) flour
½ teaspoon baking powder
¼ teaspoon salt
65g butter, at room temperature
60g pork lard, at room temperature
110g caster (superfine) sugar
40g icing (confectioner's) sugar
1 egg, at room temperature
½ teaspoon vanilla extract*
2 teaspoons lemon juice
1 tablespoon caster (superfine) sugar, extra
1 teaspoon ground cinnamon

Method

Preheat oven to 180°C. Line two large baking trays with kitchen baking paper.

Sift flour and baking powder into a large bowl, add salt and set aside.

Place the butter, lard, caster and icing sugars, egg and vanilla into a large bowl. Beat with electric beaters until the mixture is light and creamy.

Fold in half the flour mixture, all the lemon juice, then add enough of the remaining flour to form a firm dough. Divide the dough in two.

Roll out half the dough between two sheets of kitchen baking paper to about 5mm thick. Cut dough into assorted rounds with a biscuit cutter (4 or 4½ cm). Repeat with remaining dough. Place biscuits 2cm apart on the prepared trays and bake in preheated oven for 10-12 minutes or until lightly browned.

Transfer to a wire rack, sitting on a piece of kitchen baking paper. Combine extra sugar and cinnamon and sprinkle onto hot biscuits.

Tip: Any remaining dough can be re-rolled and used for more biscuits.

* Refer to Glossary – Page 482

Alfajores
Alfajores

Originally a roll of nuts and fruits held together with honey, alfajores was introduced to Spain during the Moorish period. The name now extends to biscuits held together with a sweet fruit paste. These alfajores can also be filled with quince paste on page 400.

Ingredients

1 egg, at room temperature
100g caster (superfine) sugar
½ teaspoon vanilla extract*
50ml water
40g butter, melted
200g plain (all-purpose) flour, sifted
100g self-raising flour, sifted
1/3 cup jam (such as strawberry)

Method

Place egg, sugar and vanilla into a large bowl and mix well with a wooden spoon. Add water and butter to the egg mixture, then gradually add the flour stirring with a wooden spoon until the ingredients form a firm dough. If the dough is a little sticky add a little extra flour.

Start to knead the dough until it comes away from the side of the bowl and turn it out onto a lightly floured work surface and lightly knead until smooth.

Preheat oven to 180°C. Line two large baking trays with kitchen baking paper.

Roll out the dough on the lightly floured work surface to a thickness of about 5mm. Cut dough into star or circle shapes using a biscuit cutter (about 3cm). Place shapes onto prepared trays. Collect the remaining dough into a ball and roll out again to then cut more biscuits from the dough. Bake in preheated oven for 12-15 minutes or until lightly golden, swapping trays halfway through baking. Cool on the trays.

Sandwich two biscuits together with a little jam.

Tip: Choose a firm jam to use as the filling; if it is too thin, it will run out of the middle.

436
gourmetpilgrim Spain

* Refer to Glossary – Page 482

Migas dulces con pasas
Raisin crumb and sweet bread bake

Ingredients

20g butter, at room temperature

100g raisins

125ml warm water

150g caster (superfine) sugar

100g fresh breadcrumbs*

4 free-range eggs*, at room temperature

300ml milk

Pinch of ground cinnamon

Method

Preheat oven to 180°C. Grease a square 18cm baking pan with butter and line with kitchen baking paper.

Soak raisins in warm water for 10 minutes and drain.

Reserve two tablespoons of the sugar in a small bowl. Place remaining sugar, drained raisins, breadcrumbs, eggs, milk and cinnamon into a large bowl and mix well.

Pour mixture into the prepared pan, then sprinkle with the reserved sugar.

Bake in preheated oven for 20 minutes or until set and lightly golden. Cool, then remove from the tray and cut into pieces.

* Refer to Glossary – Page 482

Andaluciá

Sevilla

In many ways Andalucia embodies all the elements generally associated with romantic, archetypal Spain. This sun-bleached region facing Africa across the Mediterranean is the birthplace of flamenco, thought to have evolved from the passionate *zambra* dances performed by gypsies in caves above Granada.

Bullfighting is observed with an almost religious fervour, especially in the capital, Seville, where its 12,000-seat bullring erupts with excitement during the annual *corrida* season. Seville is also, famously, the inspiration and setting for Georges Bizet's comic opera *Carmen*, and the legend of Don Juan. Towering over all is the red fortress in Granada, the Alhambra, crowning glory of the Moorish kingdom Al-Andalus and an enduring reminder that Andalucia is the product of a richly textured past.

Spain's second largest autonomous community is a land of snowy mountains and sunburned beaches, of Mediterranean meets Atlantic, of vast tracts of pasturelands or *dehesas* perfect for fattening *pata negra* pigs, and foothills carpeted in olive trees.

It has always had a starring role in Spanish and world history, no matter who ruled its lands. Under the Romans, Córdoba became capital of the province of Betica and no fewer than three emperors – Hadrian, Trajan and Claudius – hailed from the corner of Europe now known as Andalucia. The Moorish reign from 711 until 1492 was a golden age of flourishing art, culture and architecture when Islam left its indelible imprint on the Iberian Peninsula. The Christian era was even more prosperous. After Columbus embarked on his voyage of discovery from Andalucia, the spoils of the New World began sailing up the Guadalquivir River to Seville, transforming it into one of the richest cities of the 16th century world.

Portal of flavor and riches

In both its Moorish and Christian heyday, Andalucia was the entry point through which Arab and later American influences filtered into Spain and forever altered its character and its flavour. But the cornerstone of the Andalucian diet – olives – was laid much earlier by the Phoenicians and Romans. This region is the world's largest producer of olive oil and has no fewer than 12 DO (*Denominación de Origen*) varieties.

Vested with a strategic location since the dawn of mankind, birthplace of three Roman emperors, seat of the enduring Moorish kingdom, gateway to the New World; influential Andalucía is the origin of many elements of Spanish culture and identity.

Right: The cliff-hugging town of Casares, Andalucia, boasts a sulfuric spring supposed to have cured Julius Caesar of a liver complaint, bestowing special status on the town under the Roman Empire.

This region has always had a starring role in Spanish history, which is evident in its diverse cuisine.

Above: Arabesque decoration typical of Moorish architecture in Andalucia – seen here in the Court of the Myrtles, Palace of the Alhambra, Granada.

Opposite: Fishing harbour at Cadiz, Andalucia. Established by the Phoenicians some 1000 yrs BC, Cadiz is the oldest continuously inhabited city on the Iberian peninsula. The Cadiz fishing fleet harvests tuna migrating to the Mediterraean thrrough the Strait of Gibraltar using the age-old Andalucian practise of *almadraba*, utilizing a maze of nets to corral schools of tuna in a central pool, the floor of which is then raised for the fish to be caught.

The Arabs brought with them sophisticated agricultural and irrigation techniques that greatly increased the amount of arable land, which in turn allowed new crops, such as aubergines and almonds, and spices, such as cumin and cinnamon, to be introduced. The New World delivered further gastronomic windfalls to Andalucia through tomatoes, potatoes, corn, chillis and cacao.

It seems impossible to imagine Andalucia without *gazpacho*, the chilled soup of tomato, bread, garlic and peppers eaten during the region's typically scorching summers. But before Columbus brought tomatoes to Spain, Andalucians kept their cool with *ajoblanco*, a cold soup of garlic, oil, almonds and grapes. Córdoba is known for a thicker, more elaborate *gazpacho*-style soup called *salmorejo*, which often has eggs, ham or rabbit added.

Fish and ham – dietary staples of a fortunate region

Andalucia has the good fortune to fish from two seas, the Mediterranean and the Atlantic, so fish and crustaceans have always been central to the local diet. It was the Arabs who taught them the joys of deep-fried fish (*pescaíto frito*), which is available from takeaway shops known as *freidurías*. In the coastal resort city of Malaga the locals have a taste for *chanquetes*, mounds of tiny, deep-fried anchovies.

In Cadiz and Huelva the specialty is *mojama*, tuna that is salted and air-dried using techniques learned from the Romans and Arabs. Hake (*merluza*) and shrimp feature on almost every menu, often simmered simply but deliciously in garlic and olive oil.

Stews are central to the Andalucian diet and go by the name of *guiso, olla, cocido* or *puchero*. Mini casseroles (*cacerolas*) might blend clams and shrimp with ham and sherry. *Ollas cortijeras* is a common inland stew of chickpeas, cabbage and ham.

Walk into any bar and the *tapas* menu will offer excellent *jamón Serrano* or *Iberico*, sliced finely and fresh with the *jamonero* and served on crusty bread. Andalucians maintain they make the best hams in Spain at Jabugo in Huelva, closely followed by those from Trévelez near Granada. Cured sausages or *embutidos* are also central to the regional diet, such as the chorizo-style *morcón* or Ronda's *morcilla* blood sausage.

Pork seems to be everywhere in Andalucia, where even vegetable dishes such as green beans (*judías verdes*) arrive at table with a liberal helping of ham. The practice is a hangover from the expulsion of Muslims and Jews in the 15th century, when Christians indiscriminately added pork to dishes to flush out any non-Christians. A typical dish of Christian Granada is *habas fritas con jamón*, fried beans with ham, which is far more palatable than the city's infamous *tortilla de sacramonte* – an omelette filled with offal (lamb or veal generally), crumbed brains and assorted vegetables.

And for dessert...

For dessert, Andalucia makes some memorable cheeses such as *payoyo*, produced in a small mountain village using the milk of indigenous goats. Baked pastries like *alfajores* and sweet *pestiños* fritters, echoing traditions introduced by Jews and Muslims, are also popular.

Andalucian wines can be collectively grouped under the heading sherry, though they are far more sophisticated than the sticky sweet version sipped by English aunts. These unique white wines, most made from the palomino grape, range from light and fragrant finos to the ultra-dry manzanilla and the unctuous, dark and syrupy *Pedro Ximénez*. The four DO wine regions are the venerable Jerez, Montilla-Moriles, *Montes de Málaga* and *Condado de Huelva*.

But in the blistering Andalucian summers a smarter choice than wine might be a flute of *agua de Sevilla*, a frozen blend of *cava*, lemon juice, pineapple and triple sec served like a granita and sipped through a straw.

gourmet
pılgrım

Vinos y bebidas

Wine & beverages

There is a Spanish
wine or local
beverage for every
occasion and every
type of meal.

Historia del vino Español
(The story of Spanish wine)

A vast land, encompassing many and varied terroirs, has produced a super talented and diverse wine industry that's going from strength to strength.

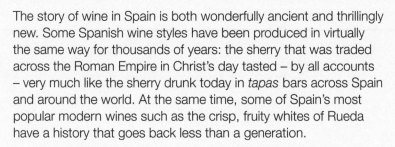

The story of wine in Spain is both wonderfully ancient and thrillingly new. Some Spanish wine styles have been produced in virtually the same way for thousands of years: the sherry that was traded across the Roman Empire in Christ's day tasted – by all accounts – very much like the sherry drunk today in *tapas* bars across Spain and around the world. At the same time, some of Spain's most popular modern wines such as the crisp, fruity whites of Rueda have a history that goes back less than a generation.

From pre-Roman times, Spanish wine has been dominated by the production and export of sherry: deliberately oxidized, fortified wines from the south, capable of withstanding the journey in barrel to England and the Spanish colonies. Until recently, winemaking in the rest of the country was mostly a very rustic affair, with grapes fermented and stored in *tinajas* – earthenware amphora-like vessels that have changed little over 1000 years.

French disaster, Spanish opportunity

Fortunes started to change for Spanish wine in the 19th century, when France's vineyards were decimated first by mildew and then the vine louse, phylloxera. French vignerons and merchants crossed the border looking for wine, and winegrowers in Rioja such as the Marqués de Murrieta and Marqués de Riscal were only too happy to oblige. Suddenly, new vineyards were planted, new *bodegas* (wineries) were built, and 225-litre American oak barrels started to appear in Rioja's cellars. Spain's quintessential red wine style was born: the combination of ripe red fruit flavours from the local *garnacha* and *tempranillo* grapes and sweet vanilla from the American oak is remarkably seductive.

Another classic French-wine style also inspired winemakers in Penedès in the late 19th century, when Josep Raventós started making sparkling wines using the champagne method at Codorníu in Sant Sadurní d'Anoia, outside Barcelona. Many other *bodegas* followed his lead and the region quickly established itself as the centre of production of *cava*, Spain's very own sparkling wine.

Emboldened by the success of these and other new regional wine styles, Spain developed its first official wine appellation system – the *Denominación de Origen* or DO – in the 1920s. But when the country descended into civil war – followed by World War II – the fast pace of wine development ground to a halt.

Spain's wine industry started to revive in the 1950s and '60s with a surge of interest in sherry, and over the past couple of decades the pace of change has picked up some furious momentum.

Back to the future – *viva la revolución!*

New generations of enterprising and innovative Spanish winemakers have introduced international grapes, such as chardonnay and cabernet – and rediscovered the value of obscure, ancient indigenous grape varieties, such as *mencia* and *bobal*. Once dominated by large, conservative co-operative wineries, Spain is now home to a huge number of smaller, privately owned and progressive *bodegas* – and some of the most striking modern winery architecture in the world.

And in the mid-90s, Spanish wine authorities legalised the use of irrigation in vineyards: prior to that, all the country's vines had been very low-yielding because they had been dry-grown (this is why, despite having the world's largest vineyard area of over one million hectares, Spain is only the third-largest producer, after France and Italy) and the ability to irrigate has resulted in some exciting new wines from previously struggling, drought-prone regions in the country's hot south.

A plethora of regional styles

Today, Spain is unquestionably one of the most exciting wine countries on the face of the planet, boasting an incredible diversity of distinctly regional wine styles.

The northwest of Spain is surprisingly wet and green. Galicia is home to the perfumed, seafood-friendly white wines of Rías Baixas, and the spicy, sinewy red wines from the steep hilly country of Bierzo León are enjoying a huge revival of interest.

A gaggle of top wine regions are clustered across the high country of Old Castille, including Ribera del Duero and Toro, with their solid, dark red wines and Rueda, with its crisp dry whites. Staying in the north, but further east, the heartland of oaky, traditional Spanish reds and whites, Rioja and Navarra, is now also home to some of the most modern, fruit-focused wines.

In Catalonia, the country around Barcelona can boast a number of top wines and regions, including the progressive whites and reds and sparkling Cava of Penedès, and the stoney higher-altitude vineyards and black wines of Priorat.

The hot, dry country in the country's southeast was once the source of vast quantities of fairly rough plonk, but some superbly modern, intensely flavoured reds are now produced in regions such as La Mancha, Jumilla, Yecla and Alicante.

Andalucia in the south-east is home to the great sherries and fortified wines of Jerez and Montilla as well as the once-famous and now revived sweet mountain wines of Málaga.

The wine revolution has also spread to the Canary and Balearic islands, where indigenous grapes, such as *listán negro* and *negramoll*, are producing some uniquely flavoured wines.

Today Spain is arguably one of the most exciting wine producers in the world.

Opposite and previous page: Cellar tunnels of La Bodega El Fabulista beneath the medieval town of Laguardia, Rioja Alavesa, Basque Country.

Above: Bodegas Ysios, by Santiago Calatrava, Rioja Alavesa, Basque Country.

Familia Torres

For the last half-century, the *Torres* have been perhaps the most influential wine family in Spain. Miguel Torres Snr was among the first to adopt modern technology such as temperature-controlled fermentation in stainless steel back in the 1960s; a 1970 *Torres* red wine thrust the Spanish new wave into the global spotlight when it beat Chateau Latour in a tasting in Paris in 1979; in the same year, Miguel Torres Jnr, the current patriarch, embraced the New World and expanded the family business to Chile; and in the new millennium, *Torres* has been at the cutting edge of sustainable viticulture, reviving old, indigenous Catalan grape varieties and expanding into other Spanish regions such as Priorat and Rioja.

www.torres.es

Above: The barrel rooms of Bodegas Torres, Pac del Penedes, Barcelona, Catalonia.

Following: The original vineyards & bodega of Marques de Riscal and the *Cuidad del Vino* (City of Wine) – pictured with the town of Elciego, Rioja Alavesa, behind.

Spanish wine words

Spanish wine regulations are quite convoluted, and involve various quality classifications. You will encounter the following phrases on the back labels of Spanish wine bottles:

Vino de Mesa	This is the basic classification, like France's *vin de table* or Italy's *vino di tavola*, used mostly for cheaper wines, or 'table wines' that can come from anywhere in the country.
Vino de la Tierra	Like the French term *vin de pays* – literally 'country wine' – this is used to indicate the wine comes from a certain part of Spain, indicated on the label.
Denominación de Origen (D.O.)	Best-known and most common classification, covering wines from specific high-quality regions such as Rías Baixas and Navarra.
Denominación de Origen Calificada (D.O.C.)	A superior classification awarded to wines from Spain's most prestigious regions, such as Rioja and Ribera del Duero. In fiercely Catalan Priorat, it's known as *Denominación de Origen Qualificada* or DOQ.
Denominación de Pago	A relatively recent addition to already crowded list of classifications, this indicates the wine comes from a *pago*, or single notable vineyard.

There is a very old and noble (but dwindling) tradition in Spain of maturing wines – particularly red wines – first in oak casks and then in bottle for a long time before releasing them to the market. The following words, regulated by Spanish wine law and found on wine labels, indicate how long the wine has been matured for:

Joven	Literally 'young': *joven* wines are bottled without any maturation in cask, usually just a few months after vintage. The modern reds encountered in many tapas bars are usually *joven* style.
Crianza	This means the wine has been matured for at least two years before release, with a minimum of six months in barrel.
Reserva	Matured for at least three years, with one year in barrel.
Gran Reserva	The wine is matured for no less than five years before release, with at least 18 months in barrel.

International grapes

Small pockets of so-called 'international' (i.e., non-Spanish) grape varieties have existed in vineyards across Spain for well over a century: cabernet franc has long been grown in Galicia (it is thought to be related to the Spanish red grape, *mencia*), and *Vega Sicilia*, Spain's most famous red wine, has long been a blend of *tempranillo*, cabernet, merlot and malbec.

Since the 1970s, though, the planting of international grapes has increased: the classic Champagne varieties chardonnay and pinot noir have made their presence felt in *cava*; sauvignon blanc is helping to lift the perfume of the white wines of Rueda; cabernet sauvignon is increasingly common in the red wines of Penedès, Priorat, Navarra and even Rioja.

Some of Spain's most important grape varieties

White grapes

Albariño

The grape responsible for the perfumed, pulpy-textured dry whites of Rías Baixas in Galicia, sometimes blended with other high-quality grapes, such as *godello*.

Moscatel

Rich and raisin-flavoured grape variety used to produce sweet wines – mostly fortified – in Andalusia.

Palomino

Lean and chalky-tasting grape used to make dry sherry.

Pedro Ximénez

Similar to *moscatel*, at its best PX produces some of the most luscious and intensely sweet of all sherries.

Verdejo

Newly fashionable grape used to make the fresh, fruity dry white wines of Rueda.

Viura/macabeo

The traditional grape used for the oaky white wines of Rioja (where it's called *viura*), also – with *xarel-lo* and *parellada* – the main grape used to make cava (where it goes by the name *macabeo*).

Red Grapes

Alicante

A red-skinned, red-fleshed grape grown in the hot southeastern regions of Spain, often blended with other varieties to produce dark, fleshy wines.

Bobal

A traditional red grape in Valencia and other south-eastern regions; once thought to be inferior, careful winemaking has revealed a grape with great potential.

Cariñena/mazuelo

This robust, tannic grape provides a solid backbone to red blends from Priorat (where it's known as *carinyena*) to Rioja (where it's called *mazuelo*).

Garnacha

A widely planted grape traditionally responsible for the bulk of many Spanish reds such as Rioja, where it was once commonly blended with *tempranillo* and others.

Graciano

A minor but important grape in Rioja: dark, tart and perfumed, a little *graciano* can really add depth of flavour when blended with *garnacha* and *tempranillo*.

Mencia

A recently rediscovered, high-quality red grape from Bierzo in Spain's northwest: the wines have marvellous spicy perfume.

Monastrell

Like *garnacha*, traditionally used in cheap wines, but extremely high quality, dense and flavoursome examples are now emerging from hot south regions such as Jumilla.

Tempranillo

Spain's most important red grape, planted from the south (where it's called *cencibel*) right up through the north (*ull de llebre* in Catalonia, *tinto fino* in Ribera del Duero, *tinto de toro* in Toro, and so on). It's the dark-fruited, generous, flavoursome grape at the heart of most of Spain's great wines.

Herederos del Marques de Riscal (Elciego, Rioja Alavesa)

In the year 1858, Camilo Hurtado de Amezaga – the Marques de Riscal, commissioned a French winemaker to establish the Bordeaux vinification techniques among the vignerons of Rioja, and began cultivating French varieties at his own vineyard in Elceigo, Rioja Alavesa, building a winery & cooperage to accommodate the Bordeaux methods.

His vision was vindicated within 7 years, when his Rioja wines began winning a run of medals at Europe's top wine exhibitions, culminating in the Diplome d'Honneur at the Bordeaux exposition of 1895 – whereby Marques de Riscal become the first winery outside of France to receive the highest accolade for wine.

In 1974 the Marques de Riscal company pioneered the cultivation Sauvignon Blanc in Rueda, leading to the establishment of the Rueda D.O., now rated at the pinnacle of Spanish white wine regions.

Today, Herederos del Marques de Riscal remains devoted to the highest quality and latest advancements in the world of wine. This is perhaps most graphically displayed at the company's original winery in Elceigo, where Frank Gehry's incredibly futuristic 'Cuidad del Vino' (world of wine) resides. The original bodega and modern underground cellars – the oldest winery in the La Rioja wine region, ages some 7 million bottles of Reserva and Grand Reserva wines and hold the company's crown jewels – bottles of every wine produced in the winery's 140 year history.

www.marquesderiscal.com

Sangría blanca
White sangria

Ingredients

300ml water

125g caster (superfine) sugar

1 small bunch fresh mint, leaves removed

3 cinnamon sticks

800ml dry white wine

1 medium peach, peeled, pitted and chopped

1 large pear, cored, quartered and chopped

1 medium orange, thinly sliced

1 medium lemon, thinly sliced

750ml sparkling apple cider*, chilled

Extra fresh mint leaves, to serve

Ice cubes, to serve

Familiarity breeds contempt, and the ubiquity of rough, too-sweet sangria that's too-often found in Spain's overcrowded tourist traps has cheapened the image of what should be a bright, light, utterly thirst-quenching drink.

The tradition of adding sweetener and other flavourings to wine dates back to the Romans and beyond, to times when the sharp, harsh tastes of often-oxidised wine needed amelioration in the form of honey or herbs. Modern, well-made red wine doesn't need the same kind of tricking-up, of course: the point of sangria is to enhance the refreshment value of red wine for a hot day.

As with mulled wine, the fresher the ingredients that go into the sangria jug, the more delicious the end result. Here's a recipe:

Pour a chilled bottle of light, young red wine (a joven, unwooded garnacha or monastrell, from La Mancha or Jumilla) into a big jug. Add some slices of orange and lemon (common in the south) or peaches or nectarines (found in northern versions of sangria), a spoonful of sugar or honey, a slug of Brandy de Jerez, a small bottle of soda water and a couple of handfuls of ice. Stir well and drink immediately.

While sangria has been enthusiastically embraced by tourists, many Spaniards are more likely to drink tinto de verano during summer (verano); it's a much simpler but no less refreshing blend of red wine (tinto) and a local, not-too-sweet lemonade, served in a simple tumbler, over ice.

Method

Place water, sugar, mint leaves and cinnamon into a medium saucepan and bring to the boil over medium heat. Reduce heat and simmer, uncovered, for 5 minutes. Remove from heat and cool to room temperature. Remove and discard the mint leaves and cinnamon sticks.

Transfer liquid to a large serving bowl. Add wine, peach, pear, orange and lemon slices and mix well. Cover bowl and refrigerate overnight.

Just before serving, add the apple cider and extra mint leaves, then stir well to combine. Ladle the sangria into a jug filled with ice cubes and serve.

* Refer to Glossary – Page 482

Sangría roja
Red sangria

Ingredients

750ml dry red wine
500ml sparkling apple juice
125ml gin
60g caster (superfine) sugar
1 large orange, juiced
1 large lemon, juiced
1 small lime
1 medium orange, extra
1 medium lemon, extra
Ice cubes, to serve

Method

Place the wine, apple juice, gin, sugar, orange and lemon juice into a large bowl and mix well.

Thinly slice the unpeeled lime, orange and lemon and add the slices to the sangria.

Ladle the sangria into a jug filled with ice cubes and serve.

Mojito
Mojito

serves 1

Ingredients

8 large fresh mint leaves
½ lime, cut into 4 wedges
1½ tablespoons caster (superfine) sugar
1 cup ice cubes or roughly crushed ice
40ml white rum (such as Bacardi)
125ml soda water

The mojito cocktail originated in the Spanish colony of Cuba, and its main ingredients – rum, sugar and limes – reflect the agricultural legacy of the island.

The cocktail is inextricably linked with the legendary novelist Ernest Hemingway, whose appetite for mojitos was matched only by his appetite for guns and fishing.

The drink is very popular in Spain, especially in beachside bars, thanks to its ultra-refreshing blend of white rum, sugar syrup, limes, mint and fizzy water. The origin of the name is unclear, but it probably comes from the Spanish word mojado, which loosely translates as 'soaked' – a seductive image for a summer cocktail.

Method

Place the mint leaves and only one lime wedge into a wide-rimmed glass.

Use a *muddler* (a wooden stick used for making cocktails) to gently crush the mint and lime together to release the lime juice and aromatic oils.

Add two more lime wedges and the sugar, then 'muddle' them to release the lime juice. Do not strain.

Fill the glass almost to the top with ice. Pour the rum over the ice and fill the glass with soda water. Garnish with the remaining lime wedge.

Denominación de Origen
(Denomination of Origin)

Devised to safeguard the integrity of the national pantry – the Spanish *Denominación de Origen* scheme denotes produce that is the 'real deal'.

Spain's Denomination of Origin scheme operates very much like a trademark to protect the integrity of the country's most treasured produce. The Spanish classification system, identified by the initials DO (*Denominación de Origen*) in the product name, is similar to schemes operating in France (where such products are labeled AOC) and Italy (DOC). The schemes safeguard a nation's agricultural pride and ensure no impostors can trade off its natural heritage.

DO regulations dictate the region, the provenance and the process of each protected product. Some are explicitly detailed. The DO laws for Cantabria's *Picón Bejes-Tresviso*, for example, stipulate which natural limestone caves this stinky blue-green cheese must be left in to mature and the minimum time it should be kept there. The Spanish DO system leaves very little to chance.

There are many dozens of unique Spanish foods and wines patented under the DO scheme, from cheeses, meats and vegetables to honey, oil, butter and vinegar. There are even DO spices – *pimentón de la Vera* DO, the smoky paprika exclusive to Extremadura, is so highly prized in Iberian cuisine that it is protected by statute.

A product must be region-specific in its character and preparation to warrant the DO trademark, which ensures it cannot be replicated anywhere else in the world. Very much like – and sometimes the same as – the appellations governing European wine production.

Spanish winemaking has been protected by a French-style appellation system since the 1920s, when laws were enacted to protect the unique La Rioja wines. As Spain's wine industry has become more sophisticated, so have the rules governing it.

Today there is a complex caste system that sorts wine regions into a five-tier league table, ranging from renowned single-estate wineries (*Denominación de Pago* or *DO de Pago*), down to simple table wines, *vinos de mesa*, with DO labelled wines falling in the middle. While DO foods are deemed to be the finest produce in the country, when it comes to wine the DO stamp indicates only decent quality – not the best.

Chacolí/Txakoli

One of the great strengths of Spanish gastronomy is its proud regionalism. While some grape varieties, such as tempranillo, have found a home in many different regions, most of Spain's grapes and wine styles are found only in very specific areas, where they have been cultivated over the centuries because they are perfectly adapted to both local growing conditions and local cuisine.

There is no more extreme example of this than the refreshing dry white wine called *chacolí*, found in the green Basque Country right up on the northern coast, near the French border. The Basque spelling is *txakoli*, and given the inextricable link between wine and place, it seems appropriate to use that here.

Txakoli is made from the spectacularly named indigenous *hondarribi zuri* grape, traditionally grown on high pergolas on steep coastal slopes. Picked early, when the grapes are low in sugar and high in acid, the resulting wine is light (less than 10 per cent alcohol), sometimes mouth-puckering in its lemony tartness and with a slight prickle of carbon dioxide – encouraged by pouring the wine from a height, in a similar fashion to traditional *sidra*.

Perfect for washing down the local seafood on a hot summer's day, *txakoli* is a wine that is unequivocally best drunk in situ: indeed, it's virtually impossible to find a bottle outside the region.

When visiting the Basque Country, enjoy this light, refreshing and unique wine – because you're unlikely to find it anywhere else.

Jerez (Sherry)

An ancient fortified wine from Southern Spain – sherry is making a global comeback.

After many centuries of production, sherry has fallen out of favour with many young, modern wine drinkers. But a visit to the remarkable country where it's made is guaranteed to make anyone fall in love all over again with the exquisite diversity of the region's fortified wines.

The light is what you notice first: the impossibly clear, almost painfully bright sunshine that pours down on Andalucia. It shimmers on the sea off the ancient port of Sanlúcar de Barrameda; it soaks into the *albariza*, the dry chalky soil found in so many vineyards here; it bounces off the stark white walls of the sherry houses in Jerez, old *bodegas* storing thousands of barrels of slowly maturing wine in their cool, dark, temple-like interiors.

Most of the different styles of sherry – such as *fino* or *oloroso* – start life in the same way. White *palomino* grapes are harvested from the region's sun-baked vineyards and fermented to produce a neutral-tasting, light (12 per cent alcohol), dry white wine. Spirit (distilled from grapes) is then added to the wine to fortify it up to around 14.5 per cent alcohol and the wine is put into old 500-litre barrels or *botas* to mature for many years.

Flor and the solera

The barrels are not quite filled to the top on purpose, to encourage the growth of a special yeast called *flor* on the surface of the wine. This layer of yeast both protects the wine from the air and contributes its own distinctive, lip-smacking flavour.

The light, dry sherries matured under *flor* are called *fino* or *manzanilla*, depending on where they're made: in cooler Sanlúcar, on the coast, the yeast covering remains thick all year and the resulting *manzanilla* sherry is lighter and more delicate, whereas in warmer Jerez, where the level of the *flor* thins out in summer, the *fino* sherry is more tangy and intense.

If the *flor* doesn't grow in a barrel of young sherry it is fortified again up to around 17 per cent alcohol, matured for many more years and becomes a fuller-bodied, more complex style called *oloroso*. If the *flor* grows and then dies off towards the end of the wine's maturation, exposing the wine to some oxidation, it is called an *amontillado*.

Below: Bodega Domecq, Macharnudo sherry district, Jerez, Andalucia.

Opposite: Blending sherry in the solera of the Gonzalez Byass company (of Tio Pepe fame), Jerez de la Frontera, Andalucia.

Following left: A taster proves a sample of sherry drawn from a barrel in the cellars of the Osborne Company, El Puerto de Santa Maria, Jerez, Andalucia.

Following right: Harvesting grapes for sherry, vineyards of Jerez, Andalucia.

The sherry revival

Equipo Navazos is one of the most important and exciting developments in sherry for many, many years. Unlike most of the region's venerable *bodegas*, which have a long history dating back to the 19th century, *Equipo Navazos* was launched in 2008, the personal project of a small group of passionate sherry-lovers, led by wine writer Jesús Barquín.

Over many years, these experts had stumbled across lots of outstanding single barrels – or *botas* – of sherry lurking in the darkest corners of various cellars in Jerez, Sanlúcar and Montilla: both in the large and well-known commercial *bodegas* and the private collections of small winegrowers. These extraordinary individual casks of sherry are traditionally lost when they become components of larger blends, so *Equipo Navazos* resolved to 'rescue' them, bottle them individually and sell them around the world.

Because of their extremely high quality and incredible rarity (being the contents of just one *bota*, each release is both extremely limited and unrepeatable) these wines have inspired a frenzy of critical acclaim and demand. Simply put, the La Bota series from *Equipo Navazos* is the most extraordinary range of sherries you will ever find.

www.equiponavazos.com

Whichever style it ends up as, all the top sherries are matured using the *solera* system of fractional blending, first developed in the region hundreds of years ago to ensure consistency of quality and complexity of taste.

Rows of barrels (called *criaderas*) of maturing sherry are stacked on top of each other, with the oldest at the bottom, the youngest at the top. Each time some sherry is drawn from the bottom row to be bottled, it is replaced with sherry from the row above, which in turn is topped up from the row above that and so on, with the top row being filled with new sherry from the most recent vintage. Some *soleras* in Spain's oldest *bodegas* have been maintained since the mid-19th century – and therefore still contain a tiny fraction of wine from that time.

The different styles of sherry

Sherry is a wine best enjoyed with food. As it sits for many years in barrel, sherry develops complex flavours rich in *umami*, the so-called 'fifth taste' that can be loosely described as 'a deep sense of savoury satisfaction'. This *umami* quality is also found in cheese (especially blue cheeses, such as *cabrales*, and salty sheep's cheese, such as *manchego*), tomatoes, paprika, roasted meat and slow-braised dishes – all stalwarts of the Spanish kitchen. So it's useful to explain the different styles of sherry in terms of the food that matches well with each.

Fino	A dry, yeasty pale sherry, with a nutty, even sometimes salty tang. Fino is fabulous with seafood, such as mussels and sardines.
Manzanilla	Like a more refined version of *fino*, drier, sometimes with a delicate green-apple edge to the yeasty tang. Excellent with garlicky, salty shrimp (prawns).
Amontillado	Off-dry to medium-dry sherry, bronze-coloured, often with a distinct flavour of hazelnuts. Superb with *jamón* and other smallgoods, such as *morcilla*.
Palo Cortado	A rare style of sherry that tastes like a cross between the light nuttiness of an *amontillado* and the savoury seriousness of an *oloroso*. Another great match for *jamón*.
Oloroso	Because it spends more time in barrel than other sherries, without the covering of *flor*, *oloroso* has more rounded, spicy, walnutty flavours. Great matched with deeply savoury dishes, such as braised rabbit.
Cream	Made by adding PX (see below) to young *oloroso* to sweeten it, cream sherry is mellow and sweet, like soft raisins. Good with custardy desserts and soft, creamy, blue cheeses.
Pedro Ximenez	Also known as PX, the famous black sherry is made from extremely ripe, shriveled grapes and is a luscious, syrupy and stunning match for dark chocolate.

Sidra (Cider)

Before they get a chance to explore Spain properly, many visitors expect the whole country to be hot, dry and dusty. So travelling through the northwest, through Asturias and Galicia, can come as quite a shock – this part of the world isn't called 'Green Spain' for nothing. While the summers can be hot, the strong maritime influence ensures that there's plenty of rain and proper cold winters – perfect for growing apples and making cider, or *sidra* as it's known here.

Spanish *sidra* is quite different to the sweet, strong, scrumpy styles of the United Kingdom or the cloudy, perfumed, sparkling farmhouse cider of France Quite rustic in appearance and aroma, *sidra* is usually sold as a still, medium-strength (around 6 per cent alcohol) cider that's often quite dry and astringent in style. It's a great accompaniment for both the local seafood and the hearty, rib-sticking local stews featuring beans and various cured pork products – apples and pork were meant to be together.

In an Asturian *sidrería*, or cider bar, *sidra* is traditionally served using a technique called *el escanciado*: the *sidra* is poured in a thin stream from a bottle held high above the glass, creating a temporary fizziness in the drink, as though it had been bottle-fermented (like sparkling wine) or carbonated (like mineral water). Because the bubbles soon dissipate, though, the drinker is encouraged to finish the glass as quickly as possible. And order another glass immediately.

Distinct from its better known European cousins, *sidra* is a still cider brewed from apples in ancient traditions – and adored across the northwest of Spain.

Brandy de Jerez

Less familiar than its famed French associates, brandy from southern Spain possesses its own unique distinctiveness.

The unique taste and character of brandy is strongly influenced by the barrels it is matured in. Brandy starts life as a raw, colourless spirit, freshly distilled from wine. As it matures inside oak casks, the flavours of the wood, and whatever has previously been stored inside those barrels, slowly seep into the liquid.

In the case of *Brandy de Jerez* – the name given to brandy made in the sherry country of southwestern Spain – the spirit is distilled from very lightly flavoured local wine; the 500-litre American oak casks (known as butts) have previously held *fino, amontillado, oloroso* or *pedro ximenez* sherry; and the maturation process can last for more than 10 years before the finished brandy is bottled.

Like sherry, *Brandy de Jerez* is aged in a *solera* system: rows of barrels of maturing spirit are stacked on top of each other, with the oldest at the bottom, the youngest at the top. Each time some brandy is drawn from the bottom row to be bottled, it is replaced with brandy from the row above, which in turn is topped up from the row above that and so on, until the top row is filled with newly distilled spirit.

There are three different types – *Brandy de Jerez* aged for an average of one year before being bottled; *Brandy de Jerez Solera Reserva* aged for an average of three years and tastes finer and more complex; and *Brandy de Jerez Solera Gran Reserva* aged for more than 10 years and the most profound expression of the spirit.

Not surprisingly, you can often taste entrancing echoes of fine sherry in a top *Brandy de Jerez*: subtle notes of yeastiness and cracked wheat, of grilled nuts and spiced fruit, of toasty, even smoky oak.

Opposite: Harvesting apples for *sidra*, Manzanova, Galicia.

Above: Classic *bodega* architecture of the Jerez region, Andalucia.

Cava

Cava is Spain's own renowned sparkling wine – very fitting for a nation given to regular celebrations.

Cava is the 'champagne' of Spain, but, of course, they can't call it that. So the story goes that when Catalan winemaker Josep Raventós i Fatjó of *Bodega Codorníu* first brewed this distinctive Iberian bubbly in 1872 he named it after the cellars, or *cava*, that nurtured it. Nice story, but *cava* was generally known as *xampany*, *champán* or *champaña* until just a few decades back when Spanish producers agreed on *cava* as a suitable new name that would not offend the French.

Codorníu still makes *cava* today in the town of Sant Sadurní d'Anoia, where around 80 per cent of Spain's *cava* producers are based – including the globally renowned Freixenet, one of the world's largest private wine corporations and the single biggest exporter of *cava*. The majority of Spain's *cava* makers are also in this same Penedès region, sandwiched between Barcelona and Tarragona where the Montserrat mountains shelter vine plantations from the humidity of the sea and the strong levanter winds.

Cava production is proscribed by *Denominación de Origen* (DO) regulations but, unlike most DO standards, the one for *cava* does not tie its production to a specific region. The DO regulates the winemaking process, not the place of production. Penedès is undeniably the soul of *cava* – more than 90 per cent of global output is produced here – but Spanish sparkling wines are also made in small quantities in Aragon, Valencia and Navarra.

Iberian varieties, international style

The trinity of grapes popularly used to produce the wine is *Parellada, Xarel-lo* and *Macabeu* (aka *Viura*), but these days *bodegas* are experimenting with other varieties like *Subirat* and the traditional French Chardonnay. Red grapes including *Garnacha* and *Monastrell* are used to create a rose version of *cava*.

Wines are made in the *méthode champenoise* style, though Catalan producers can't legally say that either. *Cava* is aged at least nine months in the bottle before sale; the more distinguished Reserva and Gran Reserva blends are left to mature for double and almost triple that time. It is made in various styles, ranging from extra brut through to *seco* (dry) and *dulce* (sweet).

The Spaniards drink a lot of *cava* at Christmas-time, when it is customary to indulge in a little luxury. Germany and the United Kingdom are the biggest overseas *cava* drinkers, each importing more than 30 million bottles a year.

Left: The cellars of Bodegas Codorniu in Sant Sadurni d'Anoia, Catalonia. Bodegas Codorniu boasts more than 30kms of underground cellars beneath the winery and vineyards.

Cava D Agustí Torelló S.A.

If there is one *cava* that comes closest to Champagne it is the *Kripta Gran Reserva Brut Nature* (preferably the 2003 vintage). Produced on an idyllic estate of sloping, vine-striped hillsides beside the Mediterranean coast, about 40 kilometres south of Barcelona, it is the elite drop of the family-owned and managed *Cava Agustí Torelló Mata*. While bulk-produced *cava* can have a reputation for being cheap fizz, the influential US wine writer Robert Parker rated the 2003 Kripta 94 out of 100 points, the highest *cava* ranking ever, and the leading French wine critic Michel Bettane described it as rivalling the finest champagnes.

Chocolate caliente
Hot chocolate

Ingredients

20g cornflour

40g white (granulated) sugar

500ml cold milk

50ml pure (single) cream*

¼ teaspoon ground cinnamon

pinch of salt

200g dark chocolate (60-70 per cent cocoa content), grated

Spanish drinking chocolate comes in a bar. It's made with sugar, cocoa, flour and spiced with a little cinnamon. One breaks it up into a saucepan of milk and then cooks it until it becomes wonderfully thick, perfect for dunking churros into. If you can't find Spanish drinking chocolate here's the very next best thing.

Method

Place cornflour and only half the sugar into a medium saucepan. Add milk, cream, cinnamon and salt. Bring to the boil over medium heat, stirring occasionally.

Add the chocolate and stir until combined and thick. Add some or all of the remaining sugar to taste.

Bring to a gentle boil, stirring constantly, and serve.

Chocolate helado
Iced chocolate

Ingredients

500ml ice-cold milk

5 large scoops chocolate ice cream

Grated chocolate, to serve

Method

Place milk and ice cream into a blender and mix until well combined. Serve directly into a tall glass or over ice in warmer weather.

Top with grated chocolate.

Café (Coffee)

Café robusta and the national caffeine fix.

Drinking coffee in Spain is an institution, and cafés are an integral part of the Spanish way of life. Tiny rooms in the bottom of an old building, perhaps once used as blacksmith shop or a hole in the old medieval wall, can be found in the smallest of towns serving coffee from early in the morning.

At the base of every apartment building in the big city suburbs will be found a similar café with the same offering – coffee, a few pastries, perhaps a shot of liquor and cigarettes.

Coffee catch-up

Coffee in Spain in general is perhaps not the world's greatest. While the Italians are famous for espresso and the northern Europeans filter some superb roasted coffee, the Spanish have a slightly more complex relationship with quality coffee.

During the Franco era, Spaniards underwent a period of economic internalisation where they didn't reach out into the world. While the rest of Europe enjoyed the flavour of more expensive Arabica beans, poorer Spain focused on getting bang for its buck from the cheaper *robusta* – now commonly used to make instant coffee.

Robusta doesn't pack a flavoursome punch, so Spanish roasters increased the flavour by roasting the beans more – even spraying them with sugar syrup for darker taste and more flavour extraction.

Changes are brewing

Today there's a strong movement to change the coffee culture in Spain, with some great coffee houses opening up that reflect the tastes of the greater global population.

Coffee is an essential part of the Spanish city life, often ordered in large ornately decorated cafés that may also have a kitchen or bakery, serving pastries and small cakes, such as *magdalenas*, which are dunked into the coffee – the first meal of the day for many city dwellers. The café owner may pour stronger drinks later in the day, but coffee will be the core of the business.

Workers may start the day with a strong black coffee, *a café solo*. Older, factory workers, enjoy a *café solo* and a shot of anise or a brandy, particularly in winter on the chilly plateaus. Many prefer *café con leche* – a milky coffee, while *café cortado* is a smaller cup 'cut' with a little milk. A *carajillo* is *café solo* with a shot of strong liquor and a piece of scorched lemon rind.

To focus on the perceived quality of coffee in Spain would be to miss the point – it's the social congregation that takes place around coffee that makes it a foundational ingredient of Spanish social life.

Café varieties

Café solo: A small black coffee enjoyed first thing in the morning or often after a main meal.

Cortado: The same as café solo but with a little splash (cut) of cream.

Carajillo: A small black coffee with a splash of Spanish brandy that's often enjoyed along with the mid-morning snack or breakfast.

Café con hielo: A hot black coffee with ice, often served in a glass – sometimes with a slice of lemon, too.

Café con leche: A medium-size mug of coffee and milk – usually about half coffee, half hot milk.

Café carajillo

Café cortado

Café con hielo

La Rioja

Logroño

La Rioja is one of the smallest of Spain's 17 autonomous communities by population and by size (it's a fraction larger than the Balearic Islands) but it has a towering reputation. It is named after the *Rio Oja*, a tributary of the mighty Ebro River that bisects the region and irrigates its fertile plains famed for their market gardens, orchards and, above all, their wines.

La Rioja has the densest concentration of wineries in Spain and is home to its oldest vineyards, many of them dating to the Roman era. Their reputations were secured in medieval times when pilgrims following the Way of St James, fortified themselves for the journey with Riojan reds. Naturally, word of La Rioja's wonder wines spread far and wide throughout Europe.

Today it remains the best-known Spanish wine region, producing around 270 million litres of vintage *vino* each year, more than 80 per cent of it rich red blends anchored in the native *tempranillo* grape. The wines are partly aged in *barricas* of American oak and partly in the bottle; two-year-old wines are known as *crianza*, three-year-olds fall into the *reserva* category, while wines aged for five years merit *gran reserva* status.

Cultivation is divided by the flow of the Ebro into Rioja Alta, which produces more elegant reds in the wetter, milder north of the region, and Rioja Baja, the drier, hotter southern region known for its robust, alcoholic wines. A third wine territory, Rioja Alavesa, follows the Ebro into Basque Country.

Signature dishes

All great wine-growing regions have a complementary food culture and La Rioja's is centred on its wealth of fresh vegetables. White asparagus, artichokes, garlic, tomatoes and aubergines are all typical of the region but the flavour that defines Riojan cuisine is the red *piquillo* pepper. This small, sweet capsicum is served with everything from salads to *lechal*, the signature Riojan roasted suckling lamb dish inherited from the Moors. Any dish described as *a la riojana* is guaranteed to contain *piquillo* peppers and, usually, chorizo.

Another quintessential local meal is *chuletas al sarmiento*, lamb chops roasted over an open fire fuelled by vine prunings. Mirroring the distinction in its wines, dishes from the north bank of the Ebro tend to be heartier – such as thick soups and robust *cocido* stews – and lighter in the south to complement the milder weather.

Widely regarded as the leading producer of fine Spanish wines, La Rioja is a small region with a huge and ancient impact on the world reputation of Spanish gastronomy – via the fruit of the vine, and hungry pilgrims.

Opposite: *Piquillo* peppers and fruit for sale in the ancient streets of Haro, La Rioja.

La Rioja – home to Spain's oldest vineyards, many dating back to the Roman era.

R. López de Heredia Viña Tondonia (Haro, La Rioja)

Established in 1877, *López de Heredia* is the oldest bodega in Haro, at the heart of Rioja. From the exquisite 19th century labels to the extended maturation of the top wines in the *Viña Tondonia* range, there is a proud commitment to preserving traditional Rioja winemaking here: the Reserva and Gran Reserva reds are not released until they are at least eight years old (even the Gran Reserva *rosato*, or pink wine, spends four years in barrel!), and old vintages dating back to the early years of the 20th century can still be bought direct from the *bodega*.

www.lopezdeheredia.com

Opposite: The barrel rooms of R Lopez de Heredia Vina Tondonia, Haro, La Rioja.

Right: Pilgrims walking the Camino de Santiago, La Rioja.

Wine and cheese: perfect partners

Cheese is a natural partner for wine and the Riojans have myriad choices (courtesy of their regional neighbours) such as *Azul de Valdeón*, also known as the DO Picos Blue, produced in Leon and the ubiquitous *manchego*. La Rioja's celebrated homegrown cheese is the pasteurised goat's milk, cottage cheese-style *Camerano* made in the *Sierra de los Cameros*. Awarded DO status in 2009 it is one of the newest additions to Spain's pantry of protected food products.

Crossroads of the Camino

Its position astride the route of pilgrims on the *Camino de Santiago de Compostela* means La Rioja has for centuries been at the crossroads of European cultures and at the vanguard of the Christian revival. The Moors left a legacy of lamb but the Christians ensured their preferred meat, pork, had a central role in La Riojan cuisine. The mountain villages, particularly, are known for their sweet but spicy black pudding, and chorizo is ubiquitous, most commonly simmered with potatoes and paprika. The Riojan version is renowned as the spiciest of Spanish sausages.

Caparrones is a common stew of chorizo and red kidney beans that is famous – or perhaps infamous – for its flatulence-inducing properties. Quails star in preparations such as *pochas con codornices*, quail cooked with white beans, piquillo peppers and tomatoes. Various recipes using snails and mushrooms are typical of the rustic, simple appeal of the village cuisine.

Being landlocked hasn't stunted the Riojans' appetite for fish. Salt cod or *bacalao* is found on menus everywhere, most commonly served a *la riojana* with tomato, garlic and liberal use of peppers including roasted red pepper flesh, paprika and cayenne. River trout is another aquatic option, especially popular when it is stuffed with ham and fried. Fresh seafood trucked in from the Bay of Biscay feeds local appetites with dishes such as hake in a green sauce of asparagus and parsley.

For those who prefer to end the meal on a sweeter note, La Rioja does a lovely version of pears poached in red wine, *peras al vino*, spiced with cinnamon sticks, cloves and ground black pepper.

gourmet
pilgrim

Referencias
Reference

A celebration of fresh
ingredients along
with tried-and-tested
methods, Spain has
a recipe for every
occasion.

Glosario
(Glossary)

Allioli	Also known as alioli, or as aioli in French cuisine. It is a strong-flavoured garlic mayonnaise widely eaten in Spain with tapas, vegetables or to accompany seafood.
Anchovy Fillets	Salted and bottled or canned in oil. Available from supermarkets. Drain well on kitchen paper towel before using.
Artichoke hearts or quarters	Are first cooked then preserved in oil, vinegar or brine and sold bottled or in bulk from supermarkets or speciality food stores. They need to be drained on a kitchen paper towel before use. Fresh globe artichokes cannot be substituted.
Aubergine (eggplant)	The most common varieties used in Mediterranean cooking are the large aubergines, which range from purple to black-skinned, or the slender or finger aubergine. They are available cooked and marinated in oil. Barbecued, marinated aubergine can be bought from delicatessens.
Bake blind	This is when a pastry shell is pre-baked with weights, such as rice, dried beans or baking beads (purchased from a kitchenware shop), before placing a filling into the pastry shell. It prevents the base of the tart from becoming too doughy once the filling is added. To bake blind, line the pastry that is in the tart or quiche tin with kitchen baking paper. Fill with rice, dried beans or baking beads until two-thirds full. Bake at 180°C for 15 minutes or until pastry is firm. Remove weights and paper. Bake for five minutes or until pastry is light golden.
Blue cheese	The most famous of the Spanish blue cheeses is the Cabrales. It has a distinctively strong flavour and originates in the northern regions of Spain where it is allowed to mature in caves. Traditionally wrapped in chestnut, fig or vine leaves, it is now sold wrapped in foil with pictures of leaves printed on it and stamped with the logo, showing proof of origin.
Bouquet garni	A bundle of herbs used to flavour a stock, soup, casserole or stew, tied with kitchen string or in a piece of muslin. Using kitchen string, tie up a fresh bay leaf, a sprig or two of fresh thyme and fresh flat leaf (Italian) parsley stalks. To stop the leaves from coming apart in the dish, tie up in muslin and add a few peppercorns.
Breadcrumbs	'Fresh' crumbs are made from bread (preferably woodfired bread or sourdough) that is one to two days old and therefore a little stale (drier). Process chunks of bread (with or without crusts) in a food processor until fine. Use as needed or store in a sealed bag or container in the freezer. Alternatively, dry packaged breadcrumbs are very fine and available from supermarkets. The two types of breadcrumbs are not interchangeable.
Butterflied (anchovies and sardines)	Remove the head, with a sharp knife just behind the side fin and discard. Using a small, sharp knife, open the sardines by cutting through the gut to the tail, then open out flat and carefully snap the backbone at the tail end. Starting from the tail end, gently pull away the backbone. Wipe over with damp kitchen paper towel.

Capers	These are the grey-green buds from a warm climate shrub prevalent in the Mediterranean. They are sold dried and salted or pickled in a vinegar brine. Rinse away the salt or brine before using. They can be found at delicatessens and most supermarkets. Capers come in a baby (small) size, regular (medium) size and as caper berries with the stalks still attached.
Cava	Spanish sparkling wine. French champagne or other sparkling white wines may be substituted.
Chicory	A plant with long, leafy stems. Also known as dandelion chicory.
Chilli paste	Sold bottled from supermarkets. For Spanish dishes, choose a paste made from red chillies with salt, vinegar and/or sugar added to preserve, as opposed to the Asian-style chilli pastes that can have quite a different flavour.
Chillies (fresh red)	Generally the smaller the chilli, the hotter it is and the seeds are the hottest part of the chilli. When preparing chillies, always wear rubber gloves and wash the knife and board well after use.
Chipolatas	A small, thin, highly seasoned sausage.
Chorizo sausage	A pork sausage, flavoured with spices, garlic and paprika. Chorizo is available fresh, where it needs to be cooked before eating – either pan fried or chopped and added to dishes for flavour. It is also sold dry cured or 'cooked' and ready to eat.
Cream	Single (pouring) cream contains 35 per cent saturated fat and can be whipped or used unwhipped. Thickened cream contains 35 per cent saturated fat with a thickening agent, such as gelatine, added to act as a stabiliser. It has a thick pouring consistency and is ideally used for whipping.
Crème fraiche	A slightly fermented cream, which causes it to thicken. It has a much richer and more refined taste than sour cream and is available at most supermarkets or speciality stores.
Dry fry	Often used for toasting spices or herbs in a hot dry frying pan without fat or oil for a short time to release their natural oils. Foods with a naturally high fat content, such as jamon*, can also be dry fried to crispen without adding extra fat or oil to the pan.
Egg mayonnaise	If using bought mayonnaise, choose an egg mayonnaise, as it is naturally thicker with a much better flavour. Alternatively, see recipe in the Sauces chapter for an easy, homemade mayonnaise.
Eggs	If using for sweets and baking, they should be at room temperature. Unless otherwise stated, cold eggs taken from the refrigerator are fine to use in savoury dishes. Free-range (open range) eggs come from hens allowed to roam freely. The eggs have a better flavour than regular eggs from caged hens. Free-range eggs are preferred in egg-based dishes, such omelettes and custards.
Emmental cheese	A yellow, medium-hard cheese with holes in it from Switzerland. It is usually used in gratins.
Endive	Also known as curly endive or frisee. It has green frilly leaves and can be eaten raw or cooked.
Eschalots	Also known as French shallots or scallions.

French trimmed	This technique is often used to prepare lamb cutlets, lamb shanks or chicken legs. Ask your butcher to French trim the meat for you. Alternatively, use a small, sharp knife to scrape and cut away all the skin, meat and fat from one end of the bone, making it more decorative and easier to pick up. Also trim away the excess fat.
Fried bread croutons	Cut day-old bread into cubes and shallow-fry in olive oil. (Alternatively, place onto an oven tray, lightly spray with olive oil and bake in a preheated 180°C oven until lightly golden).
Goat's cheese	There are many types of goat's cheeses from Spain, with each region having its own speciality. The more mature hard goat's cheeses include Murcia al Vino, which is rubbed with red wine, or the Montsec from the Catalonia region, which is rubbed with wood ash. Less mature, soft or fresh goat's cheeses are paler in colour, more crumbly and spreadable; they're often used in tapas, crumbled into soups or used in sweet or savoury tart fillings.
Green peppercorns	Immature peppercorns that are picked and then packed in brine. They are available in jars or tins from supermarkets.
Hard-boiled eggs	Place eggs in a saucepan and cover with cold water. Bring to the boil and cook for 10 minutes, then cool in cold water before peeling. To cook quail eggs, boil for just one minute then cool before peeling.
Jamon (Spanish ham)	Jamon comes in two varieties – jamón serrano or jamón iberico. They are both salt-cured and air-dried, giving them their characteristicly dry and strong ham taste and dark-red flesh. The serrano is hung to dry for at least 12 months and the iberico can be left to dry for two or more years, giving it a more intense flavour. The jamón iberico comes from a different pig that is much fatter, producing jamon with more marbling through it. A sub-category of the iberico is the highly prized jamón iberico bellota. For this variety, pigs are allowed to roam freely in the meadows, and in autumn allowed to feed on acorns, which creates even more marbling. An alternative would be prosciutto, which is also an intensely flavoured salt-cured ham. The paper-thin slices of jamon are eaten raw or used to flavour cooked and uncooked dishes. Available from most speciality food stores, butchers and supermarkets.
Julienne	A method of cutting vegetables, such as carrots, leeks and parsnips, into long, thin strips of about 2mm thick and 3cm long. To julienne a carrot, use a mandolin* or a sharp knife to cut it into 3cm sections. Thinly slice lengthways into 2mm thick slices then cut each slice into 2mm thick strips.
Knock back	Also known as 'punching down' a dough, meaning to re-knead a proven dough after the first rise. It involves punching down the dough (literally, one punch) to expel the air and knead again briefly for one minute or until smooth. The dough is now ready for shaping. Handle carefully, avoiding excessive reshaping. Cover dough and allow to stand in a warm place until doubled in size – this is the final rise for the dough before baking.
Lamb's lettuce (mâche)	Also known as corn salad or field lettuce. It has a soft and velvety tongue-shaped leaf and can be eaten raw or cooked.
Langoustine (scampi)	Also known as 'Norway lobster', is very similar to Dublin Bay prawns. If using fresh live langoustine, ask your fish merchant to kill them humanely for you. If using frozen, uncooked langoustine, defrost in the refrigerator overnight before cooking.

Manchego cheese	A famous Spanish cheese made from the milk of Manchego sheep. It can be sliced but has a crumbly texture with a piquant, nutty flavour. Delicious simply served with bread, membrillo (quince paste)* or jamon*.
Mandolin	A very sharp slicing tool, mostly used to cut vegetables or fruit.
Manzanilla sherry	A very fine (fino) and light sherry that is the driest and lightest in colour of all sherries produced in Spain. Manzanilla sherry is only produced in the Sanlúcar de Barrameda region of Spain and bottles bear the seal of origin. If unavailable, use another fine sherry.
Mascarpone	A cultured cream cheese. It is creamy yellow in colour with a soft, smooth texture and delicately sweet, slightly acidic flavour. Mascarpone is available in tubs from the dairy section of the supermarket.
Membrillo (quince paste)	A sweet, very dense fruit paste made from quinces. It is often served as a dessert, or sliced and served with bread and manchego cheese. Available in tubs from the supermarket or can be purchased in blocks by the kilo from delicatessens or speciality food stores.
Mortadella	A large, cooked pork sausage originating from Bologna, Italy. The pork is lightly spiced and finely ground with characteristic squares of fat, pistachio nuts and peppercorns visible throughout the sausage. Usually served thinly sliced and available from supermarkets, butchers and speciality food stores.
Mussels, cleaned and debearded	To prepare uncooked mussels, scrub the mussel shells with a stiff brush and remove the fibrous beards.
Nasturtium flowers	Both nasturtium flowers and leaves are edible. With a peppery taste, similar to watercress, they're often used in salads to add colour and flavour.
Orange blossom water	Also known as orange flower water. It is made from distilled water containing the essential oils of the orange blossom. Orange blossom water is used extensively in Mediterranean and Middle Eastern dishes and is available from kitchen grocery stores. The much stronger orange essence cannot be used as a substitute.
Paella rice	Calasparra is Spanish short-grain rice, widely available in good kitchen grocery stores. Arborio may be used instead.
Pamplona cured sausage	A large, cured, chorizo-style sausage, with a distinctive smoky flavour from the smoked paprika. It is usually served thinly sliced with tapas.
Pancetta	Thinly sliced rounds of salt-cured pork belly, often eaten raw, as in tapas or antipasto, or cooked like bacon. Expect it to be rather fatty.
Paprika (all varieties)	In Spain, paprika is known as Pimentón, and is available in numerous varieties (sweet smoked, mild, hot); pimentón ahumado, for example, has a distinct smoky flavour and aroma as it is dried by smoking, typically using oak wood. It is available in three versions; mild, moderately spicy and very spicy. Outside of Spain, pimentón ahumado is often referred to as simply "smoked paprika" and can be found in varying intensities from sweet and mild (dulce), medium hot (agridulce), or very hot and spicy (picante).
Pastry (pre-rolled puff and shortcrust)	These pastries can be bought frozen in blocks or in ready-rolled sheets from the freezer section of supermarkets.
Peppers (capsicums)	Also known as bell peppers, mainly available in red, green and yellow. Banana peppers are long with a pointy end and are also available in red, green and yellow. See *Roasted peppers (capsicums)* for roasting.

Pomegranate	To prepare the pomegranate, use a sharp knife to cut it in half. Holding the pomegranate skin side up over a large bowl, use the back of a large spoon to firmly tap the skin until all the seeds have fallen into the bowl. The seeds can be stored for two days in the refrigerator or frozen until needed.
Quail eggs	About an eighth the size of chicken eggs but with a much thinner mottled shell, they need to be handled carefully. See hard-boiled eggs for cooking instructions.
Quark	A soft and smooth fresh cheese that's very similar to creamed cottage cheese but with a more tangy flavour. It is sold in tubs in the dairy section of good supermarkets or speciality food stores.
Roasted peppers (capsicums)	To roast peppers, quarter peppers and remove seeds and membranes. Place under a preheated grill and cook until skin blackens and blisters. Transfer to a bowl and cover with a tea towel for a few minutes until cool enough to handle. Remove the skin and use as required. Roasted peppers are also readily available from good supermarkets and grocery stores.
Roasted sunflower seeds, pine nuts, almonds and hazelnuts	Preheat oven to 180°C. Place seeds or nuts on a baking tray and bake, tossing occasionally, for 10-15 minutes or until lightly golden. After roasting the hazelnuts, tip them onto a clean tea towel and rub off the skins.
Rucola	Also known as arugula, rugula and rocket; a peppery-tasting green leaf that can be eaten raw in salad or used in cooking. Baby rocket leaves are smaller and milder in taste.
Saffron threads	Dried stigmas handpicked from the saffron crocus flower. Available in strands/threads or ground (powdered) form, saffron imparts a yellow-orange colour to food once infused. Quality varies greatly – the better quality saffron adds a unique flavour, too. It is considered one of the most expensive spices in the world.
Salted cod	Traditionally, the fish salted and dried and known as baccalà or bacalao is cod. However, in other countries, such as Australia, ling is also used. Although quite strong smelling, the flesh is quite soft and flaky after soaking. It needs to be soaked in water, with the water changed every 8-12 hours to remove the excess salt.
Semolina	A type of wheat flour, semolina is the coarse particles left when wheat is milled, then sifted. Semolina sprinkled in the base of a fruit tart will soak up any excess juice. Generally sold in fine, medium or coarse texture from most supermarkets and speciality food stores.
Sherry vinegar	Also know as sherry wine vinegar, it's made from sherry and produced in Spain.
Shrimp (prawns)	Green shrimp are uncooked and are usually peeled and deveined before use. To devein a shrimp, remove the head then pull out the digestive tract or vein, which can be quite gritty if not removed. Alternatively, make a shallow cut along the back of the shrimp and remove the vein. Uncooked shrimp shells are often reserved to make a strong-tasting stock.
Smoked sea salt	Salt crystals infused with a mild, yet distinctly smoky aroma and flavour. Considered a gourmet product, it is available from speciality food stores.
Spagattini pasta	Also known as spaghettini. It is very long, thin strands of pasta that are thinner than spaghetti but thicker than vermicelli. Available dried in packets from most supermarkets.

Spanish black olives	Spain is one of the world's largest producers of olives. The black olives are large and round (Hojiblanca variety), cured in brine and available at supermarkets and speciality food stores.
Spanish white sausage	Also known as butifarra sausage, famous in the Catalan region of Spain.
Sparkling apple cider	Also known as sparkling apple juice.
Spring onions	Also known as green shallots, they are an immature, mild-tasting onion with a straight stem. Often used raw in salads or cooked to impart a mild onion flavour.
Sterilised jar	To sterilise jars or bottles, first wash jars and lids in hot soapy water; rinse well. Place jars and lids into a large saucepan and fill with water. Cover, bring to the boil and simmer over medium heat for 10 minutes. Use tongs to carefully remove jars and lids and drain upside down on a clean tea towel. Transfer to a large baking tray and dry in a 150°C oven for 15 minutes. For bottling hot jams or preserves, use jars while hot. For bottling cold preserves, such as liqueurs, allow the jars or bottles to cool on the tray before using. Avoid touching the inside surface of the jars or lids.
Strong (baker's) flour	Wheat flour with a higher gluten content; ideal for making breads, pastries and pasta. Also known as bread flour.
Tomato paste	A very thick concentrated paste of tomatoes used in small quantities to add a rich tomato flavour and colour to sauces, soups and stews.
Tomato puree	Also known as passata. It's strained, crushed tomato pulp, added to soups, pasta sauces, pizzas and other savoury dishes. It can be chunky or smooth and is readily available from the supermarket, usually in bottles or jars. You can make your own using fresh, ripe tomatoes by simply removing the skin and pressing through a sieve to remove the seeds.
Vanilla bean	The true form of vanilla is a thin dark bean or pod from a wild orchid that grows in the tropics. The bean is often used in cooking, either whole or slit through the middle to reveal the fragrant seeds nestled inside. The seeds can be scraped out using the tip of a sharp knife.
Vanilla extract	Vanilla extract is made from finely chopped vanilla beans that have been soaked in alcohol to extract flavour and fragrance. Imitation vanilla should be avoided, as it is inferior in flavour and aroma.
Vanilla paste	A thick paste with a high concentration of vanilla seeds. Often corn syrup is added and sometimes blended vanilla pods are also used to add flavour.
Veal jus	A more concentrated form of veal stock, available in butchers and speciality food stores.
Water bath	To do this, place the cake pan into a large baking dish then into the preheated oven. Carefully pour boiling water into the baking dish until it comes halfway up the sides of the cake pan. Bake as instructed in recipe.
Zucchini (courgette/s)	Available in dark green, light green or yellow. Zucchini flowers are edible and often stuffed and cooked before serving.

Following page: Traditional ribbon dance at the 'Festival of the Phyloxera', Sant Sadurni d'Anoia, Catalonia.

Pesos y medidas
(weights & measures)

Volume conversions

1 teaspoon = 5ml

1 Italian tablespoon = 15ml

1 UK, US & NZ tablespoon = 15ml

1 Australian tablespoon = 20ml

1 cup = 250ml (8 fl oz)

Liquid conversions

Metric	Imperial	US cups
30ml	1 fl oz	⅛ cup
60ml	2 fl oz	¼ cup
80ml	2 ¾ fl oz	⅓ cup
125ml	4 fl oz	½ cup
185ml	6 fl oz	¾ cup
250ml	8 fl oz	1 cup
375ml	12 fl oz	1½ cups
500ml	16 fl oz	2 cups
600ml	20 fl oz	2½ cups
750ml	24 fl oz	3 cups
1 litre	32 fl oz	4 cups

Oven temperature conversions

	C°	F°	Gas mark
Very cool	110-120	225-250	¼-½
Cool	140-150	275-300	1-2
Moderate	160-180	325-350	3-4
Moderately hot	190-200	375-400	5-6
Hot	220-230	425-450	7-8
Very hot	240	475	9

Cross of the Order of Santiago

Template – see recipe page 380

Índice
(Index)

A

Aceitunas negras maceradas con ajo y chili 100
Aceitunas verdes maceradas con especias 100
Acknowledgement 02
Ajoblanco 66
Albariño 452
Albóndigas con salsa de tomate 276
Alcachofas con pinones y aceitunas 182
Alfajores 436
Alicante 196, 452
Alioli 154
Almendras Saladas 86
Almond & pine nut balls 432
Almond bars 424
Almond pudding with honey 382
Almonds 72-73, 258
    Almond & pine nut balls 432
    Almond bars 424
    Almond pudding with honey 382
    Chilled almond & garlic soup 66
    Romescu sauce 150
    Salted almonds 86
    Soft almond & rosemary nougat 426
    St James tart 380
Anchovies 143, 208, 482
    Asturian rice & seafood salad 20
    Calamari with anchovy, lemon & thyme stuffing 214
    Manchego stuffed zucchini flowers 88
    Marinated anchovies 110
    Pastry sticks with manchego & anchovies 98
    Romaine lettuce, tuna & anchovy salad 16
    Sardine & caramelised onion coca 236
    Stuffed tomatoes 180
    Tostada with tomato & anchovies 94
Andaluciá 14, 39, 44, 54, 83, **440-443**
Andulacian chilled tomato & garlic soup 54
Apple cider sauce
    Hake & shrimp in apple cider sauce 212
Apple tart 384
Apples
    Apple tart 384
    Beetroot, apple & pomegranate salad 26
    Cabrales & apple pinchos 128
    Sweet Catalan flatbread 346
Aragón **327-329**
Aranjuez 44

Aromatic braised kid (or lamb) 300
Arroz con leche 390
Arroz de carne 280
Arroz negro con sepia y langostins 244
Artichokes 192, 482
    Artichokes with pine nuts, olives & thyme 182
    Braised octopus with tomato & artichokes 224
    Green olive, artichoke & salmon pinchos 104
    Spiced meat & rice dish 280
    Roast potatoes with artichokes & thyme 184
Artichokes with pine nuts, olives and thyme 182
Asador Etxebarri 254
Asparagus
    Jamon-wrapped asparagus with fennel salad 86
    Mediterranean seafood salad 30
    White asparagus with hazelnuts & manchego 170
Asturian pasta 278
Asturian rice & seafood salad 20
Asturias 20, 368-369
Asturias rice pudding 390
Atún a la brasa 242
Atún fresco con cebollitas 84
Aubergine 482
    Catalan-style roast vegetables with herbs 186
    Mediterranean dip 110
    Roasted red pepper & aubergine soup 70
    Samfaina bake 168
Avant-garde Spanish cuisine 09, 143

B

Bacalao, see also cod 88, 200, 204
Bacalao al ajoarriero 112
Balearic Islands **160-161**
Balsamic onions 242
Balsamic vinegar 128
Banana fritters 402
Banderillas 78, 110
Barbeque grill **254**
Barcelona 124, 188, 255, 412
Basque Country 10, 83, **140-143**, 461
Beef 199, 324
    Beef sausages in white wine 132
    Catalan Escudella 56
    Fillet of beef with blue cheese 316

Savoury filled peppers with tomato sauce 176
Slow cooked beef cheeks 314
Stuffed onions 174
Beef sausages in white wine 132
Beetroot, apple & pomegranate salad 26
Beverages **445-479**
Biscuits, see sweets & biscuits
Black rice with squid, shrimp & chorizo 244
Bobal 452
Bocadillo 336
Bocados de manchego 114
Bodega Codorníu 468
Boquerones en vinagre 110
Bouquet garni 482
Braised octopus with tomato & artichokes 224
Braised oxtail 312
Brandy de Jerez **468**
Brazo de gitano 388
Bread 331-353
Andulacian chilled tomato & garlic soup 54
Bocadillo 336
Cabrales & apple pinchos 128
Campestre bread 346
Catalan tomato bread 124
Chilled almond & garlic soup 66
Chilli cornbread 346
Coca dough 346
Fried bread, chorizo & black olives 130
Fried breadcrumbs with chorizo 334
Green pepper & tortilla canapes 122
Jamon & egg canapés 122
La Rioja caramelised bread 342
Montadito 338
Romescu sauce 150
Rustic bread 346
Sardines on toast 130
Savoury Catalan flatbread 344
Smoked salmon & radish pinchos 96
Sweet Catalan flatbread 346
Sweet Mallorcan bread scroll 340
Tomato with calamari soup 58
Tostada with tomato & anchovies 94
Breadcrumbs 482
Veal cutlets with warm potato salad 310
Fried breadcrumbs with chorizo 334
Raisin crumb 438
Broad beans with jamon 90
Broquetas de cordero a la plancha 304
Broquetas de pollo con salsa de yogur 286
Butifarra 413
Butter beans
Asturian pasta 278
Butter bean, tomato & jamon soup 50
Spicy sausage with butterbeans & tomato 274

C

Cabrales & apple pinchos 128
Cabrito estofado 300
Café con hielo 472
Café con leche 472
Café solo 472
Calamares relleno 214
Calamares con mayonesa de ajo 94
Calamari, see also squid
Tomato with calamari soup 58
Calamari with anchovy, lemon & thyme stuffing 214
Calasparra rice 40
Caldereta 75, 160
Caldero 41
Campestre bread 348
Canapés de cebolleta 134
Canapés de jamón y huevo 122
Canapés de pescadito y pimientos del piquillo 134
Canapés de tortilla y pimento verde 122
Canary Islands 152, 156, **158-159**
Cangrejos a la Riojana 234
Canónigos con jamón y queso 32
Cantabria 16, 20, 264-265
Capsicum, see peppers
Caracoles 132
Carajillo 472
Caramelised Catalan custard 406
Carinena/mazuelo 452
Carrilleras 314
Carquinyolis 424
Casa Botín 263
Casseroles 270
Braised oxtail 312
Chicken casserole 284
Garlic chicken with a touch of cava 124
Nun's casserole, the 250
Castilla-La Mancha **364-367**
Castilla-León **324-326**
Castillian mussels 222
Catalan Escudella 56
Catalan salad 36
Catalan tomato bread 124
Catalan-style roast vegetables with herbs 186
Catalonia 10, 56, **412-415**, 432
Cava 446, **468-469**, 483
Egg custard with cava 404
Fresh fruit salad with cava syrup 410
Garlic chicken with a touch of cava 124
Pheasant with red fruits & cava 294
Shrimp with cava 90
Cava D Agustí Torelló S.A. 469
Cebollas rellenas 174

Chacoli 461
Champinones rellenos 118
Char-grilled lamb skewers 304
Char-grilled tuna with balsamic onions 242
Cheese 74, 143, 159, 200, 265, 329, **359-363**, 364, 366, 368, 443, 479, 482, 483, 484, 485
    Cabrales & apple pinchos 128
    Fillet of beef with blue cheese 316
    Jamon, cheese & date salad 32
    Cheese mint tart and aniseed 408
Cheese, goats
    Creamy zucchini soup 62
    Tasty cherry tomatoes 84
    Tomato, goat's cheese & pine nut salad 24
Cheese, Manchego
    Bocadillo 336
    Chilli cornbread 346
    Chorizo & herb-stuffed mushrooms 118
    Creamy zucchini soup 62
    Empanadilla of olives & jamon 116
    Fried breadcrumbs with chorizo 334
    Lamb meatloaf 104
    Manchego bites 114
    Manchego stuffed zucchini flowers 88
    Montadito 338
    Mushroom & cheese-topped sole 230
    Pastry sticks with manchego & anchovies 98
    Samfaina bake 168
    Valencian orange & manchego cheese salad 18
    White asparagus with hazelnuts & manchego 170
Cheese – varieties
    Asturian 368
    Blue 482
    Cabrales 128, 368
    Camerano 479
    Emmental 32, 483
    Flor de Guia 159
    Gamonedo 368
    Goats 159, 484
    Idiazabal 143
    Mahón 360
    Majorero 159
    Manchego 360, 364, 366, 485
    Murcia al Vino 363
    Palmero 159
    Payoyo 443
    Picón Bejes-Tresviso 265
    Roncal 200
    San Simón 363
    Tetilla 363
    Torta del Casar 74, 363
    Tronchón 329
    Valdeón 362

Chestnut and mushroom soup 52
Chicken
    Catalan Escudella 56
    Chicken casserole 284
    Chicken skewers with yoghurt mint sauce 286
    Chicken with red peppers & jamon 288
    Crisp spiced chicken with red pepper jam 282
    Garlic chicken with a touch of cava 124
    Paprika & herb-coated chicken 120
Chicken casserole 284
Chicken liver pâte
    Stuffed leg of lamb 302
Chicken skewers with yoghurt mint sauce 286
Chicken with red peppers and jamon 288
Chickpeas
    Catalan Escudella 56
    Chickpeas with chorizo 172
    Nun's casserole, the 250
Chickpeas with chorizo 172
Chilled almond and garlic soup 66
Chilli & garlic marinated black olives 100
Chilli cornbread 350
Chillies, red 483
    Chilli & garlic marinated black olives 100
    Crabs a la rioja 234
    Crisp spiced chicken with red pepper jam 282
    Garlic chilli shrimp 228
    Liver in sherry-vinegar sauce 308
    Romescu sauce 150
    Spicy fried mushrooms 120
Chocolate 354
    Chocolate filled doughnut logs 430
    Hot chocolate 470
    Iced chocolate 470
Chocolate helado 470
Chorizo and herb-stuffed mushrooms 118
Chorizo and potatoes 106
Chorizo, Spanish 323, 483
    Asturian pasta 278
    Black rice with squid, shrimp & chorizo 244
    Catalán salad 36
    Chickpeas with chorizo 172
    Chorizo & herb-stuffed mushrooms 118
    Chorizo & potatoes 106
    Fried bread, chorizo & black olives 130
    Fried breadcrumbs with chorizo 334
    Lamb cutlets in chorizo tomato sauce 306
    Rabbit & potato stew 298
    Spiced meat & rice dish 280
    Spicy sausage with butterbeans & tomato 274
Chuchos 430
Chuletas de cordero en salsa 306

Chuletas de ternera con ensalada de patatas 310
Churros 354, 421, 422
Cider 369, **466**
Cinnamon 372
    Asturias rice pudding 390
    Caramelised Catalan custard 406
    Cinnamon ice cream 392
    Fried milk 378
    La Rioja caramelised bread 342
    Orange custard flan 374
    Pears cooked in red wine 374
    White sangria 454
Cinnamon ice cream 392
Citrus **39**, 372
Coca de sardinas 236
Coca dough
    Coca dough 346
    Sardine & caramelised onion coca 236
    Savoury Catalan flatbread 344
    Sweet Catalan flatbread 346
Cocas dulces 346
Cocas saladas 344
Cocido de la monja 252
Cocido esto fado 298
Cocidos 07, 44, 261, 265, 270
Cod 204
Cod, salt 200, 325, 486
    Salt cod potato cakes with roasted red pepper 112
    Salted cod & orange salad 246
Codornices al vino tinto 292
Coffee **472**
Colifor con puerros y ajos 178
Comida de pueblo (food of the people) 298
Comino de Santiago de Compostela 479
Compango 369
Conejo al jerez 296
Cortado 472
Courgettes, see zucchini
Crabs Riojan style 234
Creamy zucchini soup 62
Crema Catalána 406
Crisp spiced chicken with red pepper jam 282
Croquetas de jamón 126

Custard
    Caramelised Catalan custard 406
    Egg custard with cava 404
    Heaven's bacon 394
    Natillas custard 396

D

Deliciosos tomates cherry 84
Denominación de Origen 166, 199, 258, 327, 446, **460**
Desserts 371-411
    Almond pudding with honey 382
    Apple tart 384
    Asturias rice pudding 390
    Banana fritters 402
    Caramelised Catalan custard 406
    Cinnamon ice cream 392
    Cream cheese mint tart 408
    Egg custard with cava 404
    Fig cake 386
    Fresh fruit salad with cava syrup 410
    Fried milk 378
    Galician pancakes 398
    Gypsy's Arm rolled sponge cake 388
    Heaven's bacon 394
    Natillas custard 396
    Orange custard flan 374
    Pears cooked in red wine 374
    Quince paste 400
    St James tart 380
Dips 159
Dough
    Alfajores 436
    Churros 422
    Filled doughnut logs 430
    Shortbread cookies 434
Drinks **445-479**
Duck with mushrooms and potatoes 290
Dulce de membrillo 400

E

Egg custard with cava 404
Egg mayonnaise, see also mayonnaise 483
Eggs on pisto 96
Eggplant, see aubergine
Eggs 483, 484
    Almond pudding with honey 382
    Andulacian chilled tomato & garlic soup 54
    Banana fritters 402
    Caramelised Catalan custard 406
    Cinnamon ice cream 392
    Cream cheese mint tart 408
    Egg custard with cava 404
    Eggs on pisto 96
    Empanadilla of olives & jamon 116
    Fig cake 386

Filled doughnut logs 430
Fried milk 378
Garlic sauce (Allioli) 154
Green dipping sauce (Mojo verde) 152
Gypsy's Arm rolled sponge cake 388
Heaven's bacon 394
La Rioja caramelised bread 342
Magdalenas 428
Mayonnaise 148
Natillas custard 396
Navarra-style eggs 114
Orange custard flan 374
Potato tortilla 102
Raisin crumb 438
Soft almond & rosemary nougat 426
St James tart 380
Eggs, quail 486
Green bean salad with quail eggs 22
Jamon & egg canapés 122
Russian salad 28
El Celler de Can Roca 10, 254
El salpicon 364
elBulli 09, 10, 413
Empanadilla of olives and jamon 116
Empanadillas de aceitunas y jamón 116
Ensaimada 340
Ensalada Asturiana de arroz 20
Ensalada Catalána 36
Ensalada de atún, anchoas e hinojo 16
Ensalada de bacalao con naranjas 248
Ensalada de judías con huevos 22
Ensalada de patata y anchicoria 34
Ensalada de remolacha con manzana 26
Ensalada de tomate 24
Ensalada Mediterránea de marisco 30
Ensalada Valenciana 18
Ensaladilla Rusa 28
Equipo Navazos 463
Escabeche de pescados 250
Escalivada de verduras (Catalána) 186
Escudella Catalána 56
Esparrágos blancos con avellanas 170
Esparragos enrollados con jamón 86
Extremadura 14, 73, **74-75**, 193

F

Fabadas 278, 368
Faisán con furtos rojos 294
Fideua 232

Fig cake 386
Figs & jamon pinchos with balsamic glaze 128
Fillet of beef with blue cheese 316
Filloas Gallegas 398
Fish and seafood 07, 40, 143, 159, 196, **203-253**, 258, 265, 369, 413, 442
Asturian rice & seafood salad 20
Black rice with squid, shrimp & chorizo 244
Braised octopus with tomato & artichokes 224
Calamari with anchovy, lemon & thyme stuffing 214
Castillian mussels 222
Char-grilled tuna with balsamic onions 242
Crabs a la rioja 234
Fish stew 238
Fresh tuna with baby onions & olives 84
Garlic chilli shrimp 228
Hake & shrimp in apple cider sauce 212
Hake in green sauce 220
Lemon sole strips with dill mayonnaise 98
Lobster with tomato & olive salsa 246
Mackerel, pasta & paprika soup 60
Marinated anchovies 110
Mediterranean seafood salad 30
Monkfish, tomato & hazelnut bake 240
Mushroom & cheese-topped sole 230
Pickled fish with olives & vegetables 248
Piquillo pepper & whitebait canapés 134
Potato and mushroom stuffed turbot 226
Potato, chicory & tuna salad 34
Romaine lettuce, tuna & anchovy salad 16
Sailor s seafood soup 46
Salt cod potato cakes with roasted red pepper 112
Salted cod & orange salad 246
Sardine & caramelised onion coca 236
Sardines on toast 130
Sardines with paprika tomato sauce 216
Seafood fideua 232
Seafood paella 210
Shrimp with cava 90
Smoked salmon & radish pinchos 96
Squid with garlic mayonnaise 94
The nun's casserole 250
Tomato with calamari soup 58
Tuna & potato stew 218
Whitebait with allioli 118
Flan de almendra 382
Flan de naranja 376
Flao 408
Flor 462
Flores de calabacín rellenas 88

Free-range farming 319
Freixenet 468
Fresh fruit salad with cava syrup 410
Fresh tuna with baby onions & olives 84
Fried bread, chorizo and black olives 130
Fried breadcrumbs with chorizo 334
Fried milk 378
Fruit and vegetables 163-186
    Artichokes with pine nuts, olives & thyme 182
    Catalan-style roast vegetables with herbs 186
    Chickpeas with chorizo 172
    Fresh fruit salad with cava syrup 410
    Roast cauliflower with leek and garlic 178
    Roast potatoes with artichokes & thyme 184
    Samfaina bake 168
    Savoury filled peppers with tomato sauce 176
    Stuffed onions 174
    Stuffed tomatoes 180
    White asparagus with hazelnuts & manchego 170

G

Galicia 92, 222, **257-259**, 398
Galician pancakes 398
Gambas al ajillo 228
Gambas al cava 90
Game 272, 322
Garbanzos con chorizo 172
Garlic
    Andulacian chilled tomato & garlic soup 54
    Castillian mussels 222
    Catalan tomato bread 124
    Catalan-style roast vegetables with herbs 186
    Char-grilled lamb skewers 304
    Chicken casserole 284
    Chilled almond & garlic soup 66
    Chilli & garlic marinated black olives 100
    Chorizo & herb-stuffed mushrooms 118
    Garlic chicken with a touch of cava 124
    Garlic chilli shrimp 228
    Garlic sauce (Allioli) 154
    Garlic snails 132
    Herb-marinated green olives 100
    Roast cauliflower with leek & garlic 178
    Slow cooked beef cheeks 314
Garlic chicken with a touch of cava 126
Garlic chilli shrimp 228
Garlic sauce (Allioli) 154
Garlic snails 132

Garlicky bread 58
Garnacha 452
Gazpacho 54, 66, 198
Gazpacho a la Andaluza 54
Glossary **482-487**
Graciano 452
Green bean salad with quail eggs 22
Green dipping sauce 152
Green olive, artichoke & salmon pinchos 104
Green pepper & tortilla canapés 122
Green sauce 220
Gypsy's Arm rolled sponge cake 388

H

Habas con jamón 90
Hake & shrimp in apple cider sauce 212
Hake in green sauce 220
Ham, see also jamon 268, 325, 442
    Andulacian chilled tomato & garlic soup 54
    Butter bean, tomato & jamon soup 50
    Catalán salad 36
Hazlenuts
    Apple tart 384
    Monkfish, tomato & hazelnut bake 240
    Romescu sauce 150
    White asparagus with hazelnuts & manchego 170
Heaven's bacon (Toffee Custard) 394
Helado de canela 392
Herb-marinated green olives 100
Hígado en vinagreta 308
History of Spanish food **04-11**
Honey 372
    Almond pudding with honey 382
    Banana fritters 402
    Magdalenas 428
    Soft almond & rosemary nougat 426
Hot chocolate 470
Huerta 40, 164, 196
Huevos a la Navarra 114
Huevos con pisto 96
Hunger years, the **356**
Hunting 272, **322**

I

Iberico hams 319
Ice cream, cinnamon 392

J

Jamon 09, 50, 268, **318-321**, 325, 442, 484
    Bocadillo 336
    Broad beans with jamon 90
    Chorizo & herb-stuffed mushrooms 118
    Empanadilla of olives & jamon 116
    Figs & jamon pinchos with balsamic glaze 128
    Jamon & egg canapés 122
    Jamon-wrapped asparagus with fennel salad 86
    Jamon, cheese & date salad 32
    Navarra-style eggs 114
    Russian salad 28
    Spicy fried mushrooms 120
    Stuffed onions 174
Jamon and egg canapés 122
Jamon, cheese & date salad 32
Jamon croquettes 126
Jamón ibérico de bellota 74, 325
Jamon, serrano 319, 327
    Asturian pasta 278
    Basque eggs on pisto 96
    Chicken with red peppers & jamon 288
    Jamon croquettes 126
    Lamb cutlets in chorizo tomato sauce 306
    Lentil, tomato & jamon soup 64
    Spiced meat & rice dish 280
    Veal cutlets with warm potato salad 310
Jamon-wrapped asparagus with fennel salad 86
Jerez, see also sherry 443, 461, **462-465**
Judías blancas con chorizo picante y tomate 274
Julián Martín 321

K

Kid
    Aromatic braised kid (or lamb) 300

L

La Rioja **476-479**
La Rioja fried bread 342
Lamb 75, 199, 270, 328, 476
    Aromatic braised kid (or lamb) 300
    Catalan Escudella 56
    Char-grilled lamb skewers 304
    Lamb cutlets in chorizo tomato sauce 306
    Lamb meatloaf 104
    Stuffed leg of lamb 302
Lamb cutlets in chorizo tomato sauce 306
Lamb and red pepper meatloaf 104
Langostinas con salsa de tomate 246

Langoustine 484
    Catalan fish stew 238
    Seafood paella 210
Lard 270
Leche frita 378
Leek
    Chestnut & mushroom soup 52
    Leek & potato soup with croutons 48
    Roast cauliflower with leek and garlic 178
    Slow cooked beef cheeks 314
Leek & potato soup with croutons 48
Lemon sole strips with dill mayonnaise 98
Lemons
    Caramelised Catalan custard 406
    Cream cheese mint tart 408
    La Rioja caramelised bread 342
    Natillas custard 396
    Pears cooked in red wine 374
    Quince paste 400
    Red sangria 456
    St James tart 380
    White sangria 454
Lenguado con setas y queso 230
Lentil, tomato & jamon soup 64
Liver in sherry-vinegar sauce 308
Lobster with tomato & olive salsa 246
López de Heredia Viña Tondonia 449

M

Macedonia al cava 410
Mackerel, pasta & paprika soup 60
Madrid 28, 78, 83, 222, **260-263**
Magdalenas 428
Mahón 148, 160
Manchego bites 114
Manchego stuffed zucchini flowers 88
Manzanilla sherry 485
Mar i muntanya 413
Marie biscuits 258, 357
Marinated anchovies 110
Markets **188-189**, 322
Marzipan 418
Masa de coca 346
Mayonnaise 160, 483
    Beetroot, apple & pomegranate salad 26
    Lemon sole strips with dill mayonnaise 98
    Mayonnaise 148
    Potato, chicory & tuna salad 34
    Russian salad 28
    Smoked salmon & radish pinchos 96

Squid with garlic mayonnaise 94
Veal cutlets with warm potato salad 310
Meat 267-323
Aromatic braised kid (or lamb) 300
Asturian pasta 278
Beef sausages in white wine 132
Braised oxtail 312
Catalan Escudella 56
Char-grilled lamb skewers 304
Chicken casserole 284
Chicken skewers with yoghurt mint sauce 286
Chicken with red peppers & jamon 288
Crisp spiced chicken with red pepper jam 282
Duck with mushrooms & potatoes 290
Fillet of beef with blue cheese 316
Garlic chicken with a touch of cava 124
Lamb cutlets in chorizo tomato sauce 306
Lamb meatloaf 104
Liver in sherry-vinegar sauce 308
Meatballs in spicy tomato sauce 276
Paprika & herb-coated chicken 120
Pheasant with red fruits a& cava 294
Quail in red wine 292
Rabbit & potato stew 298
Rabbit in sherry sauce 296
Slow cooked beef cheeks 314
Spiced meat & rice dish 280
Spiced roast pork 272
Spicy sausage with butterbeans & tomato 274
Stuffed leg of lamb 302
Veal cutlets with warm potato salad 310
Meatballs in spicy tomato sauce 276
Mediterranean dip 110
Mediterranean seafood salad 30
Mejillones a la Castellana 222
Membrillo (quince paste) 400, 485
Bocadillo 336
Manchego bites 114
Montadito 338
Mencia 452
Merluza en salsa verde 220
Merluza y gambas a la sidra 212
Migas 74
Migas con chorizo 334
Migas dulces con pasas 438
Milk
Almond pudding with honey 382
Asturias rice pudding 390
Banana fritters 402

Caramelised Catalan custard 406
Cinnamon ice cream 392
Fried milk 378
La Rioja caramelised bread 342
Raisin crumb 438
Mojito 458
Mojo colorado 156
Mojo rojo 159
Mojo verde 120, 152, 159
Mojos, see also sauces 159
Monastrell 41, 452
Monkfish, tomato & hazelnut bake 240
Montaditos 338
Moorish influence 04, 74, 160, 166, 192, 196, 256, 306, 418, 440
Mortadella 485
Moscatel 452
Movida social revolution 260
Mugaritz 10
Murcia 39, 40-41, 193
Murcia al Vino 363
Mushroom & cheese-topped sole 230
Mushrooms 190-191, 200, 326
Asturian pasta 278
Chestnut & mushroom soup 52
Chicken casserole 284
Chorizo & herb-stuffed mushrooms 118
Duck with mushrooms & potatoes 290
Mediterranean seafood salad 30
Mushroom & cheese-topped sole 230
Potato & mushroom stuffed turbot 226
Spicy fried mushrooms 120
Mussels 485
Castillian mussels 222
Sailor's seafood soup 46
Seafood fideua 232
Seafood paella 210

N

Naranjas y cíticos 396
Natillas 396
Natillas custard 396
Navarra **199-20**1
Navarra-style eggs 114
New World influence 07, 74, 164, 192, 442
Nose-to-tail butchery 10
Nun's casserole, the 252

O

Octopus 255, 258
    Braised octopus with tomato & artichokes 224
    Slow-cooked Galician octopus 92
Olive oil 36, 66, **138**
    Garlic sauce (Allioli) 154
    Mayonnaise 148
Olives 138, 440, 486
    Valencian orange & manchego cheese salad 18
    Asturian rice & seafood salad 20
    Fresh tuna with baby onions & olives 84
    Jamon-wrapped asparagus with fennel salad 86
    Manchego stuffed zucchini flowers 88
    Herb-marinated green olives 100
    Chilli & garlic marinated black olives 100
    Green olive, artichoke & salmon pinchos 104
    Empanadilla of olives & jamon 116
    Green pepper & tortilla canapes 122
    Fried bread, chorizo & black olives 130
    Pincho of marinated sardines with olives 136
    Stuffed tomatoes 180
    Artichokes with pine nuts, olives & thyme 182
    Sardine & caramelised onion coca 236
    Salted cod & orange salad 246
    Lobster with tomato & olive salsa 246
    Pickled fish with olives & vegetables 248
    Spicy sausage with butterbeans & tomato 274
Onions
    Catalan-style roast vegetables with herbs 186
    Char-grilled tuna with balsamic onions 242
    Crisp spiced chicken with red pepper jam 282
    Fresh tuna with baby onions & olives 84
    Montadito 338
    Sardine & caramelised onion coca 236
    Stuffed onions 174
    Tuna and potato stew 218
Orange custard flan 376
Oranges 39, 196
    Jamon, cheese & date salad 32
    La Rioja caramelised bread 342
    Magdalenas 428
    Orange custard flan 374
    Quail in red wine 292
    Red sangria 456
    Salted cod & orange salad 246
    St James tart 380
    Valencian orange & manchego cheese salad 18
    White sangria 454

P

Pa amb tomàquet 124
Paella 04, 41, **194-195**, 196
Paella Marinera 210
Paella rice 485
Palitos de hojaldre con manchego y anchoas 98
Pan campestre 348
Pan de grano con chilis 350
Pan fried potatoes with tomato sauce 108
Pan frito con chorizo y aceitunas 130
Pan rústico 352
Pancakes, Galician 398
Panellets 432
Paprika 74, 120, **193**, 485
    Braised octopus with tomato & artichokes 224
    Chicken casserole 284
    Crisp spiced chicken with red pepper jam 282
    Mackerel, pasta & paprika soup 60
    Paprika & herb-coated chicken 120
    Sardines with paprika tomato sauce 216
    Spicy red dipping sauce (Mojo colorado) 156
Paprika and herb-coated chicken 120
Pasta Asturiana 278
Pasta 44, 486
    Catalan Escudella 56
    Asturian pasta 278
    Mackerel, pasta & paprika soup 60
    Seafood fideua 232
Pastel de carne de cordero 104
Pastry sticks with manchego & anchovies 98
Patatas asadas con alcachofas y tomillo 184
Patatas Bravas 108
Patata y atún a la cazuela 218
Pato con papas y setas 290
Pears cooked in red wine 374
Peasant cooking 357
Pedro Ximenez 452
Peppers 485, 476, 486
    Savoury filled peppers with tomato sauce 176
Peppers, green
    Aromatic braised kid (or lamb) 300
    Asturian pasta 278
    Basque eggs on pisto 96
    Black rice with squid, shrimp & chorizo 244
    Crabs a la rioja 234
    Green pepper & tortilla canapes 122
    Mackerel, pasta & paprika soup 60
    Pincho of marinated sardines with olives 136
    Rabbit & potato stew 298

Peppers, red

    Basque eggs on pisto 96

    Black rice with squid, shrimp & chorizo 244

    Catalan fish stew 238

    Catalán salad 36

    Catalan-style roast vegetables with herbs 186

    Chicken with red peppers & jamon 288

    Crisp spiced chicken with red pepper jam 282

    Green pepper & tortilla canapes 122

    Lamb meatloaf 104

    Mediterranean dip 110

    Nun's casserole, the 250

    Piquillo pepper & whitebait canapés 134

    Potato, chicory & tuna salad 34

    Rabbit & potato stew 298

    Roasted red pepper & aubergine soup 70

    Romaine lettuce, tuna & anchovy salad 16

    Romescu sauce 150

    Salt cod potato cakes with roasted red pepper 112

    Samfaina bake 168

    Sardines on toast 130

    Seafood paella 210

    Spiced meat & rice dish 280

    Spicy red dipping sauce (Mojo colorado) 156

Peppers, yellow

    Catalan fish stew 238

    Mediterranean seafood salad 30

Peras al vino 374

Pescadito frito con alioli 118

Pheasant with red fruits and cava 294

Pickled fish with olives & vegetables 250

Pierna de cordero rellena 302

Pimentón ahumado 193

Pimentón de La Vera 74

Pimientos rellenos 176

Pincho de sardinas marinadas y olivas 136

Pincho of marinated sardines with olives 136

Pinchos de higos con jamón 128

Pinchos de manzana y queso azul 128

Pinchos de salmón ahumado y rábanos 96

Pinchos de salmón y aceitunas 104

Pine nuts 372

    Valencian orange & manchego cheese salad 18

    Tomato, goat's cheese & pine nut salad 24

    Manchego stuffed zucchini flowers 88

    Artichokes with pine nuts, olives & thyme 182

    Stuffed leg of lamb 302

    Savoury Catalan flatbread 344

    Almond & pine nut balls 432

Pintxos 10, 78, 83, 110, 143, 199

Piquillo pepper & whitebait canapés 134

Pisto 168, 364

Plasencia 193

Plátanos fritos 402

Pollo a la cazuela 284

Pollo al ajillo con un toque de cava 126

Pollo con especias y páprika 120

Pollo con pimentos rojos y jamón 288

Pollo crujiente con pimentos rojos 282

Polvorones 434

Pork 74, 161, 268, 442

    Catalan Escudella 56

    Meatballs in spicy tomato sauce 276

    Savoury filled peppers with tomato sauce 176

    Spiced roast pork 272

    Stuffed leg of lamb 302

Potato and mushroom stuffed turbot 226

Potato salad, warm 310

Potato tortilla 102

Potato, chicory and tuna salad 34

Patatas bravas 108

Patatas con chorizo 106

Potatoes

    Chorizo & potatoes 106

    Creamy zucchini soup 62

    Duck with mushrooms & potatoes 290

    Leek & potato soup with croutons 48

    Pan fried potatoes with tomato sauce 108

    Potato & mushroom stuffed turbot 226

    Potato tortilla 102

    Potato, chicory & tuna salad 34

    Rabbit & potato stew 298

    Roast potatoes with artichokes & thyme 184

    Russian salad 28

    Salt cod potato cakes with roasted red pepper 112

    Spicy sausage with butterbeans & tomato 274

    Tuna and potato stew 218

    Veal cutlets with warm potato salad 310

Prawns

    Asturian rice & seafood salad 20

    Mediterranean seafood salad 30

Prawns, king, see shrimp

Preserves **38**

Prosciutto, see jamon

Pulpo a la Gallega 92

Pulpo con tomate y alcachofas 224

Q

Quail eggs, see eggs, quail
Quail in red wine 292
Quark 486
    Cream cheese mint tart 408
Quince paste 400
Quince paste, see also membrillo 114, 400

R

Rabbit and potato stew 298
Rabbit in sherry sauce 296
Rabo de buey estofado 312
Radishes
    Mediterranean seafood salad 30
    Smoked salmon & radish pinchos 96
Raisin crumb and sweet bread bake 438
Rape asado con tomate y avellanas 240
Red pepper and onion jam 282
Red pepper cream 70
Red pepper sauce 130
Red sangria 456
Regions
    Andalucia **440-443**
    Aragon **327-329**
    Asturias **368-369**
    Balearic Islands **160-161**
    Basque Country **140-143**
    Canary Islands **158-159**
    Cantabria **264-265**
    Castilla-La Mancha **364-367**
    Castilla-Leon **324-326**
    Catalonia **412-415**
    Extremadura **74-75**
    Galicia **257-259**
    La Rioja **476-479**
    Madrid **260-263**
    Murcia **40-41**
    Navarra **199-201**
    Valencia **196-198**
Rice
    Asturian rice & seafood salad 20
    Aromatic braised kid (or lamb) 300
    Asturias rice pudding 390
    Black rice with squid, shrimp & chorizo 244
    Seafood paella 210
    Spiced meat & rice dish 280
Rioja 446
Roast cauliflower with leek & garlic 178
Roast potatoes with artichokes & thyme 184

Roasted red pepper & aubergine soup 70
Rodaballo relleno 226
Romaine lettuce, tuna & anchovy salad 16
Roman influence 04, 160, 196
Romescu sauce 150
Rosemary
    Catalan-style roast vegetables with herbs 186
    Fillet of beef with blue cheese 316
    Herb-marinated green olives 100
    Soft almond & rosemary nougat 426
Rum, white
    Mojito 458
Russian salad 28
Rustic bread 352

S

Sabayón de Cava 404
Saffron **256**, 486
    Braised oxtail 312
    Sardines with paprika tomato sauce 216
    Seafood fideua 232
    Seafood paella 210
    Spiced meat & rice dish 280
    Veal cutlets with warm potato salad 310
Sailor's seafood soup 46
Salads 12-37
    Asturian rice & seafood salad 20
    Catalán salad 36
    Green bean salad with quail eggs 22
    Jamon, cheese & date salad 32
    Mediterranean seafood salad 30
    Potato, chicory & tuna salad 34
    Romaine lettuce, tuna & anchovy salad 16
    Russian salad 28
    Tomato, goat's cheese & pine nut salad 24
    Valencian orange & manchego cheese salad 18
Salami
    Empanadilla of olives & jamon 116
    Spiced meat & rice dish 280
Salchichas de ternera al vino 132
Salmon, smoked
    Green olive, artichoke & salmon pinchos 104
    Mediterranean seafood salad 30
    Montadito 338
    Smoked salmon & radish pinchos 96
    Tasty cherry tomatoes 84
Salpicón de mariscos 14
Salsa mayonesa 148
Salsa Mediterránea 110

Salsa romescu 150
Salsa verde, see green sauce
Salsas, see also sauces
Salt cod potato cakes with roasted red pepper 112
Salted almonds 86
Salted cod & orange salad 248
Samfaina 168
Samfaina bake 168
San Simón 363

Sangria
    Red sangria 456
    White sangria 454
Sangría blanca 454
Sangría roja 456
Sardinas con pan tostado 130
Sardinas con salsa de tomate 216
Sardine & caramelised onion coca 236

Sardines
    Montadito 338
    Pincho of marinated sardines with olives 136
    Sardine & caramelised onion coca 236
    Sardines on toast 130
    Sardines with paprika tomato sauce 216
Sardines on toast 130
Sardines with paprika tomato sauce 216

Sauces 145-157
    Garlic sauce (Allioli) 154
    Green dipping sauce (Mojo verde) 152
    Mayonnaise 148
    Romescu sauce 150
    Spicy red dipping sauce (Mojo colorado) 156
Sausage, chorizo, see chorizo, Spanish
Sausage, sobrasada 161

Sausages 09, 161, 413, 487
    Beef sausages in white wine 132
    Catalan Escudella 56
    Navarra-style eggs 114, 485
    Spiced meat & rice dish 280
    Spicy sausage with butterbeans & tomato 274
Savoury Catalan flatbread 344
Savoury filled peppers with tomato sauce 176
Seafood, see fish and seafood
Seafood fideua 232
Seafood paella 210
Setas fritas picantes 120
Seville 83, 440

Sherry 443, 446, 461, **462-465**
    Rabbit in sherry sauce 296
    Slow cooked beef cheeks 314

Sherry – varieties
    Amontillado 465

    Cream 465
    Fino 465
    Manzanilla 465
    Oloroso 465
    Palo Cortado 465
Shortbread cookies 434

Shrimp 486
    Asturian rice & seafood salad 20
    Black rice with squid, shrimp & chorizo 244
    Catalan fish stew 238
    Garlic chilli shrimp 228
    Hake & shrimp in apple cider sauce 212
    Mediterranean seafood salad 30
    Seafood fideua 232
    Seafood paella 210
    Shrimp with cava 90
Shrimp with cava 90
Sidra, see cider 466
Slow cooked beef cheeks 314
Slow-cooked Galician octopus 92
Smoked salmon & radish pinchos 96
Snails 328
Snails, Garlic 132
Sobrasada 161, 340
Soft almond & rosemary nougat 426
Solera 463
Solomillo de ternera al queso azul 316
Sopa de caballa 60
Sopa de calabacín 62
Sopa de castañas 52
Sopa de pimiento rojo y berenjena 70
Sopa de puerros 48
Sopa de tomate 68
Sopa de tomate con calamar 58
Sopa de tomate con lentejas y jamón 64
Sopa de tomate y jamón 50
Sopa marinera 46

Soups 43-71, 366
    Andulacian chilled tomato & garlic soup 54
    Butter bean, tomato & jamon soup 50
    Catalan Escudella 56
    Chestnut & mushroom soup 52
    Chilled almond & garlic soup 66
    Creamy zucchini soup 62
    Leek & potato soup with croutons 48
    Mackerel, pasta & paprika soup 60
    Roasted red pepper & aubergine soup 70
    Sailor s seafood soup 46
    Tomato soup 68
    Tomato with calamari soup 58
Spiced meat & rice casserole 280

Spiced roast pork 272
Spicy fried mushrooms 120
Spicy red dipping sauce 156
Spicy sausage with butterbeans & tomato 274
Spicy tomato sauce 276
Spring onion canapés 134
Squid, see also calamari **255**
    Black rice with squid, shrimp & chorizo 244
    Calamari with anchovy, lemon & thyme stuffing 214
    Catalan fish stew 238
    Seafood paella 210
    Squid with garlic mayonnaise 94
    Tomato with calamari soup 8
Squid with garlic mayonnaise 94
St James 199, 258, 380, 479
St James Cross, template 488
St James tart 380
Street food **354**
Stuffed leg of lamb 302
Stuffed onions 174
Stuffed tomatoes 180
stuffing 214, 302
Suquet 238
Sweet Catalan flatbread 346
Sweet Mallorcan bread scroll 340
Sweets and biscuits 326, 366, **417-439**
    Alfajores 436
    Almond & pine nut balls 434
    Almond bars 424
    Churros 422
    Filled doughnut logs 430
    Magdalenas 428
    Shortbread cookies 434
    Soft almond & rosemary nougat 426

T

Tapas 09, **77-137**, 354, 443
    Basque eggs on pisto 96
    Beef sausages in white wine 132
    Broad beans with jamon 90
    Cabrales & apple pinchos 128
    Catalan tomato bread 124
    Chilli & garlic marinated black olives 100
    Chorizo & herb-stuffed mushrooms 118
    Chorizo & potatoes 106
    Empanadilla of olives & jamon 116
    Figs & jamon pinchos with balsamic glaze 128
    Fresh tuna with baby onions & olives 84
    Fried bread, chorizo & black olives 130
    Garlic chicken with a touch of cava 124

Garlic snails 132
Green olive, artichoke & salmon pinchos 104
Green pepper & tortilla canapes 122
Herb-marinated green olives 100
Jamon & egg canapés 122
Jamon croquettes 126
Jamon-wrapped asparagus with fennel salad 86
Lamb meatloaf 104
Lemon sole strips with dill mayonnaise 98
Manchego bites 114
Manchego stuffed zucchini flowers 88
Marinated anchovies 110
Mediterranean dip 110
Navarra-style eggs 114
Pan fried potatoes with tomato sauce 108
Paprika & herb-coated chicken 120
Pastry sticks with manchego & anchovies 98
Pincho of marinated sardines with olives 136
Piquillo pepper & whitebait canapés 134
Potato tortilla 102
Salt cod potato cakes with roasted red pepper 112
Salted almonds 86
Sardines on toast 130
Shrimp with cava 90
Slow-cooked Galician octopus 92
Smoked salmon & radish pinchos 96
Spicy fried mushrooms 120
Spring onion canapés 134
Squid with garlic mayonnaise 94
Tasty cherry tomatoes 84
Tostada with tomato & anchovies 94
Whitebait with allioli 118
Tarta de higos 386
Tarta de manzana 384
Tarta de Santiago 258
Tarta de Santiago 380
Tasty cherry tomatoes 84
Tempranillo 452
Thyme 184
    Artichokes with pine nuts, olives & thyme 182
    Garlic chicken with a touch of cava 124
    Herb-marinated green olives 100
    Roast potatoes with artichokes & thyme 184
    Slow cooked beef cheeks 314
Tiras de lenguado con mayonesa 98
Tocinillo asado 272
Tocino de cielo 394
Toffee custard ('Heaven's bacon') 394
Tomates rellenos 180
Tomato & olive salsa 246
Tomato paste 487

Tomato puree (passata) 487
Tomato soup 68
Tomato & calamari soup 58
Tomato, goat's cheese & pine nut salad 24
Tomatoes
  Andulacian chilled tomato & garlic soup 54
  Aromatic braised kid (or lamb) 300
  Asturian rice & seafood salad 20
  Basque eggs on pisto 96
  Braised octopus with tomato & artichokes 224
  Butter bean, tomato & jamon soup 50
  Catalán salad 36
  Catalan tomato bread 124
  Catalan-style roast vegetables with herbs 186
  Chicken with red peppers & jamon 288
  Crabs a la rioja 234
  Empanadilla of olives & jamo 116
  Garlic snails 132
  Green bean salad with quail eggs 22
  Lamb cutlets in chorizo tomato sauce 306
  Lamb meatloaf 104
  Lentil, tomato & jamon soup 64
  Lobster with tomato & olive salsa 246
  Mediterranean dip 110
  Mediterranean seafood salad 30
  Monkfish, tomato & hazelnut bake 240
  Pan fried potatoes with tomato sauce 108
  Rabbit & potato stew 298
  Rabbit in sherry sauce
  Roasted red pepper & aubergine soup 70
  Romaine lettuce, tuna & anchovy salad 16
  Samfaina bake 168
  Sardines with paprika tomato sauce 216
  Savoury Catalan flatbread 344
  Savoury filled peppers with tomato sauce 176
  Shrimp with cava 90
  Spicy sausage with butterbeans & tomato 274
  Stuffed tomatoes 180
  Tasty cherry tomatoes 84
  Tomato soup 68
  Tomato with calamari soup 58
  Tomato, goat's cheese & pine nut salad 24
  Tostada with tomato & anchovies 94
  Tuna and potato stew 218
  Valencian orange & manchego cheese salad 18
Torres family 450
Torrijas 342
Torta del Casar 363
Tortilla de patatas 102
Tostada con tomate y anchoas 94
Tostada with tomato & anchovies 94

Truffles **190-191**, 328
Tuna 205
  Asturian rice & seafood salad 20
  Char-grilled tuna with balsamic onions 242
  Fresh tuna with baby onions & olives 84
  Potato, chicory & tuna salad 34
  Romaine lettuce, tuna & anchovy salad 16
  Tuna and potato stew 218
Tuna and potato stew 218
Turrón 418
Turrón de Jijona 426
Txakoli **461**
Txokos – the Basque gastronomic club 142

V

Valdeón 362
Valencia 39, 80, 188, **196-198**, 232
Valencian orange & manchego cheese salad 18
Veal cutlets with warm potato salad 310
Veal jus 487
Veal
  Meatballs in spicy tomato sauce 276
  Veal cutlets with warm potato salad 310
Vegetables, see fruit and vegetables
Verdejo 452
Vi Ranci 432
Viura/macabeo 452

W

Weights and measures **488**
White asparagus with hazelnuts & manchego 170
White sangria 454
Whitebait
  Piquillo pepper & whitebait canapés 134
  Whitebait with alioli 118
Wine 10, 41, 143, 159, 196, 198, 200, 258, 326, 329, 366,
443, **445-453, 460-469, 476-479**
  Beef sausages in white wine 132
  Braised oxtail 312
  Castillian mussels 222
  Duck with mushrooms & potatoes 290
  Pears cooked in red wine 374
  Quail in red wine 292
  Rabbit & potato stew 298
  Red sangria 456
  Slow cooked beef cheeks 314
  Veal cutlets with warm potato salad 310
  White sangria 454
Wine, Txakoli de Getaria 143

Wine – varieties
Albariño 92, 452
Alicante 452
Bobal 452
Carinena/mazuelo 452
Cava 446, 468-469, 483
Chacoli 461
Garnacha 452
Graciano 452
Mencia 452
Monastrell 452
Moscatel 452
Palomino 452
Pedro Ximenez 452
Rioja 446
Tempranillo 452
Txacoli 143, 461
Verdejo 452
Viura/macabeo 452

Y

Yoghurt mint sauce 286

Z

Zucchini 88
Basque eggs on pisto 96
Braised octopus with tomato & artichokes 224
Creamy zucchini soup 62
Hake in green sauce 220
Samfaina bake 168
Zucchini flowers
Manchego stuffed zucchini flowers 88

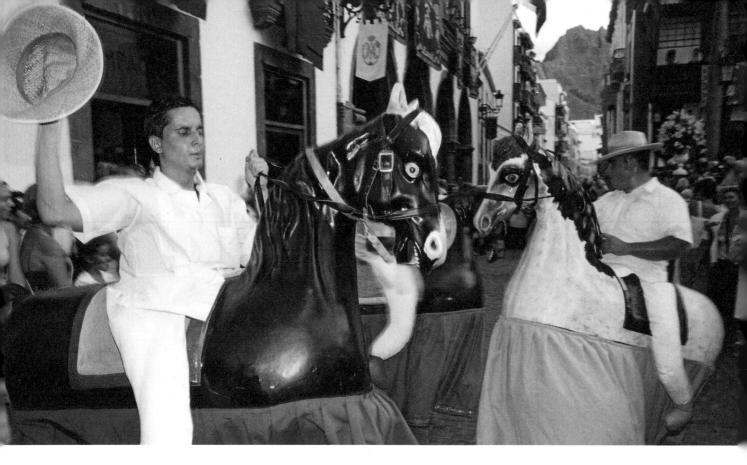

Additional Photography: Andre Martin - Pages: 8, 78, 80, 82, 139, 140, 142, 262, 263, 318, 320, 413, 446, 447, 448, 450, 453, 461, 469, 476, 478. Page 5; Gavin Hellier / Photographer's Choice / Getty Images. Page 6; Ruth Tomlinson / Robert Harding World Imagery / Getty Images. Page 7; Bridgeman Art Library / Getty Images. Page 9; Ken Welsh / Workbook Stock / Getty Images. Page 10; Scott R Barbour/ The Image Bank/ Getty Images. Page 11; Erik van Hannen / Flickr ? Getty Images. Page 39; Michael Newton/ Robert Harding. Page 40; Travel Ink / Gallo Images / Getty Images. Page 41; Hidalgo & Lopesino / age fotostock / Robert Harding. Page 72; Thomas Dressler / Gallo Images / Getty Images. Page 73; M A Otsa de Alda / age fotostock/ Robert Harding. Page 74; Mikel Bilbao / age fotostock / Robert Harding. Page 75; Ruth Tomlinson / Robert Harding World Imagery / Getty Images. Page 81; Jean Brooks / Robert Harding. Page 141; Juan Carlos Munoz / age fotostock / Robert Harding. Page 158; Neil Emmerson / Robert Harding World Imagery / Getty Images. Page 160; Jon Davison / Lonely Planet Images / Getty Images. Page 161; Jose Fuste Raga / age fotostock / Robert Harding. Page 166; Coto Elizondo / Stone / Getty Images. Page 167; JMN / Cover / Getty Images. Page 188; Federico Meneghetti / Cubo Images / Robert Harding. Page 189 (top); Annie Griffiths Belt / National Geographic / Getty Images. Page 189 (bottom); Davis McCardle / The Image Bank / Getty Images. Page 191; Santos Fernandez / age fotostock / Robert Harding. Page 192; Allison Michael Orenstein / The Image Bank / Getty Images. Page 193; Franc & Jean Shore / National Geographic / Getty Images. Page 195; Mickael David / Authors Image / Robert Harding. Page 196; Simon Greenwood/ Lonely Planet Images / Getty Images. Page 197; Marco Simoni / Robert Harding World Imagery / Getty Images. Page 198; Juan Carlos Minoz / age fotostock / Robert Harding. Page 199; Tino Soriano / National Geographic / Getty Images. Page 200; Arni Vitale / Getty Images. Page 201; Xavi Gomez/ The Image Bank / Getty Images. Page 206; Panoramic Images / Getty Images. Page 207; Ruddy Gold / age fotostock / Robert Harding. Page 208; Miguel Riopa / AFP / Getty Images. Page 209; J D Dallet / age fotostock / Robert Harding. Page 256; Luis Castaneda / age fotostock / Robert Harding. Page 258; Duncan Maxwell / Robert Harding World Imagery / Getty Images. Page 259; Xulio Villarino / The Image Bank / Getty Images. Page 260; EyesWideOpen / Getty Images. Page 261; Cristina Arias / Cover / Getty Images. Page 264; John Miller / Robert Harding World Imagery / Getty Images. Page 265; Cesar Lucas Abreu / Cover / Getty Images. Page 268; Yadid Levy / age fotostock / Robert Harding. Page 270; Anna Watson / Axiom Photographic Agency / Getty Images. Page 271; Tono Labra / age fotostock / Robert Harding. Page 321; Jeronimo Alba / age fotostock / Robert Harding. Page 322; Manuel Montero/ Cover / Getty Images. Page 323; Eric Futran / Chefshots / Getty Images. Page 324; Xorxo Lobato / The Image Bank / Getty Images. Page 325; Michael Busselle / Stone / Getty Images. Page 326 (top); Felipe Rodriguez / age fotostock / Robert Harding. Page 326 (bottom); Juan Jose Pascua / age fotostock/ Robert Harding. Page 327; JMN / Cover / Getty Images. Page 328; Sites and photos / Samuel Magal / Getty Images. Page 329; Joe Sohm / The Image Bank / Getty Images. Page 355; Neil Emmerson / Robert Harding World Imagery / Getty Images. Page 357; Hulton Archive / Getty Images. Page 362; Tolo Balaguer / age fotostock / Robert Harding. Page 363; Hidalgo & Lopesino / age fotostock / Robert Harding. Page 364; Luis Castaneda inc / The Image Bank / Getty Images. Page 365; Toyohiro Yamada / Taxi / Getty Images. Page 366; Sofia Moro / Cover / Getty Images. Page 367; JMN / The Image Bank / Getty Images. Page 368; Gonzalo Azumendi / age fotostock / Robert Harding. Page 369; Xulio Villarino / The Image Bank / Getty Images. Page 412; Max Alexander / Dorling Kindersley / Getty Images. Page 414 (bottom); Jordi Cami / age fotostock / Robert Harding. Page 414 (top); Carlos Sanchez Pereyra / Workbook Stock / Getty Images. Page 415; Carlos Sanchez Pereyra / Workbook Stock / Getty Images. Page 420; Sofia Moro / Cover / Getty Images. Page 421; Jasper Juinen / Getty Images. Page 441; Jose Fuste Raga / age fotostock / Robert Harding. Page 442; Javier Larrea / age fotostock / Robert Harding. Page 443; J.D. Dallet / age fotostock/ Robert Harding. Page 450 (main image); Familia Torres . Page 453 (main image); Thomas Vilhelm / Cover / Getty Images. Page 460; Anthony Lee / OJO Images / Getty . Page 462; George Rose / Getty Images. Page 463; JMN / Cover / Getty Images. Page 464; Pepe Franco / Cover / Getty Images. Page 465; Jose Luis Roca / AFP / Getty Images. Page 466; Xurxo Lobato / Cover / Getty Images. Page 467; Travel Ink / Gallo Images / Getty Images. Page 468; Pepe Franco / Cover / Getty Images. Page 478 (small image); Thomas Vilhelm / Cover / Getty Images. Page 479; OSOmedia / age fotostock / Robert Harding. Page 488-489; Jordi Camy / age fotostock / Robert Harding. Page 506; Javier Larrea / age fotostock / Robert Harding.

506
gourmetpilgrim Spain

Gourmet Pilgrim Spain 1st edition [English / Metric]

Published by Gourmet Pilgrim Pty Ltd. 181 Station Street, Corio VIC 3214 Australia.
www.gourmetpilgrim.com

First published 2011.

Commissioning Editor: Jay Stewart
Food Editor: Anna Phillips
Recipe Editors: Kristen Colvin, Nicole Robinson
Sub Editors: Fiona Baker, Emma Cayley, Nicole Robinson
Feature Writers: Max Allen, Richard Cornish, Kendall Hill
Design: Jamie Lamshed / Juice Visual Communications
Food Styling: Anna Phillips
Recipe Testing & Food Preparation: Julie Ballard, Anna Phillips, Dimitra Stais
Food Photography: Andre Martin
Cover Design: Jamie Lamshed / Juice Visual Communications
Cover Photography: Jamie Lamshed, Andre Martin, Anna Phillips
Thanks to: Carlos Linares, madridandbeyond.com, Inaki Rubios

Printed in China

National Library of Australia Cataloguing-in-Publication Entry Data
Title: Spain: Recipes, culture and stories from the kitchen tables of Spain / food editor, Anna Phillips; photographer, Andre Martin; texts, Kendall Hill, Richard Cornish, Max Allen.
Edition: 1st ed.
ISBN: 9780980768213 (hbk.)
Series: Gourmet Pilgrim; 2
Notes: Includes index.
Subjects: Cooking, Spanish.Other Authors/Contributors: Phillips, Anna Martin, André, Photographer Hill, Kendall Cornish, Richard, 1967-Allen, Max, 1968-Dewey Number: 641.5946

Opposite: Wooden horses on parade during the celebration of the *Descent of Our Lady of Snows fiesta*, Santa Cruz de la Palma, Canary Islands.